THE POLITICS OF EXTERNAL INFLUENCE
IN THE DOMINICAN REPUBLIC

Copublished with Hoover Institution Press,
Stanford University, Stanford, California

POLITICS IN LATIN AMERICA
A HOOVER INSTITUTION SERIES

General Editor, **Robert Wesson**

THE POLITICS OF EXTERNAL INFLUENCE IN THE DOMINICAN REPUBLIC

MICHAEL J. KRYZANEK
HOWARD J. WIARDA

New York
Westport, Connecticut
London

The Hoover Institution on War, Revolution and Peace,
founded at Stanford University in 1919 by the late President
Herbert Hoover, is an interdisciplinary research center for
advanced study on domestic and international affairs in the
twentieth century. The views expressed in its publications
are entirely those of the authors and do not necessarily
reflect the views of the staff, officers, or Board of Overseers
of the Hoover Institution.

Library of Congress Cataloging-in-Publication Data

Kryzanek, Michael J.
    The politics of external influence in the Dominican Republic /
Michael J. Kryzanek, Howard J. Wiarda.

        p.   cm.—(Politics in Latin America)
    Bibliography: p.
    Includes index.
    ISBN 0–275–92992–2 (alk. paper)
        1. Dominican Republic—Politics and government—1961–
2. Dominican Republic—Economic conditions—1961–   3. Dominican
Republic—Dependency on the United States.   I. Wiarda, Howard J.,
1939–   . II. Title. III. Series.
F1938.55.K77   1988
972.93′054—dc19   87–38481

Library of Congress Catalog Card Number: 87–38481
ISBN: 0–275–92992–2

First published in 1988

Praeger Publishers, One Madison Avenue, New York, NY 10010
A division of Greenwood Press, Inc.

Printed in the United States of America

∞

The paper used in this book complies with the Permanent
Paper Standard issued by the National Information Standards
Organization (Z39.48–1984).

10   9   8   7   6   5   4   3   2   1

For Our Wives, Carol and Iĕda

TABLE OF CONTENTS

FOREWORD

While not very large in terms of population (6 million) or gross national product ($7 billion), the Dominican Republic has long been a very important country in the Caribbean region, and looms large as a critical country in U.S. foreign policy. It is imperative, therefore, in this new era of crisis in the Caribbean, that the United States give the Dominican Republic a larger share of attention. It is a key nation of the Caribbean Basin, a country in which the United States has assumed more of an interventionist role than any other Latin American country, with the possible exception of Nicaragua. It is also the Latin American country to which, more than any other, it can be claimed that the United States has brought democratic institutions.

At this time, the Dominican Republic is deeply in trouble, and the ability of the United States to foster political and economic improvement within its sphere of influence is being severely tested there. Like many countries, the Dominican Republic groans under an unpayable foreign debt; even more than most deeply indebted countries, it lacks means of paying, perhaps even of keeping itself afloat. Compared to next-door Haiti, with which it shares the island of Hispaniola, the Dominican Republic is relatively prosperous and uncrowded; passengers flying from the one country to the other can tell where the border lies, as green forest contrasts with a brown and eroded landscape. But the chief crop, sugar, is almost worthless and is nearly excluded from the U.S. market; population and import needs grow relentlessly and more rapidly than exports; and the brightest hope—possibly the only apparent hope—for very many Dominicans is to join the exodus to Puerto Rico or New York.

It is to be hoped that this analysis of the Dominican situation by two persons who have given it much attention, Professors Kryzanek and Wiarda, will help toward an understanding of the Republic's deep problems to which the American government may, in its wisdom, address itself.

Robert Wesson

PREFACE

There are quite a number of good books about the Dominican Republic, despite that the country is not usually considered one of the major "players" in hemispheric affairs. Regardless of its relatively small size, the "D.R." as it is commonly called by Americans, offers a wonderful and nearby laboratory where one may study such subjects as bloody dictatorships, U.S. intervention, and revolutionary change. For that reason, and because it is at the vortex of the complex North-South and East-West currents swirling through the Caribbean Basin, we used "A Caribbean Crucible" as the subtitle of an earlier book written about the Dominican Republic.

This is an entirely new book. Not only is such a new book justified by the passage of time, changed circumstances, and the ending of one era and the beginning of another in Santo Domingo, but the book provides an entirely new interpretation as well. Heretofore, most books about the Dominican Republic have focused either on its domestic or its international situation. This is the first study that seeks to weave together in a comprehensive manner the complex interrelations between the outside world and the internal character and development of Dominican national life.

In *The Politics of External Influence in the Dominican Republic*, the main objective will be to examine the external influences—neighboring governments, foreign powers, multinational corporations, international lending agencies, world markets for critical resources, and economic and cultural forces from outside the country—and determine how they have shaped and interacted with local Dominican institutions. Our aim is to demonstrate both Dominican dependence on and interdependence with the external forces that wash over its shores. We seek to show how local institutions have been developed, public policies formulated, and socioeconomic issues addressed within an historical context of virtually constant outside intervention. But while the Dominican Republic has often been a pawn in these larger processes, the country is not without its own inner strength and capacities to absorb or manipulate the outside forces that influence it. In short, the book explores the evolution and current status of the Dominican Republic from the inside as well as from the perspective of the world outside that country.

Although the book attempts to describe internal Dominican conditions by exploring the impact of the outside world, it is also a country study that covers the usual "bases." That is, we have chapters on the history, politics, society, and economics of the country as well as other subjects. But woven through all these chapters is the theme of the interrelations between Dominican ways and institutions and the impact of the external influences that historically and to the present have played such a major role—of which the most recent is the United States. The Dominican Republic, we have found, is both dependent on these outside forces and interdependent with them at one and the same time. And while there have always been asymmetries of size and power between the Dominican Republic and the outside influences that have strongly shaped it, often making these relationships quite uneven, the country has nevertheless retained its own identity, its own nationalism, and its own ways of doing things. That is why we use the terms *interdependence* as well as *dependence*. For in the last analysis the Dominican Republic is a nation of two identities, one formed by Dominicans and one formed by powerful forces outside the country, that relate and interrelate in endlessly complex and changing ways.

As with any study, this book could not have been completed without the help and encouragement of a number of persons and institutions. We are indebted first of all to Dr. Robert Wesson and the Hoover Institution at Stanford University for suggesting this project, supporting it, and seeing it through to completion. We wish to thank the many Dominicans and Americans who talked with us and provided us with a storehouse of information, helping us to see the ways in which the Dominican Republic's dual identity has evolved. Professor Kryzanek thanks the Bridgewater State College Alumni Association and its director, Philip Conroy, who provided a travel grant; Professor Wiarda wishes to thank the American Enterprise Institute for its support of his research. We both wish to acknowledge the contributions of our wives, Carol and Iĕda, and our children—Laura, Kathy, and Ann; Kristy, Howard, and Jonathan—who in their own ways all helped take this book from ideas to print.

This work is the product of an evolving and productive series of collaborations over the years between the two authors. Professor Wiarda has been studying and writing about the Dominican Republic for some 25 years; Professor Kryzanek's interest in the Dominican Republic was sparked at the University of Massachusetts/Amherst where he completed a Ph.D. thesis on that country under Professor Wiarda's direction. In our earlier book Professor Wiarda's name was listed first as the senior author. But in this book Professor Kryzanek's name appears first, reflecting not only his contribution to the volume but also (in his collaborator's estimation, as well as those of other scholars) his major writings and scholarship on U.S.–Latin American relations.

THE POLITICS OF EXTERNAL INFLUENCE
IN THE DOMINICAN REPUBLIC

1

INTRODUCTION: A NATION WITH A DUAL IDENTITY

Because the world we live in today seems to be getting "smaller," with greater contact between peoples from different countries and regions, there is a growing sense of familiarity about what nation-states are known for and what unique charcteristics may set them apart from other nation-states. Mention almost any country in the world in everyday conversation and it often conjures up instant images of a faraway place with a distinct cultural heritage, prominent topographical landmarks, and a quality of life much different from that experienced back home. Although these images often only scratch the surface of a complex national mosaic, they do provide a rough glimpse of a people and the manner in which they have organized their society.

The Dominican Republic, despite its small size and its relatively minor position in the order of international power, is not a complete mystery or a faceless ministate in the Caribbean. When asked to respond to the name Dominican Republic, there often emerges a rather distinct image (especially among respondents from the United States) of a country of endless sugarcane fields, talented baseball players, old Spanish ruins, palm-lined beaches, and U.S. hotel chains. Some of the more knowledgeable respondents may even expand upon these images and talk about dictators, United States military intervention, and extreme poverty.

Popular images, of course, border on the stereotypical and usually provide only a rudimentary perspective on a country. But rather than dismiss these mental pictures outright, it may be beneficial to recognize that in the case of the Dominican Republic, image and reality form a close bond. The Dominican Republic is indeed much more than just a Caribbean playground for North Americans, but at the same time the Dominican Republic is a nation whose historical evolution and current condition is in large part a reflection of the common images retained in the memory of the general public. To identify the Dominican Republic with sugar is to ignore the growing mining industry and industrial sectors, and yet sugar exported to the United States is still the driving force of the economy. To see Dominicans as friendly (but sometimes hot-headed) baseball players grossly simplifies the national workforce; nevertheless, one cannot easily ignore the Dominican passion for the United States' pastime or the fact that today's national heroes are Pedro Guerrero of the Dodgers and Juan Samuel of the Phillies, and that there are now some 40 to 50 Dominicans in the U.S. major and minor leagues. Finally, to view the country as a quaint Caribbean vacation spot with a Spanish rather than British ambiance is to forget the sad legacy of violence and foreign intervention that was beset this nation—even though the Dominicans are a remarkably forgiving and resilient people.

In writing a book about any country there is a natural tendency to search for unifying characteristics that may help to explain or define the nation and the pattern of its historical evolution. This search for such a common denominator is often elusive and may even be fruitless since nations do not easily submit to grand theories, nor can their histories be traced back to any single factor. Yet despite these reservations, the link between popular image and national reality in the Dominican Republic may indeed point in the direction of a common denominator. Contained in the everyday images of sugarcane fields, baseball players, Spanish ruins, and winter playgrounds for North American neighbors are the key elements for defining a rather unique "Dominicanness."

Even though this is a country with a distinct political life, a domestic economy with its own dynamics, and a socio-cultural climate that is quite separate from that found in other Caribbean countries, the Dominican Republic is a nation with profound ties to the outside world. The Dominican Republic long ago came to grips with the fact that its internal and external affairs were intertwined. This is a nation that takes many of its cues from abroad and often organizes its internal life in response to decisions made in Washington, New York, Caracas, Madrid, Paris, and Tokyo. The Dominican Republic is quite simply a nation with a dual identity—one formed indigenously by the political, economic, and social forces that are Dominican and one formed as a result of circumstances and pressures emanating from locations beyond its borders. These two identities overlay and interrelate in all kinds of complex ways.

In our efforts to understand the Dominican Republic and describe its unique features, we need to come to grips with this dual identity phenomenon. Since this is a country that looks both inward and outward, it is essential that the totality of national life be examined in terms of this dual identity. From diplomatic negotiations and public policy to race relations and capital formation, the Dominican Republic is a nation not totally in control of its destiny. As we shall see, being a Dominican means learning how to contend with and accommodate outside influences that over the years have left an indelible mark. Indeed it is often from the interrelations between these internal and external influences that the distinct character of the Dominican Republic as a nation is derived.

GEOGRAPHY IS DESTINY

Placing any country on the map and describing its relationship to neighboring nations and distinct regions has become an increasingly critical factor in determining strategic importance and "power potential" in world affairs. In the case of the Dominican Republic it is important to move beyond the traditional perception of this country as an isolated, autonomous Caribbean ministate and recognize that its location in the center of an increasingly important region—and the fact that it serves as a kind of gateway to Central America, the Panama Canal, and the northern tier of South American states—has expanded its influence considerably and thrust it into the forefront of international and regional geopolitics. From the early colonial days when the Spanish, French, and English fought over and bargained for control of the island of Hispaniola, to the modern era when the United States engaged in economic and military intervention, the Dominican Republic has been a valuable piece of real estate to the major powers.

To begin, the Dominican Republic is situated in the Caribbean in the chain of islands called the Greater Antilles. Its immediate island neighbors are Cuba to the northwest and Puerto Rico to the east. Of more geographic significance is the fact that the Dominican Republic is in a rather unique position in that it shares the island of Hispaniola with Haiti. Due to the colonial maneuverings of Spain and France during the seventeenth and eighteenth centuries, the Dominican Republic evolved as a Spanish outpost controlling two thirds of the island, while Haiti, first a French colony and later an independent black state, occupied the remaining one third. A border of approximately 193 miles today separates these two sovereign nations.

Two nations with vastly different heritages occupying one island is certainly an oddity, but the geographic uniquenes of Hispaniola is more than just the fact that two countries share the same parcel of land. Over the years, the Dominican Republic and Haiti have not been good neighbors, and in fact have been unwilling to gloss over their racial, economic, political, and cultural differences, choosing instead to avoid contact and to keep age-old grudges at center stage. The long period of Haitian domination of the Dominican Republic during the nineteenth century, the recent exodus of illegal Haitian immigrants into Dominican territory, and the constant fear of excessive "darkening" and "Africanizing" of Dominican society by the Haitians has created a definite anti-Haitian climate in the Dominican Republic.[1]

Map 1.1
The Dominican Republic

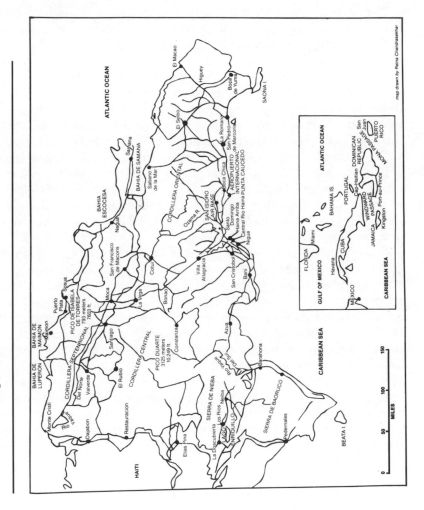

map drawn by Ratna Chandrasekhar

Table 1.1
Profile of the Dominican Landscape

Land Area 18,816 square miles
Length - East to West - 240 miles
Highest Point - Mt. Duarte - 10,417 feet (highest point in Caribbean)
Lowest Point - Lake Enriquillo - 131 feet below sea level
Average Temperature Range - Winter 64-84°F, Summer 73-95°F
Average Rainfall 53 inches Eastern region
                 82 inches Northeast region
                 17 inches Western region
Roadways - 6,306 miles of paved roads
Railways - 365 miles of public and private
Arable Land - 2,175,000 acres
Land under Permanent crops - 865,000 acres
Major Agricultural crops - sugar cane, coffee, cocoa, tobacco
Major Mineral Resources - gold, silver, ·ferronickel, bauxite

Source: Compiled by the authors.

Although the strange partition of Hispaniola is usually cited as the most important characteristic of Dominican geography, it is essential to remember that the Dominican Republic's strategic placement in the string of island nation-states has had a marked impact on regional trade and transportation and on the foreign policy concerns of the United States. The Mona Passage between the Dominican Republic and, to the east, Puerto Rico has long been recognized as the key exit channel out of the Caribbean. Oil tankers from Venezuela and Trinidad, commercial ships leaving the Panama Canal for Europe, and military vessels, whether Soviet supply ships or United States destroyers, pass through this narrow passageway. On a number of occasions the Reagan administration has talked about the Dominican Republic in strategic terms citing the importance of maintaining friendly ties to the country and ensuring stability, since the free flow of oil, military cargo, and troop ships through the Mona Passage is essential to the world economy and particularly United States security interests.[2] Some Dominicans are still convinced that the United States continues to covet Samana Bay, the best natural port in the Caribbean, which faces toward the Mona Passage.

Viewing the Dominican Republic in terms of its neighbors and its place in the region is critical but it remains only one facet of the country's geography. The Dominican Republic is also a nation unique unto itself, with an internal identity that has contributed to the patterns of population distribution, the economic utilization of available land, and the presence of foreign investors and tourists. Although the Dominican Republic is only slightly larger than New Hampshire and Vermont combined (19,332 square miles—240 miles long, 170 miles wide), it is a country of great diversity with at least three distinct regions. The regions of the Dominican Republic correspond to the presence of five mountain ranges that cut across the land from northwest to southeast. The Cordillera Central is the largest of the ranges running finger-like through the center of the country from the northwestern corner of the Dominican Republic near the Haitian border to the southern coastline. It is in the Cordillera Central that Mount Duarte, the highest mountain peak in the Caribbean, is situated. The remaining mountain ranges, the Cordillera Septentrional, the Sierra Neiba, the Sierra de Baoruco, and the Cordillera Oriental in the eastern end of the island all form rich mountainous valleys that are home to much of Dominican agriculture.[3]

One such region, the Cibão between the Cordillera Central and the Septentrional, is the largest agricultural valley in the country and famous as a center of Dominican tobacco, coffee, rice, banana, and cattle production. The presence of such rich farmland has been a natural magnet for Dominican farmers and ranchers. The second-largest city in the country, Santiago de los Caballeros, is recognized as the home of the Dominican agriculture community and as an important commercial and cultural counterforce to the capital city of Santo Domingo. The "food basket" of the country, as the Cibão is called, has been so successful as a producer of agricultural goods that it has helped the Dominican Republic become a major exporter of staple commodities to the Caribbean and of course to the United States.

Where mountainous beauty and agricultural wealth mix handsomely in the northern and central sections of the Dominican Republic, the country's identity as one of the world's major producers of sugar cane may be found in the eastern end of the island. In towns like La Romana, San Pedro de Marcorís, and Higüey one can find the huge sugar centrals that refine the Dominican Republics primary export commodity. Strangely enough, alongside the sugar fields the eastern section of the Dominican Republic also contains some of the most famous vacation resorts in the Caribbean. Initially developed by the multinational corporation Gulf Western, the world renowned La Romana complex ("Casa de Campo") has helped spur other resorts in this area, and now also along the north coast, in towns like Puerto Plata and Playa Grande. In La Romana one can see the past and the future of the Dominican economy as sugarcane, once the sole generator of foreign exchange, now competes with tourism as the country seeks to change its image and the character of the national economy.

A description of the Dominican Republic would be incomplete without mentioning the large southern region of the country which is the most populous and most diverse. With the nation's capital city of Santo Domingo at its center, the southern region is at once both heavily urban (Santo Domingo's population in 1981 was 1,313,172) and sparsely populated. Where Santo Domingo has become a financial and governmental mecca for the country, the extreme southwestern section of the country, near Lake Enriquillo and the Haitian border, is semi-desert with small villages and little agricultual activity. Not surprisingly, the southwest is the home of some of the poorest Dominicans who eke out an existence growing sugarcane and coffee. The proximity to the Haitian border and the presence of sugar and coffee plantations has made the southwest a key entry point for black migration eastward.

Of particular importance in the southern section of the Dominican Republic is the distinct pull that Santo Domingo exerts over the entire country. At one time Santiago and the Cibão were dominant, not only from an economic standpoint, but also in terms of social status and political power. The large landowenrs from in and around Santiago were the elites the country looked to for leadership, and the political "king makers" who managed national affairs. But just as the mountain ranges seem to point southward and the major rivers empty out into the Caribbean, Dominicans now look to Santo Domingo as the hub of the country. It is the focus of finance, wealth, banking development, and money, as well as being the seat of government. Santo Domingo represents the struggle going on in Dominican society between the old and the new, the developed and the underdeveloped, the dependent and the independent. In Santo Domingo the remnants of Spanish colonial rule sit beside gleaming multinational office buildings; near the Ozama River cardboard shanties compete for space with new government highrises; and along beautiful Avenida George Washington sleek Porches, Volvos, BMWs, and Mercedes-Benz limousines pass by U.S.–owned hotels, reminding Dominicans that their capital city and indeed their country is inextricably tied to the outside world.

In colonial times Santo Domingo was an international outpost as conquerers, traders, missionaries, and soldiers of fortune (Columbus, Pizarro, Cortéz, Ponce de Leon) passed through its stone walls. Today Santo Domingo is host to a different type of foreign visitor as American bankers, Japanese sales personnel, and Venezuelan oil brokers travel through the city negotiating contracts or signing agreements for goods and services vital to the Dominican economy. Santo Domingo, like most Latin American cities, mirrors the extent to which the country at large has become engulfed in the web of international dependency and interdepedency. The daily arrival of consumer products and heavy machinery from abroad; the steady stream of U.S. advisors, consultants, and tourists; the skyrocketing prices for gasoline and cooking oil; and

Table 1.2
Profile of the Dominican People

```
Population - 5,647,977    1981 Census
Population Density - 308 per square mile
Population Projection 1990 - 7,534,000
Percent of Population Urban - 53.5%
Ethnic Composition - 60% mulatto
                      5% white
                     35% black
Official Language - Spanish
Religious Affiliation - 97% Catholic
Per Capita Income, 1985 - $1,809.00
Income Distribution - Top 10% of income earners received 38.5% of
                         National Income
                     Bottom 50% of income earners received 18.5% of
                         National Income
Labor Force - 1.7 million
              47% in agriculture
              23% in industry and commerce
              16% in government
              14% in services
Unemployment - 25%
Underemployment - 25-30%
Literacy Rate - 68%
Life Expectancy - 61.4 years
```
Source: Compiled by the authors.

the increasing presence of small assembly plants owned and operated by foreigners are now commonly accepted reminders of the extent to which Santo Domingo and indeed the Dominican Republic are tied to the international economy and rely on the more advanced nations for aid, investment, and assistance.[4] Much has happened to Santo Domingo since the days of Christopher Columbus, but its status as a city with a pervasive foreign presence has not changed.

BEING DOMINICAN

Being Dominican can be approached in a purely statistical manner. As of 1981 there were 5.6 million residents in the country, up from 4 million in 1970. By 1987 the figure had changed to an estimated 7 million. The population density in 1981 was 116 people per square mile. Urban areas contain 53 percent of the population and the average annual rate of growth of the total population is 2.7 percent. Although these statistics are informative and will be helpful later on when public policy initiatives are discussed, they tell little about the Dominican people in terms of their ancestral roots, the dominant racial strains present in the country today, the extent and influence of internal migration and external immigration, and the way that social status is tied to race and ethnic composition. The answers to these concerns and a more comprehensive definition of being Dominican not surprisingly can be found by examining the colonial history of the country and the pressures and pitfalls created by economic development and decay.

Unlike many Central American and Andean countries, the Dominican Republic has little if any of a surviving native Indian tradition. When Christopher Columbus landed on Hispaniola in 1492, he made contact with an Indian population that the Spanish called Tainos. The Tainos were at first a peaceable people who had developed a fairly prosperous agricultural community on the island. Unlike the cannibalistic Carib Indians on the eastern end of the island, the Tainos initially sought to get along with the Spanish. Unfortunately as was the case elsewhere in the New World, when the colonists met the indigenous population, the result was often death and the disappearance of the Indian culture. As documented by Ian Bell, within 60 years of Spanish colonization of the Dominican Republic the population of the Tainos, which may have been as much as 2 million (but was more likely only several hundred thousand), all but disappeared. Yet despite the eradication of the Tainos through disease and harsh treatment by the Spanish, the Tainos intermarried with their Spanish conquerers and thereby left their mark on Dominican society. As Bell states, "Tainos features can be seen here and there in Dominican faces today. Tainos methods of cultivation are still used in remote areas; . . . and the Taino language lives on in local vocabulary and in countless names of districts, places and rivers all over the country."[5]

The rapid disappearance of the Indian population in the Dominican Republic forced the Spanish administrators to look elsewhere for the slave labor required to maintain the local agriculture. As a result the Spanish relied on the importation of Africans to fill the void. The infusion of black slaves and the resulting intermarriage between the Spanish and the Africans created a population that today is largely mulatto. Recent estimates of the racial composition in the Dominican Republic conclude that 60 percent of the population is mulatto with 35 percent black and 5 percent white. The 60 percent mulatto population interestingly makes the Dominican Republic the only country whose major racial grouping represents a mixture of African and European backgrounds.

But while unique to the Dominican Republic, the mulatto composition has in the view of some analysts created deep-seated psychological and social problems that have effected the national character. Pedro Andrés

Pérez Cabral, in his study *La Comunidad Mulata: El Caso Socio-Politico de la Republica Dominicana*, for example, states that Dominicans have consistently attempted to play down and disguise their mulatto background and in the process have developed an inferiority complex regarding their abilities as a people and a nation. As a result they have often sought to reject their mixed racial heritage and acquire Western or "white" values and customs. In Pérez Cabral's view, it is not surprising that Dominican mulattos have looked to Spain or the United States for leadership and have been ill at ease with their distinct racial heritage. Pérez Cabral's analysis of the mulatto character in the Dominican Republic is not shared by all, but it does point out the possible burdens that racial mixing has had historically on the self image of the nation.[6]

The portion of the Dominican population that is defined as black is largely the result in this century of substantial Haitian immigration to the east and the increasing separation of these people from the mulatto and white population. Although the blacks in the Dominican Republic are still only approximately a third of the total, they are the fastest growing racial category, a development that has caused the majority of Dominican mulattos to worry about the gradual "Haitianization" of their country. Dominicans reject the notion that they are racist when the question of Haitianization is raised, and yet there is no doubt that skin color is a factor in social, economic, and political advancement. Moreover, the extended period of Haitian domination of the Dominican Republic in the early part of the nineteenth century, and the fact that most Dominicans feel that their drive for nationhood was retarded by the Haitians, have caused them to be wary of any "darkening" of their population. There is no doubt that the Dominicans feel superior to their neighbors and fear a decline in their culture should Haitianization progress further.[7]

As to the small white population, these Dominicans are either recent immigrants or the remnants of Spanish settlers who maintained the purity of their ancestry and today occupy prominent positions either as landed aristocrats or important leaders in the financial and commercial sectors of the economy. Despite their small number the white population remains at the top of the social pyramid and is the class that is the envy of mulattos who reside in the middle and lower-middle sectors. Also adding to the strength and vitality of the white population has been the arrival of new immigrants from Europe, the Middle East, and the Orient. The Dominican Republic is no melting pot, but it is possible to see, especially in the cities, Syrian, Turkish, and Lebanese immigrants thriving in small businesses, such as restaurants and clothing stores. Since 1950 a steady stream of Japanese and Chinese have come to the country, with the Japanese taking up farming and the Chinese becoming involved in a number of financial and entertainment enterprises.[8]

Surprising to some is the presence of a Jewish community in the northern coastal town of Sosúa. Welcomed to the country by the dictator Rafael Trujillo in 1940, many of the Jews of Sosúa have largely been assimilated into Dominican society, despite the strong Catholic presence. Others, especially the younger generation, have left the Dominican Republic for the United States or Israel.

The Jewish emigrés, however, are not unique. In 1940, 5000 refugees from the Spanish Civil War came to the Dominican Republic. Six hundred Hungarians from the 1956 uprising were also given entry to the country by Trujillo. Many of these refugees have remained in the Dominican Republic and made significant contributions to the advancement of their adopted homeland.[9]

We need to get beyond these categories, lists, and statistics, however, and try to define the character and personality of the Dominican people. How does this mixture of mulattos, blacks, and whites express itself in everyday life? What can we learn about "Dominicanness" by concentrating our attention on the Dominicans as people? The answer to these questions is of course complicated and often unclear, but there are some consistent behavior patterns that give a clue as to what Dominicans are as a people. To begin, it may be instructive to examine the impressions of Christopher Columbus who in writing back to his benefactor in Spain said, "May your Highness believe that there can in all the world be no better nor gentler people . . . very open hearted people who give what they are asked for with the best will in the world and, when asked, seem to regard themselves as having been greatly honored by the request."[10]

Although Columbus was writing about his encounter with the native Indians, the description of the friendliness and openness of the Dominican people remains valid today. As Trujillo historian Robert Crassweller states, "[The Dominicans] are people of simple sweetness and goodwill, gentle and casually dignified."[11] The perceptions of Columbus and Crassweller can be easily substantiated with a visit to the Dominican Republic. Despite the obvious poverty and the continued economic sacrifices endured by the people, one is amazed at the smiles that greet foreign guests and the genuine willingness to provide assistance to those unfamiliar with the country. What is perhaps most surprising to many visitors from the United States is that Dominicans do not appear to harbor ill feelings for past U.S. transgressions, or openly express their nationalistic fervor in ways that border on anti-Yankee sentiment. To say that Dominicans love the people of the United States would be an exaggeration, but there is in the Dominican Republic an astute recognition among the people that their country has a special relationship with the United States and therefore it is not only prudent to put forward a positive image, but, more importantly, it is good for business and for the country as a whole to tie itself to the United States within limits.[12]

But as with any people who live in an impoverished and dependent environment, the Dominicans have their violent side. For example in 1984, with unemployment at 30 percent, food and gasoline prices sky-rocketing in response to International Monetary Fund guidelines, and government cutbacks in the areas of education and social services. Dominicans took to the streets to protest austerity measures that made their lives unbearable. The street demonstrations were quite violent with scores dead and millions of dollars in damage.[13] Many in the Dominican Republic were saddened by the three days of rampage, not only because of the loss of life and property but also because the violence reminded them of how vulnerable their society and new democracy are to economic and financial dislocation. Many fear such violence could again be repeated.

The juxtaposition of the Dominican people's pleasant demeanor and periodic outbursts of violence accents the tensions and frustrations present in a country that has constantly had to rely on the outside world for its livelihood. Dominicans may be no different than other people who are facing difficult times, but the recent internal instability fueled by a weak economy and foreign debt is troublesome to those who wonder whether in the future the Dominican personality will reveal its dark side with greater frequency. Unfortunately for the Dominicans, the answer to that question is dependent upon the extent to which outside circumstances and conditions—sugar prices on the one hand, oil on the other, for instance—combine again to create a climate of anger and conflict.

SPANISH TRADITIONS—AMERICAN ASPIRATIONS

Defining and describing the elements of a nation's culture are enormous and complex tasks. The ways in which a people express themselves and reveal their identity as a nation are many and cover the full spectrum of endeavors including the more public forms such as art, music, and literature, and other less discernible means of national expression, such as intellectual traditions, social mores, and political values. Where to begin and where to look for a Dominican culture is indeed a problem. Perhaps a walk down Calle Conde in the old city, or a lengthy reading of the Dominican daily newspaper *El Caribe*, or a trip to the *mercado* or the *Museo del Hombre Dominicano* in Santo Domingo are good places to begin. All would undoubtedly provide a snapshot of one facet or another of Dominican culture. But in a study such as this where the accent is on showing the influence of the outside world on the Dominican Republic, the nation's cultural traditions are best examined by narrowing the field of vision and concentrating on the political values, beliefs, and attitudes of the people—in short by examining Dominican political culture.

Because the Dominican Republic is a nation with such profound ties to the outside world and particularly to the United States, it is natural that the manner in which Dominicans view the practice of politics and establish what is acceptable political behavior would reflect the influences of foreign powers who have been involved in Dominican affairs over the years. Moreover, by concentrating attention on political culture and the influence of foreign powers on that culture it will be possible to move closer to an understanding of a unique "Dominicanness." In many respects politics and the values, beliefs, and attitudes that move politics are at the center of national life. Dominicans can take great pride in the fact that their country has been the birthplace of such men of letters as Pedro Henríquez Ureña and Héctor Inchaustegui Cabral, artists such as Paul Guidiccelli and Guillo Pérez, and the violinist Carlos Piantini.[14] But it is the political leaders like Trujillo, Bosch, and Balaguer that pique their interest and arouse their spirit, and it is debates (and sometimes fights) over political philosophy or what to do about the "Colossus of the North" that capture the attention of the public. Therefore by examining Dominican political culture it will not only be possible to explore the fundamental building blocks of this society, but also see the extent to which outside influences have contributed to the nurturance of "Dominicanness."

Dominican political culture can best be examined and understood as a tense competition between a personalistic-familial-authoritarian-caudillistic tradition brought to Hispaniola by the Spanish conquistadores, and an institutional-legalistic-democratic tradition encouraged by a series of United States "civilizers."[15] Modern Dominican history, especially since the turn of the century, is filled with examples of this tension between the two political cultures: dictators replaced by civilian politicians, but only temporarily; political parties vying for the attention and support of the public along with military caudillos, land-owning patrons and local religious leaders; elaborate attempts at rationalizing the decision-making process through constitutions; and civil service laws competing with the influence of family, clan, and personal ties. The characterization of the Dominican Republic as a country with a dual identity is perhaps seen best in this tension between an Hispanic political culture which has had over nearly 500 years to develop and is firmly entrenched in society, and one that is relatively new and offers the people an alternative, democratic way of looking at their relationship to government.

The elements of the Spanish influence on Dominican political culture derive in large part from the centralized and autocratic nature of the colonial experience. The complete and uncontested power of the Spanish monarchy; a political environment in which powerful people were more important than powerful institutions; and the accent on allegiance to God, king, and family taught by the Catholic missionaries, created a view of government as detached from the people, but always willing to take on the duty of benevolent (and sometimes oppressive) caretaker. Even today over 160 years after Madrid abandoned the Dominican Republic as a colonial outpost, it is possible to see the legacy of the Spanish system on the political culture. Dominicans continue to define their politics in personal terms and see individual political leaders as responsible not only for grand accomplishments, such as an era of national prosperity, but also for more mundane successes such as a new road, a sewing machine, or even a 20-peso handout. Periods of history are defined as belonging to Heureaux, Trujillo, or Balaguer and blame for a policy failure is hardly ever put on the legislature, the cabinet, or the opposition party. Success or failure is the possession of the individual leader.[16]

The emphasis on personalismo and caudillismo (men on horseback) in politics has led to periods of strong authoritarian rule in the Dominican Republic, as caudillo figures using the strength of their personality and a willingness to employ force have dominated Dominican politics for most of its modern history. The dictatorial reign of Rafael Trujillo from 1930–1961 is both a classic case of authoritarianism in Latin America and a revealing example of the limits of Dominican toleration for nondemocratic governance. Trujillo was perhaps Latin America's most corrupt and repressive dictator and yet his regime was not without its supporters and even today is viewed by some Dominicans as a time of internal peace (albeit enforced) and significant economic modernization. Despite his cruelty, some Dominicans continue to see in Trujillo a man who could get things done, while maintaining an ordered society. There was with Trujillo a "normalcy" in Dominican society that was comforting and familiar.[17]

Trujillo the personalistic strongman, was also Trujillo the father, brother, uncle, and cousin to hundreds of family members who benefited from the dictator's power. Estimates of Trujillo's wealth vary, but most analysts agree that Trujillo and his family controlled nearly 75 percent of the economic enterprise in the Dominican Republic during their years in power. When Trujillo was assassinated in 1961, Dominican society not only lost a leader who controlled them for over 30 years, but also a tightly knit web of family members who ran sugar centrals, cement companies, banks, auto dealerships, airlines, government bureaucracies, and local police and military garrisons. The Dominican Republic under Trujillo had become a family feifdom.

Although the Trujillo dynasty represents the worst example of family politics, it nevertheless underscores a pattern of government power and policy-making markedly different from that found in the Western tradition. Even today old family names such as Cabral, Bermúdez, Taváres, and Mejía frequently appear in prominent official positions, and those familiar with the processes of Dominican government recognize that public decisions often hinge on what families may be affected by the policy or whether there is a personal grudge that needs to be cleared up. Visitors to the Dominican Republic often marvel at how small the country is in terms of the interconnections that become obvious once business is transacted or political alliances are determined. What these visitors are experiencing is the ongoing operation of personalistic-familial, clan-based politics in a country steeped in the Spanish tradition.

Despite the fact that the Spanish colonial experience continues to exert a profound influence on the Dominican political culture, it no longer is able to completely dominate the manner in which the people choose to view their relationship with government. The efforts by Dominicans to gain their independence first from Spain and then from Haiti were initiated by persons imbued with a vision of a society modeled after the liberal democracies that were developing in Europe and in North America. Independence leaders like Juan Pablo Duarte had read the philosophies of the democratic thinkers on the continent and studied the constitutions of countries that had moved away from government by personal whim. Therefore once the Dominicans gained their independence, political leaders like Duarte set out to transform their country from one based on Spanish authoritarianism to one of Western constitutionalism.[18]

The road to democracy, however, was filled with obstacles and the vision of transforming the Dominican political culture to one that mirrors those found in Europe and the United States became blurred. Civilian political leaders in the Dominican Republic worked valiantly to establish an atmosphere where liberal democracy could flourish, but were constantly forced to function in a political climate in which the old ways seemed impossible to overcome. Dominican politicians appeared unable to develop a political system with a basic consensus about the rules of the game. As a result the country was often torn asunder by competing political groups anxious to gain power. It seemed that without the strong authority figure who could rise above politics the Dominican Republic fell quickly into disarray.

At a number of key junctures in this historical process the United States became deeply involved in the country's internal affairs and sought to advise the Dominicans on the proper way of building democracy. U.S. presidents and emissaries at times drafted constitutions, ran elections, lectured politicians, and educated the populace on the merits of adopting a system of government like that found in the United States. In most instances the United States approached this effort to transform the Dominican political culture with a mixture of missionary zeal, paternalism, and arrogance as it sought to "civilize" a country in which we had important economic and security interests. What it got in return for its efforts was often the formation of a democratic facade with a personalistic-familial-authoritarian substructure. Despite the attempts at building the institutions of democracy and encouraging the acceptance of democratic values and practices, the Dominican Republic remained a country steeped in the Spanish tradition. Constitutional principles were often ignored, elections were never final and often contested, legislatures never really functioned effectively, and the Dominican people and their leaders gave only lukewarm support to these experiments in democracy. After generations of relying on the local patron to make decisions, it was well nigh impossible to expect Dominicans to embrace a system of governance that required individual choice and responsibilities, encouraged competition, and demanded strict adherence to set procedures and legal principles.

Faced with the insecurity and unpredictability presented by liberal democracy, Dominicans on a number of occasions returned to the "normalcy" of authoritarianism. The rise of Trujillo in 1930, the fall of Juan Bosch in 1963, and the 12 years of Balaguer's civilian authoritarianism (1966–1978) are but the most recent examples of democratic weakness in the Dominican Republic. Yet despite the staying power of the authoritarian model, there are increasingly clear signs that the democratic alternative remains alive and that Dominicans are more convinced then ever that their country must move away from a system based on personalism, repression, and centralized control.

To many who study the Dominican Republic, the presidential election of 1978 was a watershed in the development of the democratic tradition. Not only did Antonio Guzmán, a moderate democrat representing a social-democratic party, the Partido Revolucionario Dominicano (PRD), defeat Joaquín Balaguer, but for the first time the Dominican Republic witnessed a peaceful transfer of power from a ruling party to the opposition. Guzmán was able to garner widespread support from urban workers, middle-class professionals, and rural campesinos. Guzmán also received welcome assistance from the administration of President Jimmy Carter who let it be known that the United States would not support a regime that ignored the democratic wishes of the people. With this kind of support, Guzmán took office and began moving the Dominican Republic away from its authoritarian past.[19] Political prisoners were released, the military was professionalized, the legislature became a working body again, the rule of law prevailed, and efforts were made to rationalize administrative decision making. Fortunately, for Dominican democracy, the tragic suicide of Guzmán at the end of his administration did not send the system into collapse, for in 1982 another social democrat, Salvador Jorge Blanco, took office and continued the traditions of liberal democracy despite mounting economic and social problems.

Although this recent "wave" of liberal democracy in the Dominican

Republic is encouraging to those who view the authoritarian model as oppressive and retarding growth, it is much too early to say that the Dominicans have accepted a new political culture and institutionalized the structures and practices of Western style democracy. In a Third World country like the Dominican Republic political culture is easily influenced by economic conditions, and democratic structures and practices can collapse in the wake of intense internal instability. Moreover, because the practitioners of democracy in a country like the Dominican Republic are new at their job and have little in the way of tradition to fall back on, there is no aassurance that such essential elements of democratic government like political parties, interest groups, the media, and popular opinion, will be able to weather the economic and social storms. A continued economic slide and an intensification of social unrest could easily make the authoritarian model look more attractive and its advocates appear to be saviors of the country.

The fact that the democratic political culture in the Dominican Republic can be compromised and that the authoritarian model lurks in the wings has helped give rise to a layered society. While the liberal democratic tradition is more recent and therefore may rest on the surface of politics, it nevertheless disguises the authoritarian values and traditions often lurking below. And because the authoritarian values and traditions have been there longer and are more established, the democratic layer is less secure and more susceptible to be swept away. Today, in the Dominican Republic, democratic politics seem to have gained a strong foothold among the people. There is substantial support for the democratic model from every sector of the country, including even the most conservative elements in Dominican society.

Moreover, the social bases for democracy are stronger: The middle class is larger, there is more affluence, literacy is more widespread, and the per capita income is higher. And yet the hurricane winds of instability and upheaval can build up quickly in this country. Oil prices, debt, inflation, unemployment, austerity, corruption, class tensions, party factionalism, and maladministration can weaken the democratic base and raises the specter of authoritarianism. The possibility of shifting layers of politics—authoritarianism and democracy—is an unavoidable fact of life in the Dominican Republic and one that most likely will recur in the future.

NOTES

1. For a thorough presentation of the relationship between the Dominicans and the Haitians see Rayford Logan, *Haiti and the Dominican Republic* (New York: Oxford University Press, 1968).

2. *Wall Street Journal*, January 7, 1983.

3. The most detailed discussion of the geography and topography of the Dominican Republic can be found in Weil, Thomas, et al., *Area Handbook for the Dominican Republic*, (Washington, D.C.: Government Printing Office, 1973), pp. 9–17.

4. For a recent view of Santo Domingo by a non-Dominican, see Shelby Coffey, "Letter from the Dominican Republic," Washington *Post*, March 30, 1984, p. E1.

5. Ian Bell, *The Dominican Republic* (Boulder, CO.: Westview Press, 1981), p. 17.

6. Pedro Andrés Pérez Cabral, *La comunidad mulata: El caso socio-politico de la Republica Dominicana* (Caracas: Grafica Americana, 1967). See also Franklin J. Franco, *Los negros, los mulatos y la nación dominicana* (Santo Domingo: Ed. Nacional, 1969).

7. See a book review by Pierre L. Hudicourt of Joaquín Balaguer, *La isla reves: Haiti y el destino dominicano*. 2d ed. (Santo Domingo: Libreria Dominicana S.A., 1984) in which he develops many of the themes of Haitianization and severely criticizes Balaguer for intensifying the antagonism between the two peoples. *Caribbean Review*, 14, Fall 1985, p. 21.

8. C. Harvey Gardiner, "The Japanese and the Dominican Republic" *Inter-American Economic Affairs* (Washington, D.C.), Vol. 25, no. 3, Winter 1971, pp. 23–38.

9. See Frances Henry, "Strangers in Paradise—The Jewish Enclave in Sosua" *Caribbean Review*, 14, Fall 1985, pp. 16, 39–40. See also Kai Schoenhals, "An Extraordinary Migration—Jews in the Dominican Republic," *Caribbean Review*, 14, Fall 1985, pp. 17, 41–43.

10. Quoted from Bartolomé de las Casas, *Historia de las Indias*.

11. Robert D. Crassweller, *Trujillo: The Life and Times of a Caribbean Dictator* (New York: Macmillan, 1966), p. 12.

12. Although out of date, the public opinion study of Lloyd Free, *Attitudes, Hopes and Fears of the Dominican People* (Princeton, NJ: Institute for International Social Research, 1965), is still revealing and points up the inner conflict of Dominicans toward the United States.

13. See the Dominican newspaper *El Caribe* for the dates April 23–May 1, 1984.

14. A classic discussion of Dominican culture, particularly from the standpoint of its literature, can be attained by reading Joaquín Balaguer's *Historia de la literatura dominicano* (Ciudad Trujillo: Editorial Libreria Dominicana, 1956).

15. See Howard J. Wiarda, "Democratic Development in the Dominican Republic: A Difficult Legacy," a paper prepared for a conference on "Democracy in Developing Nations," Stanford University and the National Endowment for Democracy, Stanford, CA, December 19–21, 1985, for a discussion of this theme.

16. Howard J. Wiarda and Michael Kryzanek, "Dominican Dictatorship Revisited: The Caudillo Tradition and the Regimes of Trujillo and Balaguer," *Revista/Review Interamericana*, VII no. 3, Fall 1977, pp. 417–35.

17. Howard J. Wiarda and Michael Kryzanek, *The Dominican Republic: A Caribbean Crucible* (Boulder, CO: Westview Press, 1982), pp. 37–38.

18. See Antonio Sánchez Valverde, *Idea del valor de la Isla Española* (Santo

Domingo: Ed. Nacional, 1971), for a more complete discussion of the movement toward democracy in the post-Haitian independence era.

19. Michael Kryzanek, "The 1978 Election in the Dominican Republic: Opposition Politics, Intervention and the Carter Administration," *Caribbean Studies*, 19, nos. 1 and 2, April–July 1979, pp. 51–73.

2

DOMINICAN HISTORY: THE SOURCES OF A DUAL IDENTITY

Describing the impact that external forces have had on the Dominican Republic is in many respects an easy task since evidence of foreign influence and domination is everywhere. What is difficult about this task is trying to organize and present the historical evidence in a manner that goes beyond a mere litany of intervention and dependency to a meaningful analysis of how major powers and institutions shaped the development of this Caribbean nation. At the same time it is important not to lose sight of the fact that there is much in Dominican history that is Dominican and not the direct byproduct of foreign presence or pressure.

The ideal goal in describing Dominican history would be to strike a happy medium and separate those events that are the result of the natural interaction of a people with their environment from those that arise because of the nation's chronic inability to control its own destiny. But even though there is a distinct and autonomus Dominican historical tradition, it is often difficult if not impossible to ignore the shadow of external forces hovering over the nation. As will be shown, the foreign influence on the Dominican Republic is more than just the usual history of military invasions, financial controls, commercial exploitation, diplomatic intimidation, and dependency; it is the pervasive and ongoing realization of the Dominican people that there are few instances in their past in which they "made" or controlled their own history.

SPANISH COLONIZATION: A BRIEF ENCOUNTER WITH GLORY

The recorded history of the Dominican Republic begins with the landing of Columbus and the Santa María on the north coast of present-day Haiti on Christmas Day, 1492. Thinking that they had reached the far east, Columbus' party erected a makeshift fort and began the process of establishing a Spanish presence in the New World. Colonization by the Spanish in this new world would not be easy as the early settlers faced numerous hardships, from disease and devastating hurricanes to uprisings by the Taino Indians who refused to be enslaved by the gold- and land-hungry *conquistadores*. Despite these setbacks, Columbus' discovery fired the imaginations and greed of the Spanish Crown. By the beginning of the sixteenth century, hundreds of fortune hunters, merchants, administrators, and members of religious orders were arriving at the newly established seat of Spanish power, Santo Domingo, the first permanent Spanish settlement in the Americas.[1]

From 1509 until 1524 Santo Domingo, under the governorship of Diego Columbus (Columbus' eldest son), became the capital of the Indies and the most influential outpost in the New World. Spanish troops and traders saw Santo Domingo as a jumping-off point for further exploration in Mexico and Central America, while representatives of the Crown used the outpost not only as a center of colonial administration but as a collection depot for the gold and other riches that were being sent back to Madrid. The importance and prosperity that came to Santo Domingo during the reign of Diego Columbus also helped to initiate a period of construction, as a crude colonial outpost turned into a center of culture. The famous Alcazar (royal palace), which stands today, was built by Diego and the first cathedral in the New World was started during his administration.[2]

The period of glory for Santo Domingo and indeed for the eastern two thirds of Hispaniola was unfortunately quite brief. With Diego's departure in 1524, Santo Domingo went into a decline. The Spanish explorers were more interested in the richer possibilities for gold and silver in Mexico and Peru, and soon there was competition from other colonial powers anxious to cash in on the enormous wealth of the New World. As with most declines, Santo Domingo did not lose power and influence as the result of one event but rather saw its dominant administrative and commercial position gradually give way as first Cuba and then Mexico became the centers of colonial interest. Santo Domingo remained a thriving city of 3500 inhabitants, but in a series of steps beginning in 1526 its administrative authority over the burgeoning Spanish holdings was greatly reduced and its attractiveness as a trading center disappeared as attention shifted to the conquest of the mainland.[3]

After a devastating earthquake in 1562, Santo Domingo became a mere way station in the vast Spanish colonial empire. The notoriety and wealth that had come with being the first settlement in the New World had all but vanished in less than 70 years. The monuments to colonization remained, but the colonists had moved on, leaving behind a land stripped of gold and without the people and resources to begin a new era of colonization. The sad conclusion of this period in Dominican history would unfortunately be repeated in the future. The cycle of avaricious or insecure foreign powers using this land, placing their mark on its development (or, in most cases, its decay), and then turning their attention elsewhere would appear again and again in Hispaniola. From such a promising beginning as the seat of colonial power in the new world, the land that would become the Dominican Republic faced an uncertain future, and worse yet, the inability to exert much influence over that future.

THREE CENTURIES OF DECLINE AND DECAY

According to most historians of the colonial period, the years from Diego Columbus' departure in 1524 to 1795, when Spain ceded all of the island to the French in the Treaty of Basle, were marked by serious depopulation (only 6000 people could be counted on the eastern or Spanish section of the island in 1730), regular attacks by British or French buccaneers anxious to plunder the Spanish settlements or benefit from the lucrative contraband trade, and a general lack of interest on the part of the Madrid government in a colony that had little left to offer but a few cattle ranches and very limited commerce. Without a firm Spanish commitment to protect or develop Hispaniola, the principal outposts of Santo Domingo and Santiago de los Caballeros were either sacked or burned to the ground. In fact, at one point the Spanish, anxious to stop the smuggling on the north coast, relocated the citizens, burned a number of towns, and declared this area off-limits.[4]

The failure or unwillingness of the Spanish to control the attacks by the French and English prompted Spain to cede the western third of the island to France under the terms of the Treaty of Ryswick in 1697. The treaty is significant because it set in place what has become a permanent separation of the island into the French-controlled western section (eventually to become modern day Haiti) and the Spanish-controlled central and eastern sections (eventually to become the modern day Dominican Republic). The separation created by the Treaty of Ryswick, however, also created another type of difference. The French-controlled western third of the island developed quickly into what many considered to be the richest colony in the world at this time. Relying upon over 500,000 slaves imported from Africa, the French led the world in the exportation of sugar, coffee, cocoa, and other agricultural commodities. Eventually the French would reap the sad rewards of their harsh slave policies in the form of a black revolt and the collapse of their richest colony, but for over one hundred years Hispaniola became an island of sharply contrasting economies.[5]

Despite the serious decline that was experienced in Spanish Hispaniola during this period, there were signs of a moderate revival by the mid-eighteenth century. The Spanish government took a greater interest in its long-forgotten colony and began programs to attract new settlers to the island. After enduring well over 50 inept governors since the time of Diego Columbus, Santo Domingo benefited from a Spanish administration that recognized the vast potential of this colony. Also the strength of the neighboring Haitian economy (known then as Saint-Domingue) eventually spilled over to Spanish Hispaniola, especially in the area of beef production. By 1785, the colony's population had risen to nearly 150,000 and the cities, particularly Santiago de los Caballeros, took on a new aura of vitality.

Although it is important to mention this modest revival, one must not lose sight of the fact that as the nineteenth century approached, Spanish Hispaniola remained a colony whose development was seriously retarded and completely overshadowed by the French colony to the west. Moreover, depopulation and the weakness of the economic base curbed any sense of independence and desire for nationhood. Where all around them there were emerging cries of independence and revolution, the inhabitants of Spanish Hispaniola remained wedded to dependence on Spain or whomever replaced Spain as the dominant colonial power.

In 1795 the colonial responsibility for Spanish Hispaniola fell on France, as the war in Europe with Spain gave the French the opportunity to take over the rest of the island. The principal architect of the French takeover of Spanish Hispaniola was a black slave named Pierre Dominique Toussaint L'Ouverture who used his small army to defeat the Spanish forces. The victory of Toussaint and the French not only brought the Spanish colony a new controlling power, but revealed the potential strength of the black slave forces on the island and set the stage for the next era of Dominican history.

THE HAITIAN INVADERS

In chronicling Dominican history, it is extremely difficult to present the evolution of this nation and its people in terms that suggest progress or development. The history of this country is rather a series of debilitating events that stunt growth, occasionally linked by short periods of peace, limited prosperity, and good government. Such is the case in the time period from the Treaty of Basle in 1795 to the final push for independence in 1844. After the brief era of revitalization at the close of the eighteenth century, Spanish Hispaniola again became a pawn in the game of regional geopolitics between the Spanish, French, and English. But the diplomatic and military machinations of the European powers paled in light of the territorial designs of the emerging black leadership in neighboring Saint-Domingue.

After his brilliant defeat of the Spanish forces which brought about complete French control of Hispaniola, Toussaint saw his influence wane as Napoleon and his representatives on the island sought to diminish the black leader's power. Sensing that the French were anxious to neutralize his movement, Toussaint in 1801 sent his army deep into the eastern section of the island and captured Santo Domingo. With victory assured and the Spanish administrative corps on a ship to Cuba, Toussaint returned to Port-au-Prince and declared himself to be the Supreme Head of the Island.

Toussaint's bold invasion of the eastern end of the island awakened the French to the strength of the black forces and brought France and Spain closer as they sought a return to the status quo ante. But while France and Spain planned their retaliation, Toussaint and his slave army turned their attention to the business of managing the affairs of Hispaniola. Contrary to some historical accounts, notably the American diplomat Sumner Welles, who wrote a highly critical version of the Haitian invasion, the administration of Toussaint in the eastern section of the island was quite benevolent if not enlightened.[6] Toussaint worked vigorously to strengthen the languishing economy and to entice Spanish farmers and merchants to return to their enterprises. Although there were instances of repression and ongoing tension between the black conquerors and the white landowners, Toussaint proved himself to be a capable leader.[7]

This brief interlude of rule by Toussaint's army came to an end when, in 1802, Napoleon sent a large military contingent to the island under his brother-in-law General Victor Emmanuel Leclerc. Although Leclerc failed to regain all of Hispaniola, he did drive the black army back to Saint-Domingue, and, more importantly, captured Toussaint. With Toussaint in prison in France, the leadership of the slave army fell to the cruel Jean Jacques Dessalines and to Henri Christophe who divided up the western end of the island. Despite having been defeated by the French forces, the black leaders tried again to take Santo Domingo in 1805, but were driven back by a combined French and local Spanish garrison. But in the meantime a black, independent Haiti had emerged.

From 1805 until 1809 the French under General Louis Ferrand controlled Spanish Hispaniola. But when news of Napoleon's losses in Europe reached the island, the Spanish in and around Santo Domingo rose up to drive the French out. In 1809, with the help of the British, the eastern two thirds of the island again was placed under Spanish rule. Driving the French out of Hispaniola can be looked upon as something of a victory since it returned the eastern section of the island back to its original rulers, but for the next 12 years (until 1821) Spanish Hispaniola entered what most historians refer to as "España Boba" or the era of "foolish Spain."[8] Spanish Hispaniola again suffered from a succession of incompetent governors and a monarchy in Madrid that had little interest in developing this sad colony. In 1821 there was a half-hearted attempt by the colonial treasurer, José Nuñez de Caceres to declare the eastern section of the island independent and to establish some relationship with Simon Bolívar's Gran Colombia, but there is no record of a response from Bolívar or any great mass movement to support the expulsion of the Spanish governor.

Instead of embracing independence and creating a new government, Nuñez de Cáceres and other leaders looked to the government of Haiti for recognition and support. The new ruler of Haiti, General Jean Pierre Boyer, responded to the request by stating, "The whole island should constitute a single republic under the flag of Haiti" and sent his army across the border to again occupy the remainder of Hispaniola. There was at first little resistance to the occupation (in fact Nuñez de Cáceres handed over the keys to Santo Domingo on a silver platter), but soon after the people recognized the Haitians not only as cruel and incompetent administrators but also as completely lacking interest in maintaining the basics of Spanish civilization in their new possession. The white plantation owners faced extermination, the male population was forced into military service, the university and secondary schools were closed, ties to the Catholic Church were broken, and the economy, especially in and around Santo Domingo, was all but destroyed. The barbarity and stupidity of the Haitian occupiers not only wreaked havoc with a colony that could ill afford another round of debilitating foreign control, but ingrained perhaps forever in the collective memory of the Dominicans the horror of black rule. Even today the enmity toward Haiti runs deep in the Dominican Republic and is directly traceable to the 22-year period when the Haitians ravaged the eastern section of Hispaniola. If there was any good that came from this era of Haitian rule, it was the formation for the first time of a Dominican national spirit.[9]

INDEPENDENCE CAUDILLO STYLE

Juan Pablo Duarte is considered by Dominicans to be the father of their country; and the secret organization that he founded called La Trinitaria is permanently enshrined as the driving force behind the expulsion of the Haitians and the establishment of an independent Dominican nation. History records, however, that the struggle to gain independence and create the Dominican Republic was not so much the work of the idealistic Duarte who spent most of his time out of the country and was viewed as a generally ineffectual leader. Rather, the Dominican nation was founded in an almost haphazard way as local caudillos such as Pedro Santana, Buenaventura Báez and José María Imbert battled selfishly for control and showed little if any commitment to the principles of constitutional democracy that so impressed Duarte and his supporters in La Trinitaria.[10]

The beginning of the end of the Haitian occupation occurred when a devastating earthquake hit the island in 1842. The government of Jean Pierre Boyer, never able effectively to administer to the needs of the island, failed miserably to bring relief to the people. Soon after the earthquake, La Trinitaria, which was founded in 1838, began to exert more influence on the direction of politics in Haitian-occupied Hispaniola. On February 28, 1844, after an attack on the Haitian garrison in Santo Domingo was almost botched, a provisional junta made up of Trinitarians declared the colony independent. Duarte, who was in Curaçao at the time, was sent for and arrived on March fourteenth to a triumphant welcome. After years of planning for independence, raising money for arms and trying to rally the spirits of his people, Duarte appeared to be on the verge of national leadership. Unfortunately for Duarte and the Dominican Republic, more aggressive and ruthless leaders were anxious to seize the moment and thrust themselves into power.

One such man was Pedro Santana, a rancher with his own private army from El Seibo. After distinguishing himself in the battles to drive the remaining Haitian forces out of Dominican territory, Santana grew tired of Duarte's idealism and maneuvered to push him out of national leadership and eventually into exile. After accepting the presidency in November of 1844 by bullying a consitutional assembly into accepting his version of executive power, Santana set about achieving his most important objective—negotiating a protectorate arrangement with the French or for that matter any other foreign power that could provide him with an attractive financial package. Although it may seem odd that after over two years of struggle to rid the country of the hated Haitians, Santana would immediately set out to establish a new colonial arrangement, the protectorate idea was not uncommon or unpopular at the time, considering the history of this young nation and its dependence on foreign powers to provide security. What was different about Santana's efforts was that he shrewdly sought out the best deal possible from the major powers and was willing to offer his country and its resources to the highest bidder.[11]

During his first presidency Santana made a number of diplomatic overtures to the French, the English, and the United States. These efforts were partially successful. In 1847 President Buchanan appointed a commercial agent for the Dominican Republic, and in 1849 the French signed a treaty of friendship, while the British agreed to appoint a consul. All three countries were increasingly interested in the Dominican Republic, in particular with the Samana Bay region, the superb natural harbor that President Santana was willing to offer for sale or lease.

The willingness of Santana to establish close relations with major European powers, even if it meant protectorate status or the sale of Dominican patrimony, cannot be easily dismissed, considering the weakness of the country and the continued threat from Haiti. From 1848 through 1855 Haiti, under a hated dictator named Faustin I, repeatedly invaded the Dominican Republic and created enormous destruction and panic in the country. Only through pressure from the British and French and the battlefield heroics of Báez and Santana were the Haitians finally repulsed. The fighting left the country in shambles and created a serious rift between the two caudillos over who was going to lead the nation and continue the efforts of attracting a foreign guardian and financial sponsor.

THE DOMINICAN REPUBLIC—UP FOR SALE

From the time of independence in 1844 to the reign of the dictator Ulises Heureaux in 1882, Dominican politics was largely controlled by two men, Pedro Santana and Buenaventura Báez. Both men entered the presidency of their country in a kind of revolving-door process with one going into exile or returning home while the other managed Dominican affairs. During this period Santana was president for three terms, while Báez occupied national office five times. Neither man could be described as a proponent of liberal democracy; rather government during this period is perhaps best described by Latin American historian Hubert Herring, who called Santana and Báez (along with the more stable dictator, Heureaux) "brazen opportunists, ready to betray their country for their own ends."[12] Although the so-called "dual caudillos" can be credited with fending off the Haitians, they were power-hungry and greedy leaders whose answer to the internal economic woes and foreign threats facing their country was actively to seek protectorate status, annexation, or at the very least some long-term economic relationship with either a European nation or the United States.

It was not long after the Haitians had given up on their quest for reunification that President Santana sought out a protectorate arrangement with the Spanish. In 1859 Santana sent his representatives to Madrid to inquire as to Spanish interest in protectorate status for the Dominican Republic. As described by Ian Bell, Santana sought assurances from Spain that it would "maintain the independence and integrity of the Republic, protect it from external attack, provide money for specified fortifications and officers to train the Dominican army and encourage the immigration of Spanish settlers."[13] To entice the Spanish, Santana pledged not to enter into an alliance with any other nation and to provide its new protector with unnamed concessions, presumably in the areas of trade and resource development.

Although the eagerness to return to colonial status on the part of Santana seemed strange in an era of increasing nationalism, the Dominican Republic was a country with severe financial difficulties (a bankrupt treasury brought on in large part by Báez) and memories of a belligerent neighbor ready to reconquer the eastern section of the island. Under such circumstances, Santana was able to assure the Spanish that there would be little if any opposition to a protectorate. For Spain the opportunity to regain a foothold in its old colonial sphere of influence was enticing, especially since Santana was actively seeking an alliance. With both sides seeing positive results of recolonization, Spain reoccupied the Dominican Republic in March of 1861.

The Spanish remained in the Dominican Republic for over four years and in that time period did little but fuel opposition to the recolonization. The Spanish administration was inept, the economy continued to falter, and there were frequent problems between the white colonists and the darker skinned Dominicans. Furthermore, trade with the United States dropped dramatically (the Spanish occupation coincided with the U.S. Civil War), thereby depriving the Dominican Republic of one of its most lucrative trading partners.

By 1863, the War of Restoration had begun to rid the Dominican Republic of the by now despised Spanish. Rebel units from in and around Santiago were successful in driving out the Spanish forces and gradually controlled most of the north. The Spanish were forced to return to their stronghold in Santo Domingo and seek a diplomatic solution. Seeing that there was little hope of regaining the military initiative, Queen Isabella II broke off the annexation agreement and the Spanish garrison returned to Cuba in July of 1865. As for Santana, he died a year earlier, after resigning his position in what was viewed as a collaborationist government. Disillusioned with Spanish rule and facing a hostile population, there is some evidence that Santana committed suicide.

With the Spanish gone, the Dominican Republic unfortunately entered another cycle of political instability, financial dependency, and continued efforts to establish some type of protectorate arrangement. This time the proponent of foreign intervention was Buenaventura Báez who occupied the presidency three more times from 1865 to 1878. In Báez' fourth term in office from 1868 until 1873 the Dominican dictator worked tirelessly to negotiate a series of loans that would bail out the troubled economy and sought out a new protector for his country—the United States.

Both Presidents Andrew Johnson and Ulysses Grant showed interest in annexing the Dominican Republic, primarily because the Samaná Bay region offered the United States a Caribbean port at a time when this country was beginning to exert more influence in the hemisphere. In 1870, the Dominican people approved the annexation (a phony plebiscite victory of 16,000 to 11 satisfied the Grant administration that there was "democratic" support), but the Senate of the United States refused to ratify the treaty.[14] Anti-annexation senators, such as Charles Sumner of

Massachusetts, led the fight in large part because of questionable land speculators who were vigorously lobbying Congress. Today a statue of Charles Sumner is the only memorial to a U.S. citizen on display in the Dominican Republic.

The failure of annexation, however, did not stop Báez from trying to attract foreign control over Dominican territory. In 1872 he negotiated a 99 year lease with a New York company for Samaná Bay. The plebiscite called to ratify the contract was so obviously rigged that opponents to Báez were successful in driving him out of power and into exile. Báez would return once more to the presidency, but the dream of U.S. annexation or the lease of Samaná Bay had disappeared. The Dominican Republic remained a bankrupt and unstable nation run by dictators, whose ony solution to financial and economic problems was to establish dependent relationships with major powers.

This sad era in Dominican history ends with the rise of the dictator Ulises Heureaux in 1882. Although there is some evidence that early on in his reign Heureaux sought to modernize the Dominican Republic by developing the nation's first telegraph system, building railroads, and strengthening the agricultural sector, there is even greater evidence of cruel repression, extravagance, and a continuation of foolish financial dealings with foreign banks. As one of the present authors earlier wrote of Heureaux, "he bought up many of his rivals and subjected most of the rest to vilification, exile or murder; employed an army of spies (including his former mistresses); sent assassins abroad; and enriched himself, his friends and his relatives at the expense of the nation."[15]

Despite Heureax's control over internal politics, his downfall came as a result of his involvement with Holland and the United States. In order to acquire more cash for the Dominican Treasury (and for himself), huge loans were signed with a Dutch bank and the lease of Samaná Bay was finally achieved. The Samaná agreement, which included preferential treatment for United States trade with the Dominican Republic, raised extensive criticism in Europe and eventually forced the abrogation of the lease arrangement. But Heaureaux needed money; and when his ties to the Dutch and other European banking houses collapsed, United States creditors gained increased influence in Dominican financial affairs. By the late 1890s, the Dominican Republic under Heureaux was bankrupt again and in debt to a number of European and U.S. creditors. The situation got so bad that Heureaux was forced to print worthless paper money, a decision that created even more serious problems for the ravished Dominican economy.[16]

Not surprisingly, such desperate circumstances fostered opposition. At least five revolts and coup attempts were planned and executed against Heureaux. The last, led by a group from the Cibão headed by Ramon Cáceres, was successful. In July of 1899 Heureaux was assassinated by Cáceres as he visited the Cibão region. With Heureaux dead, the familiar story of instability and bankruptcy continued in the Dominican Republic. It was into this political and international mess that the United States entered Dominican politics and, as we shall see, never really left.

U.S. DEBT COLLECTORS AND CIVILIZERS

The financial chaos and political turmoil that engulfed the Dominican Republic following the assassination of Heureaux coincided with a period in which the United States under President Theodore Roosevelt began exerting greater influence over the Caribbean region. As the basis for Roosevelt's desire to control events in our geographic backyard the U.S. president delivered a message to Congress on December 6, 1904, that alerted the neighboring Caribbean nations to the manner in which this country intended to respond to unrest and indebtedness. The so-called Roosevelt Corollary to the Monroe Doctrine committed the United States to the role of international policeman and warned nations that strayed from acceptable behavior that this country was ready to intervene in order to set things straight. As President Roosevelt said in his address,

Chronic wrongdoing or an impotence which results in a general loosening of the ties of civilized society may in America, as elsewhere, ultimately require the intervention by some civilized nation, and in the Western Hemisphere the adherence of the United States to the Monroe Doctrine may force the United States, however reluctantly . . . to the exercise of an international police power.[17]

With the United States now willing to intervene in the internal affairs of the region, it was not long before the Dominican Republic was touched by the Big Stick. In March 1905, Dominican President Carlos Morales signed an agreement with the United States in which this country agreed to become the collector of customs of the Dominican Republic. The receivership arrangement stipulated that 45 percent of the revenue collected was to return to the Dominican government, while the remaining 55 percent was to be used to repay the long line of European creditors. Since foreign-generated indebtedness had risen to $40 million and there were some signs that angry creditors might convince their governments to take aggressive action to make the Dominicans pay up, both the Morales regime and the Roosevelt administration felt it was not only financially sound but strategically prudent to sign a receivership agreement. After two years of the receivership the foreign debt had dropped dramatically and, as a result, the agreement was established in the form of a treaty in 1907. Unfortunately from the Dominican perspective, the treaty went beyond creating a more permanent receivership arrangement, since the United States demanded that any decision by the local government concerning the expansion of the debt would require U.S. approval.[18]

Although the Dominicans were disgruntled with the controls demanded by the United States, the positive results that were achieved in lessening the debt burden contributed to a brief period of political stability and social progress in the country. Thanks in large part to the enlightened rule of President Ramón Cáceres who occupied national office from 1908 to 1911, the Dominican Republic benefited from their leader's desire to accent reform and modernization, rather than use government for personal enrichment. But as the assassin of Heureaux and a man who presided over a country still torn asunder by competing power groups, Cáceres himself was killed in November of 1911, thus ending one of the more tranquil (however brief) eras of Dominican politics.

Sadly for the Dominican Republic, the familiar cycle of instability, violence, and indebtedness started up again with a vengeance. Few Dominicans were able to hold office for very long and the Dominican financial condition worsened considerably. While the Dominican Republic slid toward political and economic collapse, both the Taft and Wilson administrations were watching closely and becoming increasing concerned over the internal turmoil in a nation where the United States had considerable interests. As early as 1912, President Taft's Secretary of State Philander Knox thought that the answer was some form of intervention:

Only complete control by our government would permanently insure order and justice but any degree of control would be beneficial; indeed without our effective control, one administration here would be as good as another.[19]

But where the Taft administration was reluctant to employ U.S. force to bring order in the Dominican Republic, the Wilson administration did not harbor such restraint. In November of 1915, Wilson's minister to the Dominican Republic, James Mark Sullivan, handed Dominican President Juan Isidro Jiménes a series of demands that virtually turned the country into a U.S. protectorate. Jiménes balked at the proposal, which would have taken all fiscal authority away from the Dominican government, and resigned from the presidency. With the Dominican Republic leaderless and the Wilson administration convinced that only the United States could restore order, the U.S.S. *Dolphin* under the command of Rear Admiral William Caperton sailed from Haiti and with an initial contingent of 700 marines occupied the Dominican Republic. Upon landing, Admiral Caperton announced that:

It is not the intention of the United States government to acquire by conquest any territory in the Dominican Republic nor to attack its sovereignty, but our troops will remain here until all revolutionary movements have been stamped out and until such reforms as are deemed necessary to insure the future welfare of the country have been initiated and are in effective operation.[20]

The U.S. remained in the Dominican Republic for eight years, from 1916 until 1924. Although the United States encouraged a new provisional government at the outset of its occupation, the Dominican president, Francisco Henríquez y Carvajal, refused to cooperate with the U.S. personnel and left office. Therefore from November of 1916 to 1922 the United States administered the country by martial law. Much has been made of the occupation of the Dominican Republic in terms of the reforms and modernization programs introduced by the United States. Indeed there were a number of reforms made in taxation, property rights, and fiscal policy, and the country did benefit from the building of new roads, schools, and sanitation facilities (as well as the introduction of baseball!). But as historian Bruce Calder points out, many of these reforms were short-lived, relied primarily on Dominican financing, and were not well received by the local population.[21]

Very early on in the occupation the spirit of Dominican nationalism that had been dormant for so long began to develop. Rebel groups in the eastern sugar-producing regions began to challenge the marine units with effective hit-and-run tactics. In response to the armed resistance, marine units engaged in a number of instances of torture, rape, and murder. The fact that a disproportionate number of the marine officers were from the South and were charged with controlling a peasant resistance that was largely black and mulatto did little to lessen the tensions or stop the atrocities.

With the change of administration in Washington in 1921 and an increasingly hostile situation in the Dominican Republic, President Harding let it be known that the United States wanted to remove itself as an occupying force. Secretary of State Charles Evans Hughes worked with Dominican representatives to develop an agreement that would allow the United States to leave, but which maintained U.S. involvement in the financial affairs of the country. The resulting Hughes-Peynado plan accomplished those objectives and led the way or the formation of a provisional government headed by the Dominican sugar king Juan Batista Vicini in 1922. Elections were held two years later and a duly elected Dominican president, Horacio Vásquez, took power as the U.S. military quietly left the country.

The eight-year occupation of the Dominican Republic by the United States was a prime example of the approach this country took during this era toward instability and insolvency in the Caribbean. With a mixture of brute force, benevolent reform, and efficient administration, the United States occupiers sought to create a system of governance and an economic climate that the Dominicans seemed unable or unwilling to produce for themselves. This was the height of arrogance and paternalism on our part, but political leaders at the time continually pointed to the evidence of "progress" in the Dominican Republic. Bruce Calder in his exhaustive study of the occupation does not see it that way. He calls the occupation "neither wise nor just" and describes our policies as "basically unproductive."[22] What Calder saw in the intervention is a powerful nation thinking that its presence in a country would make a permanent difference. In reality what occurred in the eight years of the U.S. occupation was that the military rulers and the marines merely suppressed traditional Dominican politics and intensified nationalistic feelings among a people who had been historically complacent about matters of independence and local control. The reforms and modernization were good in themselves, but the real task of creating a nation of people that agreed on the rules of governance was largely ignored.

One lasting contribution, however, of the U.S. occupation was the creation of a national constabulary that was viewed as a means of maintaining order after the marines left. It was from this marine-trained National Guard that the Dominican Republic would see the rise of their next leader, Rafael Trujillo, who in his own repressive and avaricious way did succeed in creating a nation and establishing a common set of governing rules. Unfortunately the nation became the personal estate of Trujillo and the rules of governance were steeped in the traditions of personalism and authoritarianism. In a real sense the Trujillo dynasty is the lasting legacy of the U.S. occupation of 1916–1924.

NOTES

1. Ian Bell, in his book, *The Dominican Republic* (Boulder, CO: Westview Press, 1981), pp. 11–14, provides an excellent description of the first years of colonization.

2. The most authoritative text on this period is Frank Moya Pons, *Historia colonial de Santo Domingo* (Santiago: Universidad Católica Madre y Maestra, 1974).

3. See Troy S. Floyd, *The Columbus Dynasty in the Caribbean, 1492–1526* (Alburquerque: University of New Mexico Press, 1973).

4. Seldon Rodman, *Quisqueya: A History of the Dominican Republic* (Seattle, WA: University of Washington Press, 1964), pp. 20–22.

5. One of the few scholarly accounts of this period is Emilio Cordero Michel, *La Revolucion haitiana y Santo Domingo* (Santo Domingo: Editora Nacional, 1968).

6. Sumner Welles, *Naboth's Vineyard: The Dominican Republic, 1844–1924* (New York: Payson and Clarke, 1928).

7. Seldon Rodman, op. cit., pp. 38–39.

8. See Hugo Tolentino Dipp, "Raza y historia en Santo Domingo," Vol. 1:

Los origenes del prejuicio racial en America (Santo Domingo: Editora de la Universidad Autonoma de Santo Domingo, 1974).

9. A critical evaluation of the early founders of Dominican democracy can be found in Juan Isidro Jiménes Grullon, *El mito de los padres de la patria* (Santo Domingo: Editora Cultural Dominicana, 1971). See also Ian Bell, op. cit., pp. 35–45 for a good English language interpretation of the early movement for democracy in the Dominican Republic.

10. See Hugo Tolentino Dipp, *La traición de Pedro Santana* (Santo Domingo: Impresos Brenty, 1968).

11. Samuel Bailey, *A Diplomatic History of the United States* (New York: Appleton-Century-Crofts, 1964), pp. 382–83.

12. Hubert Herring, *A History of Latin America* (New York: Alfred Knopf, 1957), pp. 425–26.

13. Ian Bell, op. cit., p. 47.

14. Charles Tansill, *The United States and Santo Domingo 1798–1873. A Chapter in Caribbean Diplomacy* (Baltimore: Johns Hopkins Press, 1938).

15. Howard Wiarda, *The Dominican Republic: Nation in Transition* (New York: Praeger, 1968), p. 30.

16. Helen Tilles Ortiz, "The Era de Lilis: Economic Development in the Dominican Republic, 1880 to 1899," Ph.D. dissertation, Georgetown University, 1975.

17. Congressional Record, 58th Cong., 3d sess., p. 19.

18. For a Dominican perspective on this period, see Antonio de la Rosa, *Las finanzas de Santo domingo y el control americano* (Santo Domingo: Editora Nacional, 1969). See also Fred J. Rippy, "The Initiation of the Customs Receivership in the Dominican Republic," *Hispanic American Historical Review* 17, November 1937, pp. 419–57.

19. U.S. State Department, *Papers Relating to the Foreign Relations of the United States*, 1916, pp. 220–29.

20. The definitive study of the American intervention in the Dominican Republic can be found in Bruce J. Calder, *The Impact of Intervention: The Dominican Republic During the U.S. Occupation of 1916–1924* (Austin: University of Texas Press, 1984). For the Dominican perspective on this era, see Max Henríquez Ureña, *Los yanquis en Santo Domingo* (Madrid, 1929).

21. Bruce J. Calder, op. cit., pp. 242–46.

22. Calder, op. cit., p. 252.

3

THE CONTEMPORARY SCENE: TRUJILLO, REVOLUTION, AND THE STRUGGLE FOR DEMOCRACY

Rafael Leonidas Trujillo Molina is one of those leaders who seems to so dominate a nation's history that he forces the people under his rule and those who follow to be continuously preoccupied with the causes of his dictatorship and with the socio-political environment that brought him to power. There is no question that during his 31 years as the leader of the Dominican Republic Trujillo turned his country into what one of the present authors earlier called, "probably the strongest and most absolute dictatorship ever established in Latin America, and perhaps also the most personal dictatorship on either side of the Iron Curtain."[1] Although cruelty and corruption will forever remain the trademarks of his regime, it is important not to lose sight of the fact that Trujillo followed in the footsteps of a long line of Dominican dictators and conducted the affairs of state in a manner that was quite familiar, if not traditional. In 1930 when Trujillo came to power, the earlier brief experiments in democracy had failed to unify the people or to bring the country to a sound financial footing. With little in the way of a democratic model to follow, but generations of authoritarian rule, it was thus natural that someone with the means of maintaining control would eventually assume supreme power in the mold of Heureaux, Báez, and Santana.

Yet despite the historical groundwork that had been laid in preparation for the Trujillo regime, the new Dominican dictator cannot simply be characterized as just another caudillo controlling the reins of power for his own benefit. Rafael Trujillo was clearly a dictator with a grander vision of himself and a shrewd ability to manipulate both the internal political scene and the Washington connection. Trujillo's willingness to employ the armed forces and the secret police to silence his enemies, his formation of political and social organizations to improve the image of the regime and spread its power, and the near complete control that he exerted over the bureaucracy and other key institutions in the country (such as labor unions, economic enterprises, and the media) created a governing regime that can best be described as totalitarian.[2] There was little in the Dominican Republic that was not in some way connected to

Trujillo or his family. Moreover, *El Benefactor* (one of a long list of titles that Trujillo used) made sure the Dominican people understood that their lives had been made better through his personal intercession. It is safe to conclude that the Dominican Republic under Trujillo was not so much a sovereign nation as a vast and lucrative business empire with the Dominican people as employees and a governing structure that existed to control rather than to serve.

Although by the time of his assassination, in May of 1961, Trujillo had earned a reputation as the epitome of the ruthless Latin American dictator, there were clear signs during his rise to power in the early 1930s that this onetime telegraph operator and sugar plantation policeman possessed the organizational skills, the financial prowess, and the willingness to utilize force essential to control the reins of national power and amass a huge personal fortune. In the years following the withdrawal of U.S. military forces Trujillo rose quickly through the ranks of the national police force. By 1928 he was a brigadier general and chief of staff in the National Army.[3] From this powerful position Trujillo planned his takeover of the presidency from the incumbent chief executive Horacio Vásquez. Aided by a rebellion by Vásquez' enemies and a U.S. State Department that seemed unwilling to support the Dominican president in the face of another crisis, Trujillo engineered the resignation of Vásquez, forced his way onto the ballot, and won the election with a vote total that exceeded the number of eligible voters. Those who questioned Trujillo's methods or the election outcome became the first victims of the new dictator's repression.

Trujillo's capture of the presidency was quickly overshadowed by a massive hurricane that struck Hispaniola in September of 1930. With thousands dead or injured and the country in total disarray, Trujillo used this tragic event to strengthen his hold on government and to begin to lay the groundwork for his almost complete control of the Dominican economy. Emergency assistance from abroad was often misused, the government (Trujillo) bought up sizable tracts of property from landowners impoverished by the destruction, and constitutional guarantees were eliminated by a regime claiming the need for strong centralized rule. In a matter of months Trujillo had transformed the Dominican Republic and clearly established himself as a leader who would not be easily intimidated by his political opponents.

Although the hurricane had allowed Trujillo to tighten his grip on Dominican society, the devastation forced the dictator to face familiar problems—an empty treasury and foreign indebtedness. It was in this post-hurricane period that the Dominican people began to realize that Trujillo was more than just a petty caudillo and that his objectives were more complex than merely holding power. In the face of severe economic problems, Trujillo introduced a series of what today would be described as austerity policies. Budget cuts, (except in the military), import and manufacturing taxes, renegotiations of outstanding foreign debts, and sometimes heavy-handed government efforts to ensure productivity became commonplace during the 1930s and 1940s. The revenue that was saved from these belt-tightening measures was used by Trujillo to finance the growth of a new agro-industrial sector in sugar, coffee, cocoa, and tobacco, and in the development of numerous service-related enterprises, from airlines to the production of *El Presidente* beer. In most cases, these new industrial and service enterprises remained in the hands of Trujillo or one of his relatives.[4]

With the onset of World War II and the free world in need of staple commodities, the Dominican Republic evolved into a major exporter of agricultural goods and Trujillo, who controlled most of the sugar, cocoa, and tobacco production, became an enormously wealthy individual. Providing the advanced industrial countries, in particular the United States, with agricultural products had been an integral part of the Dominican economic picture, but Trujillo enlarged the export trade and relied more heavily on U.S. demand for Dominican goods. During the Trujillo era the Dominican Republic became the second-largest exporter of sugar (after Cuba) to the United States, producing nearly 1 million tons per year for export during the 1950s.

The U.S.–Dominican sugar connection was a mixed blessing for Trujillo. On the one hand, the sugar trade and the money it generated allowed the dictator to continue expanding his grip on the national economy and to engage in a public works program that brought the country some needed infrastructure projects along with a number of monuments to the megalomania of *El Benefactor*. But there was a price to pay for this dependency in that Trujillo had to sustain a public relations campaign in Washington to maintain the quota and goodwill with legislators and bureaucrats closely connected to sugar policy. There is ample evidence substantiating Trujillo's willingness to utilize unethical and illegal tactics (bribes and payoffs of U.S. officials) in order to ensure a favorable decision on the yearly sugar quota and to improve the image of his regime in Washington.[5]

Besides the sugar connection to the United States, Trujillo ingratiated himself with Washington policymakers in the 1950s by becoming the hemisphere's chief mainstay (self-appointed) against communist aggression. In the years following World War II and into the Eisenhower administration the United States and the Dominican Republic negotiated a number of military agreements that allowed Trujillo to boast about his close ties with Washington and his importance as a bulwark against communism. In particular the Mutual Security Act of 1951 allowed the Trujillo regime to make purchases of U.S. weapons and equipment. As Atkins and Wilson show in their study of U.S.–Dominican relations during this period, the Trujillo regime received over $6 million in military deliveries from 1952 through 1961. Although the amount was small in terms of what other nations in the hemisphere received under the Mutual Security Act, the effect of the assistance was that Trujillo became a valuable friend of the United States and a necessary part of its plan to stop the spread of communism.[6]

By the late 1950s Trujillo's hold on Dominican politics was beginning to wear thin. Grandiose projects that drained the treasury like the failed International Fair of Peace and Brotherhood, bold efforts to silence his opponents such as the abduction and murder of Jesús María de Galíndez off the streets of New York, an attempt to blow up a car carrying President Rómulo Bentancourts of Venezuela, and increasing criticism from Washington over his repressive tactics and the obvious corrupt nature of his regime created a climate of opposition.[7] Coup attempts, vigorous Church condemnation, and most important of all sanctions from the Eisenhower administration and the Organization of American States revealed the unpopularity of the Trujillo regime. What was especially damaging to Trujillo was the decision by the United States to place an excise tax on the Dominican sugar quota which cost the dictator 30 million dollars in badly needed revenue. The sugar tax plus the cold shoulder from the Eisenhower administration and the Latin American community of nations severely weakened his legitimacy and cast him in the role of a Caribbean outlaw who must be brought to justice or removed.[8]

With opposition growing within the Dominican Republic and Washington anxious to separate itself from the worst of Latin America's dictators, Trujillo's days as the complete leader of his country were numbered. On the night of May 30, 1961, driving home to his mistress in San Cristóbal, Trujillo's car was run off the road by seven men who shot and killed the dictator, dumped his body in the trunk of the car, and drove off. The assassins, a mixture of disgruntled military officers and businessmen, were apparently convinced that Trujillo's recent mismanagement of the financial affairs of the nation and the foreign intrigues that isolated the country justified their action.

There is also some evidence and endless rumor that the Central Intelligence Agency supplied the weapons used by the assassins as a means of encouraging the removal of the Dominican dictator. Although no direct link to the United States has been established in the death of Trujillo, it was no secret in 1961 that the Kennedy administration wanted a change of leadership in the Dominican Republic. The United States feared that Trujillo had become another Batista who might well pave the way for another Fidel Castro.[9]

Assessing the impact of Rafael Trujillo and his regime on the Dominican Republic often centers on the level of control that the dictator exerted on all aspects of national life. The enormous wealth garnered from an endless list of economic enterprises, the formation of a rather bizarre cult of personality, the intimidation of important social groups, and the enormous power of life and death over those who challenged his authority have helped to create a certain mystique about the Dominican dictator. Even today, Trujillo, despite his excesses, remains a larger-than-life figure in the Dominican Republic. Dominicans and foreigners alike continue to report on the "superlatives" of his reign, whether it is the 25,000 Haitians who were massacared in the 1930s on Trujillo's direct order, or the fact that in the 1950s he was viewed as one of the three or four richest men in the world, or that he controlled well over 50 percent of the economic activity in the Dominican Republic. Although it is difficult not to ignore the excesses of Trujillo, it is more important to talk in terms of his legacy. As Robert Crassweller states, Trujillo's major offense is his "sin against the future." In Crassweller's view, "Few men have had so splendid an opportunity to lead their people toward a new social order, . . . But Trujillo's character and the nature of the society he headed were such that he could hardly have been expected to lead the Dominican Republic to a secure and functioning democracy within his lifetime."[10] Rafael Trujillo had brought the Dominican Republic the political stability and a level of economic order that had been missing throughout its history, but sadly the Dominican dictator also created a state system and a style of personal rule that was so complete and dependent on his presence that when he was assassinated the nation was left not only without a leader, but without an alternative method of governance. A return to democracy was definitely not on the minds of many Dominicans in the days following the death of their dictator. Unfortunately for the Dominicans, 30 years of Trujillism had all but destroyed the democratic foundation and left them novices at creating a political system that catered to the wishes of the people.

TRANSITION TO DEMOCRACY

The death of Rafael Trujillo did not immediately open up the floodgates of democracy in the Dominican Republic. Trujillo may have been murdered, but Trujilloism remained in place as the dictator's son Ramfis, members of the extended family, and the last of El Benefactor's puppet presidents, Joaquín Balaguer, attempted to maintain order and stave off the forces of democratic change. Feeling pressure from the United States, both in terms of sugar quota cutbacks and public criticism, Ramfis sought to change the image of Trujilloism by instituting a series of cosmetic reforms. The so-called "democratization" efforts of Ramfis served only to heighten public opposition to the old regime and angered Trujillo's brothers, Héctor and Arismendi, who returned from exile in Bermuda to replace the dictator's son as the head of the country. Where Ramfis sought to put a more acceptable face on the Trujillo regime, the Trujillo brothers were only interested in returning to the days of complete control. But within weeks of their return to the Dominican Republic, Héctor and Arismendi faced increased public pressure from the business community and from the United States in the shape of the Atlantic fleet anchored offshore to remind them that the Kennedy administration was no friend. With this kind of opposition mounting daily, the Trujillo brothers left the country for good on November 20, 1961.

The departure of the Trujillos set off wild celebrations and massive takeovers of the dictator's property. President Balaguer, who remained in office, tried to control events by presenting himself as a friend of the people and a willing participant in the process of expropriating Trujillo's massive holdings. To his credit, Balaguer was able to survive the dismantling of the Trujillo regime and eventually headed a new seven-man Council of State that was formed to help the country move toward elections and a democratic form of government. Although the Council of State faced a brief 48-hour coup attempt by members of the old-line Trujillo armed forces, it did continue in place (reconstituted, however, without Balaguer who went into exile in New York City) until the inauguration of the country's first elected president in February of 1963.

The task of the Council of State and indeed the entire Dominican nation in moving toward democracy was enormous. Not only was the governing apparatus in disarray, but the economy was in shambles due to international sanctions that those opposed to Trujillo had imposed. Fortunately for members of the Council of State the United States poured in millions of dollars in aid and technical assistance to help smooth the way for democracy and to rebuild the economy. During this period it was estimated that the Dominican Republic received more per capita aid from the United States than any other Latin American country. Yet despite the considerable assistance from the United States and a good faith effort to lay the groundwork for democracy, the Council faced considerable criticism from those primarily on the newly emerging left who felt that the business-dominated governing body was not ridding the country of Trujillo-era bureaucrats and was insensitive to the needs for agrarian reform, greater income equality, and social welfare programs.[11]

The return of vigorous political debate in the Dominican Republic over the policy priorities of the Council of State signalled the extent to which the country had changed in a brief period of time. With exiles free to return home, political parties forming anew, and election fever gripping a country that had not seen an honest election since the days of Horacio Vásquez, the Dominican Republic was alive with the spirit of democracy. A beneficiary of this new spirit was the Partido Revolucionario Dominicano (PRD) and its charismatic leader Juan Bosch. Bosch and the PRD represented the newly enfranchised middle and lower classes in the Dominican Republic who did not benefit from Trujillo's industrialization programs and in fact had retrogressed in the 30 years of his rule. With the first opportunity in over a generation for open and free elections, Bosch and the PRD worked tirelessly to convince the Dominican people that it was possible to bring about social reform through the democratic process.[12] In light of the fact that in nearby Cuba, Fidel Castro was proclaiming the wonders of revolutionary communism as the surest road to change, the promise of liberal democracy espoused by Bosch brought world attention to the presidential elections of December 20, 1962.

In that election Bosch defeated the candidate of the business and professional class, Viriato Fiallo, by a two-to-one margin while candidates of the PRD captured both houses of the Dominican Congress by substantial majorities. The stunning victory of Juan Bosch and the reform-minded PRD set the Dominican Republic on a course that had never really been travelled before. Bosch was determined to govern as a voice of the masses and as a champion of personal liberty. As the new Dominican president said in his inaugural address,

Let us join our hearts together in the task of building institutions that will give shelter to those who never had it, that will give work to those who seek without having found it, that will give land to those farmers who need it, and security not only to those born here but to all those who wander the earth in search of refuge from misery and persecution. . . . While we govern, liberty will not perish in the Dominican Republic.[13]

The lofty dreams expressed by President Juan Bosch in his inaugural address would never reach fulfillment, as a military coup stripped the reform leader of his position after only seven months in office. The action taken by a conservative group of Dominican military officers led by Colonel Elías Wessin y Wessin reflected the mood of important business, church, professional, and landed elites who worried over Bosch's alleged courting of the communist left and his zealous (often stubborn) efforts to turn government away from past practice. Bosch, unfortunately, was his own worst enemy and did little to assuage the fears of his powerful opposition. In the name of independence, he alienated the Catholic church hierarchy by refusing to recognize Catholicism as the official state religion; to achieve his agrarian reforms objectives he mobilized the peasants and created the impression that he was forming a *campesino* militia like that found in Cuba; and, perhaps most significant of all, he refused to work closely with the U.S. Embassy and disillusioned the very people whom he would need to promote his reform program and help him to remain in power. U.S. Ambassador to the Dominican Republic during the Bosch era, John Bartlow Martin, in his book *Overtaken by Events*, criticizes Bosch's failure to work within the guidelines of the Alliance for Progress and for his romantic and ineffective approach to leadership. To Martin the Dominican experiment in democracy suffered because of Bosch's "vanity, pride, posturing, rigidity, hopelessly grandiose dreams, volatility and instability and an almost childlike refusal to assume responsibility."[14]

The seven-month presidency of Juan Bosch is often looked upon as a lost opportunity for democratic reformers in the Dominican Republic. But more importantly this experiment in democracy came at a time in which Dominicans had barely emerged from what is now viewed as Latin America's most complete dictatorship. After the death of Trujillo the Dominican Republic rushed full speed ahead toward Western-style democracy without the complete support of key social elites who had prospered under the old regime. The push for democracy and reform that Bosch and the PRD represented is a quite natural outgrowth of years of autocratic rule and the Alliance for Progress atmosphere created by the United States. But what was lost amid all the euphoria of campaigns, elections, and constitutionalism was the recognition that democracy requires more than the outward displays of participation and goodwill. Democracy had been placed atop a social, economic, and political system that was not prepared for aggressive social change, alliances with known leftists, criticism of traditional institutions, and a president whose skills at dealing with the opposition and the United States left much to be desired. The coup of September 1963 should have surprised no one—nor, for that matter, the uprising that would come two years later to restore democracy and Juan Bosch.

THE 1965 REVOLUTION

Juan Bosch was replaced as president by a triumvirate dominated by men from the National Civic Union (UCN), which had lost the 1962 election to the PRD. The triumvirate presided over a nation that was slowly coming apart. The military was clearly the power behind the throne and used its newly restored power to engage in a period of corruption and repression reminiscent of the Trujillo era. As one of the present volume's coauthors wrote at the time, "The society disintegrated to the point where a complete breakdown seemed imminent; the Dominican Republic's political system came to resemble not a single unified nation but a pattern of hateful, warring factions."[15] The chaos that gripped the Dominican Republic forced the members of the triumvirate to name a new president who would better be able to disentangle himself from the military and bring the country together. The man chosen for this difficult task was Donald Reid Cabral, an original member of the seven-man Council of State that ran the country after the assassination of Trujillo.

Although most observers of this period in Dominican history see Reid Cabral as another in the line of puppet presidents who were required to do the bidding of the military, there is evidence that this appointed president did attempt to reorganize the faltering economy, begin some limited land reform, and allow political parties to function openly in the country. One must be very careful, though, about casting Reid Cabral in too positive a light since much of the reform was cosmetic, the austerity programs devastated the urban and rural poor, and the efforts to restore democracy were viewed by opposition politicians as merely means to legitimize his own political aspirations. The Dominican Republic during the rule of Reid Cabral remained a country deeply split between the old regime and the democrats, or as they would come to be called the "constitutionalists."

In the spring of 1965 the Dominican Republic was a nation of conspiracies. A full range of anti–Reid Cabral plotters was working behind the scenes in an attempt to rid their country of a government that seemed to have alienated every group or political persuasion. The U.S. Embassy was also maneuvering, hoping to keep Reid Cabral in power. The best organized of the plotters were those within the Partido Revolucionario Dominicano (PRD), who, along with support from some Christian Democrats, middle-class professionals, and disgruntled military officers, were determined to bring back deposed president Juan Bosch and with him Dominican democracy. On April 25, 1965 Reid Cabral's efforts to head-off a pro-Bosch conspiracy set in motion a series of events that would have a profound effect on the future of the Dominican Republic and on the relationship that the country had developed with the United States.

With support from some key military officers, the Boschists captured the presidential palace, placed Reid Cabral under house arrest, and announced that a constitutionalist regime had been reestablished. Pro-Bosch radio announcements sent Dominicans into the street in support of the coup and for a return of their democratic president. The brief period of excitement created by the declaration of a new government was broken as the anti-Bosch loyalists, with at least tacit support from the U.S. Embassy, strafed the National Palace and began preparations to send military units into Santo Domingo to drive the Boschists, or "constitutionalists," out. Tensions escalated quickly as the constitutionalist forces began distributing arms to the populace and ordered them to take up positions to defend the National Palace and Dominican democracy.[16]

What occurred next can be described as one of those critical periods of decision making that influence the course of events. In the case of the Dominican conflict, the key decisions would not be made by loyalists or "constitutionalists", but rather by U.S. Ambassador William Tapley Bennett, and eventually by President Lyndon Johnson. As loyalist forces under the direction of General Elías Wessin y Wessin prepared their assault on the old section of Santo Domingo, constitutionalist leader Colonel Francisco Caamaño Deno visited the U.S. Embassy and sought to arrange a cease-fire. Fearing an attack by the vastly more powerful loyalist troops would lead to major bloodshed, Caamaño Deno was inclined to make concessions in order to ensure the safety of his fellow rebels. Ambassador Bennett's response to the cease-fire request, however, was to chastise the constitutionalists and reject any call for a cease-fire. Bennett, a staunch anti-communist, saw the constitutionalists not as democrats anxious to bring back Juan Bosch, but as revolutionaries intent on creating a "second Cuba" in a country that the United States had protected if not controlled since the days of Theodore Roosevelt.[17]

Colonel Caamaño Deno left the U.S. Embassy infuriated with the United States' position and urged his fighters to stand up to the loyalist forces as they crossed over the Duarte Bridge into the old section of Santo Domingo. In fierce fighting the constitutionalists routed the "loyalists," and pushed them out of the city. Smelling victory, the constitutionalists expanded their control of the city and prepared for the return of Juan Bosch from exile in Puerto Rico. It was at this juncture in the civil war that another critical decision was made, this time by President Lyndon Johnson.

President Johnson, upon receiving Ambassador Bennett's appraisal of the situation and the urgent pleas of the loyalist opponents to the constitutionalist revolt, on April 28, 1965, ordered U.S. Marine units to land in the Dominican Republic. Ostensibly sent to protect U.S. personnel and property, it became clear from the outset that the marines and later airborne units were there to quell a rebellion of the constitutionalists and restore order and the status quo. The U.S. military quickly moved to establish an international zone that effectively cut the rebel forces into two camps and on a number of occasions entered rebel territory with loyalists troops to engage the constitutionalists. Public pronouncements by former Ambassador John Bartlow Martin to the Organization of American States that the constitutionalists were "Communist dominated" and by President Johnson, who told the people of the United States about his fears of a "second Cuba," served to present the rebels as the enemy and the opponents of U.S. interests.

Despite the presence of U.S. troops (eventually some 23,000 would serve in the Dominican Republic), the constitutionalists fought on holding the old sections of Santo Domingo near the Ozama River and the ocean. As the fighting entered into May, it was becoming clear that the United States would be forced to deal with two governments, two arm-

ies, and a divided nation.[18] Faced with this dilemma, the Johnson administration set about to arrange a number of diplomatic contacts designed
to bring an end to the fighting and a satisfactory departure from the
Dominican Republic.[19]

The efforts by the United States to extricate itself from the Dominican
civil war are in large part an example of a major power pushing its
weight around in institutions such as the Organization of American
States. From the time the United States decided to intervene in the
Dominican crisis, the Johnson administration prodded the OAS into
supporting this country's policy. On a number of occasions OAS member
countries criticized the heavy-handed approach of the Johnson administration and its obvious preference for the loyalist forces. Perhaps the
most disturbing development in this relationship was the pressure put
on the OAS to agree to an Inter-American Peace Force made up of units
from Latin American countries that would lend an air of multilateral
involvement to the U.S. presence in the Dominican civil war. Although
President Johnson got his Inter-American Peace Force, the independence
of the OAS was compromised and our Latin American allies were out-
raged at U.S. pressure tactics. Furthermore, only countries with strong
authoritarian regimes, such as Brazil, Nicaragua, and Paraguay (Costa
Rica was the only democratic country involved), sent troops to the Dominican Republic. The Latin American democracies refused to be a party
to the U.S. intervention.

As the fighting moved into the summer, it was clear that the civil war
had stalemated with the constitutionalists increasingly being bottled up
in downtown sections of Santo Domingo. From June through August
an ad hoc committee of the OAS headed by Ambassador Ellsworth
Bunker of the United States met with both sides and fashioned an agreement for settling the dispute. The agreement, which came to be known
as an Act of Dominican Reconciliation, was reluctantly agreed to by both
sides—the constitutionalists because they realized the futility of continued fighting and the loyalists because the United States threatened to
deny them financial support and labeled them the "chief obstacle" to
peace.

The OAS agreement called for the reintegration of the Dominican
armed forces, the formation of a provisional government, and the holding of free elections in June of 1966. On September 3, 1965, Héctor García-
Godoy became the provisional president and began the difficult task of
rebuilding a war-torn and divided nation and preparing a disillusioned
population for another experiment in democracy. Although the U.S.
military left the Dominican Republic in September of 1965, the Johnson
administration was committed to making the transition to democracy a
smooth one. The task, however, would be difficult with the Dominican
military separated between constitutionalists and loyalists, with revo-

lutionary fervor and political hatreds still high, and the nation's capital and its economy in shambles from almost five months of fighting. Despite the truce and prospect of a renewal of democratic practice, the Dominican Republic was in reality a country divided into two political camps—one ascribing to an authoritarian mode of operation and owing its survival to the United States, the other a mix of leftist revolutionaries and liberal democrats disheartened over the intrusion of United States in their attempt to return the country to constitutionalism.

Much has been written in retrospect about the Dominican civil war and the U.S. intervention not only because the events of spring and summer of 1965 seemed to suggest a turning point in the manner in which the United States intended to respond to revolutionary situations in the Third World, but also because the intervention revealed the extent to which the United States was prepared to influence, if not control, the course of Dominican political development. It was only for a few days that the Dominican civil war was truly Dominican. After April twenty-eighth and the arrival of U.S. troops, the expressed motive for the intervention shifted from returning the country to constitutionalism to ensuring that another Caribbean nation would not follow the path of Cuba. The United States had not only intervened in the internal politics of a neighboring country, it had actually redefined the terms of conflict.

Those who have reflected upon this brief period in U.S.–Dominican relations often approach the analysis from the perspective of regional geopolitics or as a case study of executive decision making. But the U.S. intervention in the Dominican Republic in 1965 was also an example of how a powerful country can force its will on a weak country and in the process deprive it of the ability to control its future. As Piero Gleijeses says in his revealing account of the civil war,

[T]he Dominican revolt, a democratic movement owing nothing to Castro and in no way following the Cuban model, came close to success. It afforded a unique opportunity for the Dominican people to break the chains of oppression. It could have shown a new, non-Cuban road toward social change. Instead, the Pax Americana prevailed.[20]

THE BALAGUER ERA

Despite the apparently good faith efforts by the United States to remain on the sidelines and not appear as promoting the candidacy of any Dominican for the presidency, it became clear very early on in the campaign leading up to the June 1966 election that those political figures associated with the constitutionalist movement would face a severe handicap. Although Juan Bosch was permitted to return from exile, assume the leadership of the Partido Revolucionario Dominicano (PRD), and offer himself as a candidate for the presidency, marauding military and national police units made it difficult, if not dangerous, for him to organize the voters and speak openly in public forums. Fearing for his life, Bosch ventured from his home only a few times, while his supporters were systematically intimidated and on occasion murdered for engaging in campaign activities.

On the other hand, Joaquín Balaguer returned from exile in New York City and found unlimited opportunities for presenting his platform. Balaguer and his supporters encountered none of the dangers faced by the Boschists, and more importantly were perceived as the favorite of the U.S. Embassy.[21] In a country with a high degree of nationalism such a label could prove to be a burden, but in the Dominican Republic, which had just recently experienced a devastating civil war and a U.S. intervention, being a friend of Washington was an asset, especially if a pro–United States president could return the country to stability. Balaguer, in fact, played upon his noninvolvement in the civil war, his promise to return the country to "normalcy" and the fact that a vote for Bosch would most likely refuel the fires of revolution and interventionism.

With effective electoral competition impossible and the widely held view that a vote for Bosch would create havoc in the country, Joaquín Balaguer easily defeated Juan Bosch in the presidential elections of June 1966. Balaguer garnered 57 percent of the vote to Bosch's 39 percent. Balaguer carried 22 of the nation's 27 provinces and even got 33 percent of the vote in the constitutionalists' stronghold of Santo Domingo. Although Bosch waited two weeks to concede defeat, it was clear that the constitutionalist revolution was indeed over and that a new form of caudilloism was back in power.

Upon entering office, Balaguer shrewdly used his strong national support, his control of the armed forces and the national police, and the generosity of the United States to rebuild the country and to silence his critics. In the first two years of his administration, President Balaguer received over $132 million in economic assistance from the United States, which, on a per capita basis, again made the Dominican Republic the largest recipient of U.S. aid in Latin America. The U.S. aid coupled with a favorable sugar arrangement allowed Balaguer to begin rebuilding the Dominican economy and turn the attention of the people away from partisan politics and the 1965 revolution.[22]

Although many on the left had only contempt for Joaquín Balaguer and his administration, the shy and scholarly president of the Dominican Republic was extremely effective in providing the country with both political stability and a sense of economic progress. Balaguer was a master of balancing the various contending factions in Dominican politics and adept at attracting foreign investors to a country with a reputation for unpredictability and unrest. During his 12-year tenure (1966–1978) the Dominican Republic shifted dramatically from being a country torn asunder by revolution to one where political opposition all but disappeared, an expanded and influential middle class emerged, and foreign money and tourists changed the character of the Dominican economy.[23]

The transformation of Dominican society was only achieved at a high price. During the Balaguer years the government of the Dominican Republic was democratic in name only. Opposition political leaders were forced underground or into exile as the National Police or their agents moved freely to intimidate, injure, or murder those who dared to resume partisan politics.[24] The early 1970s were particularly dangerous for opposition leaders as paramilitary gangs with the support of the police roamed poor barrios in and around Santo Domingo beating and killing those viewed as leftists. President Balaguer publicly denounced these attacks and appointed commissions to examine the evidence, but little was done to stop the repression. It was not until international pressure mounted and the left was decimated that the repression subsided. Throughout this period, though, Balaguer remained personally unconnected to the violence and maintained his image as a successful democratic leader. The fact that he was reelected in 1970 and 1974, and then again in 1986, was used by his supporters (and the United States) as proof of his popularity and the viability of Dominican democracy. In reality, Balaguer largely ignored democratic institutions and practice and he so intimidated his opposition that his reelection became a contest against weak or nonexistant challengers.[25]

With effective opposition silenced or neutralized, Balaguer went to work to stregthen the Dominican economy. As a result of extremely favorable world prices for sugar and enormous injections of U.S. aid, Balaguer was able to achieve significant growth for the Dominican economy. For a period of about five years during the mid to late 1970s the Dominican economy grew at rates of 10 percent to 12 percent annually. Balaguer poured hundreds of millions of dollars into major public works projects, such as roads, hydroelectric dams, and facilities necessary for the growing tourist industry. The strengthening of the economy triggered a large increase in imported goods as the professional and business class felt confident enough in the future to purchase foreign cars, furnish new homes, and demand the latest in consumer and leisure goods from the United States and Europe.

But as the economy heated up and the disposable income of the middle and upper classes expanded, the so-called Dominican "Miracle" was being viewed as limited to those at the upper end of the socio-economic scale. During this period, Balaguer imposed harsh austerity measures which denied government workers pay increases, raised taxes, and did not permit social welfare programs to grow in spite of unemployment levels that remained at 20 percent to 25 percent. For the vast majority of the Dominican people the "Miracle" of Joaquín Balaguer never touched their lives.[26]

Perhaps the most lasting impact of the Balaguer years on the Dominican Republic was the manner in which the president opened the country to foreign investors and tourists. During this era the Dominican Republic attracted a number of major multinational corporations such as Gulf & Western, Alcoa, Falconbridge, and Simplot. With investment capital provided by these firms and a cooperative government providing tax breaks and other incentives, the Dominican economy moved slowly away from its dependence on sugar and expanded into the area of extractive industries with gold mining, and ferronickel and bauxite production. Tourism also enjoyed strong government support as Balaguer worked closely with Gulf & Western to develop the La Romana resort complex and to open up the undeveloped north coast region to the tourist trade. Balaguer wisely shied away from appearing too subservient to foreign interests, but it was clear this his administration welcomed U.S. and European investment capital and that he was willing to rewrite the tax laws and initiate programs that would bring not only the major multinationals to the Dominican Republic, but an increasing number of small assembly plants that could benefit from the low wage, low tax, weak union atmosphere present in the country.

Despite the enormous success that Balaguer enjoyed throughout the late 1960s and 1970s, all miracles come to an end. By the 1978 election, Balaguer was no longer above criticism. The oil price increases and drop in sugar prices had brought an end to the economic boom. With gasoline prices shooting upward and a negative balance of trade growing, Balaguer faced public anger, even from among his most ardent middle-class supporters. Moreover, the facade of democracy that Balaguer built up over the years to disguise the authoritarianism and caudilloism of his regime began to crumble as opposition leaders put aside their differences and formed a coalition to make sure that the Dominican president would face a real challenge in 1978.

But perhaps most importantly, the Dominican Republic in 1978 was a much different country than in 1966. Although the revolution was a mere memory, there was a definite longing for a working democracy and a concern that the image created by Balaguer was a negative one. These views also came at a time when the United States had a president who was openly taking positions in support of human rights and social reform. Although the United States had stayed at arm's length from the Balaguer regime for the last 12 years, the Carter administration let it be known that the *continuismo* present in the Dominican political system was not looked upon favorably. In many respects, by 1978 Joaquín Balaguer could no longer finesse his way out of trouble or ignore the pressure from the North.

THE 1978 ELECTION AND THE RETURN TO DEMOCRACY

The presidential election of 1978 can be considered one of those important turning points in the political development of the Dominican Republic. After 12 years of Balaguer's clever and sometimes ruthless depoliticization, the time seemed right to resume the quest begun in 1961 to create a legitimate and stable democratic system. The quest, however, would not be easy and was fraught with danger. Conservative and authoritarian forces in support of Joaquín Balaguer's candidacy for reelection were convinced that a return to a more liberal, reform-style democracy would threaten their interests and create the kind of political disorder that they had so effectively quashed since 1966. Despite the fact that Balaguer's opponent was PRD moderate (and millionaire rancher) Antonio Guzmán, many of those who favored a continuation of benevolent authoritarianism feared that radical forces in the opposition party were merely using Guzmán as a front in order to gain votes and respectability and would, upon winning the presidency, install a regime that was clearly leftist.

To forestall a Guzmán victory and the perceived prospect of a "leftist" regime, Balaguer and his supporters used their considerable power to turn voters away from a popular opposition candidate and political party. Pressure was placed on government workers to vote for their "boss" and their jobs, trucks appeared in poor barrios with bread deliveries, and glossy brochures with the Dominican president standing next to Jimmy Carter at the signing of the Panama Canal treaty were distributed to thousands of Dominicans.[27] Although Balaguer had given up hope of intimidating the opposition into not participating in the election, he made every effort to present his administration as responsible for stability, prosperity, and good relations with the United States.

On election day it became evident very early that Balaguer's public relations schemes were not effective with the Dominican voters. Where in the past barely 50 percent of the electorate participated in what were obviously oppositionless contests, the 1978 elections attracted over 70 percent of the eligible voting public. Moreover, early returns showed Guzmán with a sizable lead of 180,000 votes over Balaguer. It was at this juncture that conservative interests in support of President Balaguer (and perhaps Balaguer himself) entered directly into the electoral process. At 4:00 A.M., military units entered the Central Electoral Headquarters in Santo Domingo and acting on "superior orders" confiscated the ballot boxes from the crucial National District (where Guzmán's major support could be found) and hauled them off to an undetermined site.

The theft of the ballot boxes sent shock waves of disbelief through the Dominican Republic and indeed throughout Europe and Latin America. Democratic leaders in France, Germany, and Venezuela openly criticized the raid and demanded a continuation of the ballot count, Organization of American States observers urged President Balaguer to resume the democratic process, and the world press began paying attention to the struggle for democracy in this small Caribbean nation. But despite the outcry and the attention, the future of Dominican democracy lay in the hands of President Jimmy Carter and the position taken by the United States. Antonio Guzmán made it very clear in public pronouncements that only U.S. pressure could restore the ballot count, while Joaquín Balaguer warned Washington to resist intervening in Dominican affairs.

Fortunately for Dominican democracy, the Carter administration listened to Guzmán's pleas for assistance and rejected Balaguer's calls for neutrality. President Carter and the U.S. embassy in Santo Domingo forcefully notified Balaguer that the United States was displeased with the raid on the election headquarters and that the Dominican government should be mindful of the considerable economic assistance that comes from Washington. The Carter administration also reminded Balaguer of his pledge of open and free elections made at the Panama Canal signing ceremony. In a matter of a few days it was quite obvious that the United States was determined to see a resumption of the vote count and a movement toward a peaceful democratic transition.

In the face of such enormous pressure, Balaguer agreed to a resumption of the vote count and agreed that he would abide by the decision of the electorate. Although there was great relief in the Guzmán camp and a sense of satisfaction in Washington over Balaguer's decision, it would take nearly two more weeks to force the government to present a final vote tally. In those two weeks the supporters of Balaguer did all they could to delay the count or question its veracity. Rumors that military units would never permit a Guzmán victory filled the capital and talk of a general strike against the government raised the specter of a renewal of the polarization present in 1965. Luckily neither threat materialized as the government posted the ballot tally showing Guzmán clearly defeating Balaguer by over 150,000 votes. The long road to open democracy in the Dominican Republic had finally come to an end. Never before had the Dominican Republic moved from one presidential administration to another in a democratic manner. The accomplishment of Guzmán and the PRD was indeed a significant one, but could not have happened without the diplomatic and political intervention of the United States. Although the election of 1978 was a time of major change in the

Dominican Republic, the role of the United States in ensuring the integrity of the electoral process showed that perhaps little had changed, at least in terms of who possesses the ultimate power over Dominican political affairs.[28]

The ascension to power of Antonio Guzmán and his PRD backers did bring significant change to the Dominican Republic, but not so much in the areas of economic rejuvenation and social reform. Rather the Guzmán administration will be remembered for its vigorous efforts to create a freer and more harmonious political climate in the Dominican Republic and to reintroduce concepts such as human rights, military professionalization, and tolerance of opposition. This is not to say that President Guzmán was unconcerned with the plight of the urban and rural masses. In reality, Guzmán and his administrative team worked vigorously to redirect government resources toward social welfare programs, job training, health clinics, and housing. But, once in office, Guzmán faced the unavoidable nemesis of rising oil prices and falling sugar prices, which together spelled less revenue, heavier debt burdens, and fewer opportunities to move forward with more ambitious social reform programs.

As the Dominican economy continued on the downward spiral, President Guzmán faced heightened criticism not only from the vast army of the unemployed, but from his own party where leftists such as José Francisco Peña Gómez decried the government's inability or unwillingness to address the serious problems facing the poor. From the professional and business community, Guzmán was also castigated for rising inflation, restrictions on some imports, and for a faltering economy which could not match the growth rates of the Balaguer "Miracle" years. The praise that Guzmán received early on for bringing home political exiles, firing disloyal generals, and legalizing the Communist party were forgotten by a public that either wanted jobs or a standard of living reminiscent of the Balaguer era. Unfortunately for Guzmán, he could do neither.[29]

As the 1982 presidential elections neared, the mood in the Dominican Republic was one of caution and apprehension, not only because of concern over another presidential transition (Guzmán pledged not to run for reelection), but because the faltering economy was creating political unrest that could easily lead to another round of governmental instability and perhaps the end of Dominican democracy. The ruling government party, the PRD, chose as its candidate Salvador Jorge Blanco, a moderate-left lawyer who many felt would be more aggressive than Guzmán in attacking the social ills and economic injustices present in Dominican society. Pitted against Jorge were Joaquín Balaguer and Juan Bosch, who in many respects represented a reincarnation of the dual caudillos (Santana and Báez) of nineteenth century Dominican presidential politics. Bosch had by now left the PRD, gravitated toward a more avowed independent Marxist position, and founded his own party, the Party of Dominican Liberation (PLD).

Despite the economic problems that surfaced during the Guzmán administration, the PRD remained the dominant political organization in Dominican society. With strong ties to the urban working class and considerable support among the professional ranks, Jorge was an easy winner in the presidential elections, defeating Balaguer and Bosch with 47 percent of the popular vote. Moreover, the PRD was able to capture a majority in both the Dominican Senate and Chamber of Deputies for the first time, thereby solidifying its hold of the public policy process. The election of Jorge brought a sense of relief to the Dominicans who were unsure whether their country could continue the tradition of peaceful democratic transition, but their renewed confidence was shattered when in July of 1982, just one month short of the presidential inauguration, Antonio Guzmán, depressed over a corruption scandal in his administration, committed suicide in the National Palace. The man who had helped to move the Dominican Republic toward democracy, but had never gained the admiration of his people, apparently was unable to endure the embarrassment and public ridicule that a corruption investigation involving members of his own family would create.

With the cloud of the Guzmán suicide hanging over the inauguration, President Jorge informed the Dominican people that difficult times lay ahead. In his speech upon taking office Jorge promised more social reform and efforts to help the unemployed, but he also talked of austerity measures such as tax increases, pay freezes, import restrictions, oil conservation measures, and budget tightening. The picture that Jorge painted of the future was not a pleasant one since projections of foreign oil prices, trade imbalances, and debt requirements were not favorable. While the Dominican people took pride in the fact that they had elected a man who would reorder national priorities in favor of the poor, they quickly came to the realization that their new government would have great difficulty living up to its promises.

The administration of Salvador Jorge Blanco from 1982 to 1986 is best described as engaged in a constant battle with international lending organizations determined to force their debt-reducing models on Dominican society, and with angry urban dwellers who experienced directly the results of government-imposed belt-tightening. As sugar prices dropped to as low as 4¢ a pound on the world market and the public debt rose to over $4 billion, President Jorge felt it necessary to approach the International Monetary Fund for financial assistance. In early 1983 the Dominican government and the IMF agreed on a $599 million Extended Fund Facility, which would provide the country with a series of loans over three years, contingent on a number of major austerity measures and policy initiatives. In particular, the IMF wanted the Jorge administration to raise taxes, cut the budget deficit, restrict imports, and devalue the peso. The call for a devaluation of the peso caused an enormous outcry in the country, as the poor felt that a decision on the peso would raise prices on essentials such as rice, beans, cooking oil, and gasoline.

As the date for the next portion of the loan disbursement approached, the Jorge administration grew less willing to follow IMF guidelines. The Dominican president stated that abiding IMF recommendations "might cause some kind of revolution." Jorge's perception of the mood of the Dominican masses was indeed accurate for in April of 1984, when the government sought to enforce oil price increases mandated by the IMF, the capital city of Santo Domingo erupted in three days of street fighting in which 100 people died, 500 were injured, and 7000 were arrested. The fightiing in the city was the worst since the revolution of 1965 and destroyed whatever goodwill Jorge had developed as a president in favor of the poor. The government's harsh crackdown on the rioters and its seeming willingness to accede to IMF demands gave leftists in the ruling PRD and in the Dominican Communist party a issue around which to rally the disgruntled urban poor. For the first time since the 1965 revolution there was growing support for political leaders who espoused Marxist-style solutions to the Dominican economic and social dilemma.

The April 1984 uprising forced the Jorge administration to reevaluate its relationship with the IMF and determine to what extent its recommendation should be heeded, especially if such cooperation would instigate urban unrest. For over a year the Dominican government delayed agreeing with the IMF over guidelines for additional loan disbursements. But while the Jorge administration dragged its feet in order to pacify an angry political constituency, the Dominican economy worsened to the point where, in December of 1984, the country teetered on the brink of defaulting on a number of important foreign loans. Only an emergency $50 million loan from the United States kept the country afloat. Finally, in April of 1985, the government reached an accord with the IMF and received $79 million in loans, which was only one fourth of the $300 million it would have received in 1983 and 1984 had it complied with the suggested austerity measures. The accord restored confidence in the Dominican financial situation and paved the way for a number of new foreign loans. Although the debt-financing crisis was over for the moment, the twin problems of indebtedness and social disorder remain. As a result of accepting most of the IMF's guidelines the Dominican Republic strengthened its financial situation, but at the same time its people grudgingly agreed to a significantly different economic life-style.

The furor over abiding by IMF guidelines not only affected social order in the Dominican Republic, it carried over into the political realm, as well. As a result of the government's austerity measures and the angry response of the populace, the ruling PRD was wracked with factionalism as moderates and leftists fought over the future direction of the party and the choice of the presidential nominee for the 1986 election campaign. In an uproarious party convention, Jacobo Majluta, the former interim president (after the Guzmán suicide), emerged as the PRD standard-bearer. The choice of Majluta, however, was so disputed by leftists, who felt that the former president was a carbon copy of Guzmán, that the party was unable to unify behind its candidate. What was once a model social democratic party organization had become a divided and disillusioned group of politicians estranged from their constituency, having to face charges of widespread corruption under two PRD governments and unsure of what direction to take the party or the country.[30]

As the 1986 elections approached, the internal problems of the PRD were not the only important part of the Dominican political puzzle. Joaquín Balaguer, now running under the banner of a reconstituted Reformist Social Christian party (representing a union of his Reformist party with the Social Christians), was again seeking the Dominican presidency. Despite the fact that he was blind and aging (Balaguer was 78 at election time), the former president represented a time (the mid–1970s) in which the Dominican Republic was without debt, trade imbalances, and IMF austerity measures. The memory of earlier repression and limited democracy did not seem to worry most Dominicans who saw in Balaguer a return to better days. Complicating the situation even more was the revived candidacy of Juan Bosch who presented himself as the major opponent of the IMF restrictions and champion of the urban working class.

The 1986 elections thus pitted three ex-presidents against each other—one the candidate of a tarnished governing party, one a symbol of the good old days, and one a rabble-rousing revolutionary from another era. The Dominican Republic had always been a country that relished its tradition of personalismo and the election of 1986 gave the people a unique opportunity to bring back into power a familiar personality.

Democratic elections and the peaceful transfer of presidential power are relatively new to the Dominican Republic, and so the May 1986 elections were approached with a good deal of apprehension. Although there were incidents of politically motivated violence during the campaign (primarily as a result of PRD infighting), Dominicans seemed more concerned with whether the tabulation of the votes would be handled properly since preelection polls had shown that Majluta and Balaguer were both popular and could become the next president. Dominicans were also closely watching the 30 senate races and the 120 contests for seats in the Chamber of Deputies since the next president would have to deal with a legislative branch that had gained increased status and was willing to challenge the executive branch over key public policy issues.

As early returns came into the Central Election Board in Santo Domingo, it became clear that Majluta and Balaguer were virtually tied for the presidency, although Balaguer maintained a slim lead over his PRD opponent. Majluta, for his part, ignored the Balaguer lead and talked as if he was the winner and that once the vote count was complete he would be declared the victor. But the voting trends remained favorable to Balaguer. With 92 percent of the vote counted, the aging former president had a lead of over 35,000 votes and was viewed by independent election analysts as clearly the winner.[31]

With Balaguer the apparent president-elect, Majluta cast doubt on the election process and demanded a recount, claiming that his computers showed him the victor and that members of the Central Election Board should resign. This bold move by the PRD candidate caused an uproar in the country and forced the government to deploy troops in the major urban areas and around strategic locations just in case supporters of the two candidates were to take to the streets in protest. Fortunately for Dominican democracy, an independent election commission headed by the Catholic archbishop of Santo Domingo intervened in the dispute and, using its own electoral data and observations of the vote count, was able to verify the Balaguer victory and convince the Majluta camp that contesting the election was futile and damaging to the stability of the nation. Although the Central Election Board did not certify the Balaguer victory until later in the summer, by May twenty-sixth, ten days after the election, Joaquín Balaguer was recognized as the president-elect and the Majluta camp was refraining from talk of a vote recount. The unofficial final vote count gave Balaguer and his Social Christian Reform party 857,942 votes or 41.5 percent of the total; Majluta and the PRD received 812,716, or 39.4 percent; and Juan Bosch's Dominican Liberation party received a surprising 379,269 votes, or 18.3 percent. Three minor party candidates split the remainder of the vote.

There were many, especially outside the Dominican Republic, who were surprised that a nearly blind ex-president whose commitment to democracy was certainly questionable was the choice of the largest segment of the voting population. But to the Dominicans Balaguer is not to be judged solely in Western terms of physical vigor and support for democratic institutions. To many Dominicans Balaguer is a patrón, a godfather, a revered man of letters (most Dominicans refer to him as Dr. Balaguer) who is scrupulously honest, hard-working, and a master of patronage and political manipulation. Moreover, the memory of the Dominican "miracle" engineered by Balaguer in the 1970s is tempting to those who had seen their earning power decrease dramatically under

PRD presidents. But there was more to Balaguer's victory than style and past memories. The ex-president was able to build a winning coalition of rural campesinos who had seen little land reform under the Jorge administration and the new urban middle classes upset with their government's economic policies. Balaguer also owed a debt of gratitude to his old nemesis, Juan Bosch, who played upon the factionalism in the PRD to gain 18 percent of the vote and thereby seal the fate of Majluta.

The return of Joaquín Balaguer to the presidency raises questions about the future of democratic governance in the Dominican Republic. In many respects Balaguer is an old-time caudillo whose techniques of governing will differ from that found in the Jorge administration. Greater centralization of executive power, frequent personnel shifts and a less open style of governance have been trademarks of Balaguer in the past and are still present today. What remains an unknown is the climate of democracy that Balaguer will develop.

Many analysts in the United States are convinced that democracy is firmly established in the Dominican Republic and that Balaguer will continue to operate accordingly. It would be difficult, many say, for Balagauer to reintroduce a more authoritarian style of governance or to be intimidated by those in the national police or the military who want to use force as a means of quieting a restive population. Questions, however, remain, especially because of Balaguer's age and physical condition. Balaguer's vice-president, Carlos Morales Troncoso, is a well-respected administrator, but his democratic and political credentials are unknown. Appointments by Balaguer to military and national police leadership positions also provide a clearer signal as to the moderation, balancing of opposed forces, and future course of democratic practice in the Dominican Republic. And finally, should the current political and economic stability established by the Jorge administration begin to degenerate, Balaguer might be inclined (or be forced by conservative elites) to return to the harsh methods used during his past administrations to reestablish social and economic order.

There was no doubt that the election of Joaquín Balaguer to the Dominican presidency represented a desire to return to the "old days," when life in the Dominican Republic was more secure and prosperous. It remained to be seen, however, whether this return to the old days also meant a return to a style of governance that jeopardized the advances in democratic practice made under consecutive PRD administrations. Actually the Balaguer government in office sought to accommodate and reconcile these opposing trends. On the one hand, Balaguer continued to govern as the personalistic, caudillistic, patronage-oriented leader that he had always been. On the other, the climate and context in which he had to govern were much more democratic than they had been during Balaguer's earlier presidencies. As a shrewd but now aging leader, Balaguer adjusted to this new climate accordingly; but there were also signs of the other features familiar from Dominican history: fragmentation and a tendency toward political unraveling.

NOTES

1. Howard Wiarda, *The Dominican Republic: A Nation in Transition* (New York: Praeger, 1968), p. 34.

2. See Howard Wiarda, *Dictatorship and Development: The Methods of Control in Trujillo's Dominican Republic* (Gainesville, FL: University of Florida Press, 1968).

3. Robert Crassweller, *Trujillo: The Life and Times of a Caribbean Dictator* (New York: Macmillan, 1966), pp. 39–51.

4. Seldon Rodman, *Quisqueya, A History of the Dominican Republic* (Seattle: University of Washington Press, 1964), pp. 136–41.

5. G. Pope Atkins and Larman Wilson, in their book *The United States and the Trujillo Regime* (New Brunswick, NJ: Rutgers University Press, 1972), provide an excellent overview of the longstanding relationship between the Trujillo regime and the United States, which was based on sugar and later spread to hemispheric defense.

6. Ibid., pp. 79–100.

7. See especially Jésus de Galíndez, *La era de Trujillo* (Santiago, Chile: Editorial del Pacifico, 1956).

8. Bernard Diederich, *Trujillo: The Death of the Goat* (Boston: Little, Brown, 1978).

9. See "The United States and the Assassination of Trujillo," Appendix I, in Piero Gleijeses, *The Dominican Crisis: The 1965 Constitutionalist Revolt and American Intervention* (Baltimore: Johns Hopkins University Press, 1978), pp. 303–07.

10. Robert Crassweller, *Trujillo: The Life and Times of a Caribbean Dictator*, op. cit., p. 6.

11. Former Ambassador to the Dominican Republic, John Bartlow Martin, in his book *Overtaken by Events: The Dominican Crisis from the Death of Trujillo to the Civil War* (Garden City, N.Y.: Doubleday, 1966), gives an in-depth discussion of the Council of State era. See pp. 155–77.

12. Juan Bosch's views on building democracy in the Dominican Republic are contained in his book *Crisis de la democracía de América en la República Dominicana* (Mexico, D.F.: Centros de Estudios y Documentacion Sociales, 1964).

13. As quoted in John Bartlow Martin, *Overtaken by Events*, op. cit., p. 338.

14. Ibid., p. 716.

15. Howard Wiarda, *The Dominican Republic: A Nation in Transition*, op. cit., p. 61.

16. See Piero Gleijeses, *The Dominican Crisis*, op. cit., pp. 195–218. See also Dan Kurzman, *Santo Domingo: Revolt of the Damned* (New York: Putnam, 1965), and Tad Szulc, *Dominican Diary* (New York: Delacorte Press, 1965).

17. Abraham Lowenthal, in his book *The Dominican Intervention* (Cambridge, MA: Harvard University Press, 1972), gives perhaps the best account of the internal controversy in the Johnson administration concerning how to define the "constitutionalists" and how to avoid a "second Cuba."

18. José Moreno, in his book *Barrios in Arms: Revolution in Santo Domingo* (Pittsburgh: University of Pittsburgh Press, 1970), provides a firsthand account of the "constitutionalist" camp in the old city and the struggles endured by the constitutionalists in the face of mounting pressure from the United States forces.

19. The best account of the negotiation process that was undertaken during the Dominican crisis is provided by Jerome Slater, in his book *Intervention and Negotiation: The United States and the Dominican Revolution* (New York: Harper & Row, 1970).

20. Piero Gleijses, *The Dominican Crisis*, op. cit., p. 301.

21. See Edward S. Herman and Frank Brodhead, *Demonstration Elections: U.S. Staged Elections in the Dominican Republic, Vietnam and El Salvador* (Boston: South End Press, 1984).

22. James Nelson Goodsell, "Balaguer's Dominican Republic," *Current History* 53, no. 315, November 1967, pp. 298–302.

23. Michael Kryzanek, "Diversion, Subversion and Repression: The Strategies of Anti-Regime Politics in Balaguer's Dominican Republic," *Caribbean Studies* 19, nos. 1 and 2 (1979).

24. Carlos Maria Gutiérrez, *The Dominican Republic: Rebellion and Repression* (trans. Richard E. Edwards) (New York: Monthly Review Press, 1972).

25. Michael Kryzanek, "Political Party Decline and the Failure of Liberal Democracy: The PRD in Dominican Politics," *Journal of Latin American Studies* 9 (1977), pp. 115–43.

26. Jan Knippers Black, *The Dominican Republic: Politics and Development in an Unsovereign State* (Boston: George Allen and Unwin, 1986), pp. 62–63.

27. Michael Kryzanek, "The 1978 Election in the Dominican Republic: Opposition Politics, Intervention and the Carter Administration," *Caribbean Studies* 19, nos. 1 and 2, April–July 1979, p. 55.

28. Ibid. pp. 71–73.

29. Jan Knippers Black, *The Dominican Republic*, op. cit., pp. 129–36.

30. Jonathan Hartley, "A Democratic Shootout in the D. R.—An Analysis of the 1986 Election," *Caribbean Review* XV (Winter 1987).

31. See *El Caribe* for the period May 16, 1986–May 26, 1986.

4

THE POLITICS OF DEMOCRATIC DEVELOPMENT IN THE DOMINICAN REPUBLIC

The study of political development in Third World settings has often produced disappointing results for those schooled in the Western liberal and democratic tradition. Aid officials, scholars, and liberal politicians, particularly in the era of the 1960s and the ill-fated Alliance for Progress, held out great promise for those countries that followed models of governmental organization, political parties, and popular participation found in the more advanced countries. But after extensive experimentation by eager reform presidents in the Third World, fueled in large part by economic assistance from the United States, many in the West became disillusioned about the often meager developmental results and the prospects of establishing stable and functioning democratic systems.[1]

In the poorer countries the issues of food and housing seemed much more important to the people than the struggle to establish open elections and a functioning system of checks and balances. Often in abrupt power shifts the Western-oriented reformers were soon replaced by conservative generals who ignored democratic guidelines and accented development models that reenforced authoritarianism and the status quo.[2] U.S. intellectuals and politicians who felt confident that the poor countries could eventually become "like us" were forced to redefine their views on political development and also to reassess the prospect of bringing democracy to the rest of the world.

But what is perhaps most intriguing about the failure of the Western democratic model to establish a permanent hold in the political systems of the Third World is the manner in which those countries that did embrace democracy redesigned the Western pattern to fit their own unique internal circumstances and conditions. Democratic governments have emerged in quite a number of Third World countries in the 25 years since North American and European models of development and democracy occupied the frontlines of public discourse on development. The most successful governments, however, never sought to build their democracies as if the institutions and processes of popular politics were in some way prefabricated. Rather what emerged in these newly developed democracies were hybrid strains of constitutionalism, representative government, and popular involvement in national affairs that mixed and blended imported with indigenous ingredients. Democracy had indeed been established in country X, but more than likely it was a democracy that was different from that found in the advanced industrial democracies—compromises had been made, shortcuts taken, procedures eliminated, and some guarantees put off to the future. The newly developed democracies proudly displayed their systems of government as a break with the past and as a sign of emergence into the modern world, and yet the structure of these new democracies quite often revealed vestiges of the old regime and of venerated tradition as national leaders fashioned their system in a way that matched the reality of politics and local society.[3] The Dominican Republic has had a long history of authoritarian government alternating with (usually) brief periods of democratic rule. It adopted a liberal democratic constitution in 1844 (the first of 30-odd), but that quickly gave way to 30 years of man-on-horseback rule. The pattern has repeated itself at least four times in Dominican history. The theory (democratic) and the practice (authoritarian) of government have been diametrically opposed. Frequently the authoritarians themselves have adopted new constitutions providing for strong executive rule and vast emergency powers, giving rise to two constitutional traditions that are very far apart: one liberal and democratic and the other authoritarian and caesarist.

The pattern has repeated itself so often that many Dominicans have serious questions about the prospects for democracy in their country. Will democracy emerge finally or will it always be overthrown? Is the country really suitable for Western—or U.S.—style democracy or is that merely an imported (from the United States) form grafted onto an authoritarian political tradition and thus destined never to triumph? Is it possible to blend democracy with strong leadership in ways that are peculiarly Dominican? These are the questions with which many Dominicans wrestle.[4]

It is now a little over 20 years since the Dominican revolution ended with the election of June 1966 and the ascension of Joaquín Balaguer to the presidency. The election of the new Dominican president after years of upheaval and failure of earlier experiments marked a new beginning for a country which had been struggling to establish a system of liberal democracy on a social, economic, political, and cultural base that was thoroughly authoritarian and centralized. Since 1966 the Dominican Republic has seen the character of democratic governance change. While Balaguer did little to advance the principles of popular rule, he did rule constitutionally. He was replaced by two PRD reformers who made concerted efforts to institutionalize key elements of the Western democratic model. But in a kind of strange twist, the election of 1986 brought

Joaquín Balaguer back into the presidency of the Dominican Republic thereby providing a fairly defined period in which to investigate not only the progress of Dominican democracy, but the manner in which three presidents fashioned a more-or-less democratic political system pledged to a mode of operation far removed from that of Trujillo.

But evaluating the progress of Dominican democracy through the administrations of three presidents cannot be done merely by determining whether elections were fair or a peaceable transfer of power took place. Assessing the status of democracy in the Dominican Republic and its prospects for the future will be the result of a more thorough examination of institutional development and the presence of internal and external support mechanisms. Since each president, whether Balaguer, Guzmán, or Jorge, shaped their administrations, and indeed Dominican democracy, primarily through their own unique decision-making formulas and their own perceptions of political realities, it is essential to delve beneath the surface of elections and inaugurations to examine the manner in which democracy has been constructed and how it works. It is only by looking at the actual functioning of such institutions and their status within the political system that it will be possible to determine the character and effectiveness of democratic governance in the Dominican Republic.

THE CREATION OF EFFECTIVE GOVERNMENTAL INSTITUTIONS

Central to the concept of political development in the Third World, at least as it has been viewed by Western scholars, is the importance of moving away from a decision-making structure which is founded upon individual or familial power, centralized and monolithic control of government policy, and in some instances a kind of cult of personality. In its place those same Western scholars have tended to favor the creation of complex and oftentimes countervailing institutions that stress objectivity, rationality, and a more impersonal approach to the formulation of public policy. The development of a modern society, so the conventional wisdom suggests, is best nurtured and secured in an atmosphere where policy evolves through a process in which a number of institutions and individuals have a hand in shaping the final product. The model is U.S.–style checks and balances and interest group pluralism.

In the Dominican Republic the transition from the old system to the new is as yet incomplete. In fact the struggle between the personal and institutional models of governance, the caudillistic and the democratic, is ongoing and, on numerous occasions in the postrevolution era, has revealed the deepseated problems that can arise when a developing nation seeks to move away from traditional practices and implement a new system of governance. As we shall see, the old ways die hard in the Dominican Republic.

Perhaps the single most important change in Dominican government in recent years has been the development of a new, more democratic process and style of decision making during the administrations of Antonio Guzmán and Salvador Jorge Blanco. Where Balaguer epitomized the civilian caudillo who made almost all government decisions, stayed aloof from the rigors of democratic give and take, and only presided over what amounted to a mere showcase democracy, his PRD successors sought to strengthen the democratic climate by showing greater confidence in democratic institutions, tolerating regular instances of conflict between the executive and legislative branches, and building an image among Dominicans and the outside world that the Dominican Republic was becoming a country where the uncontested power of the president was giving way to a rudimentary, and even occasionally effective, checks-and-balances system.

For example, with the election of Guzmán in 1978, the Dominican Congress was elevated to a position of greater prominence in the political system. Although Guzmán and the PRD gained control of the 120-seat Chamber of Deputies as a result of the 1978 election victory, the Balaguer forces, using their control of the election commission, were able to retain a 16 to 11 margin in the Dominican Senate. Balaguer and his Partido Reformista Senate allies used their majority in the upper branch of the legislature to control judicial appointments and to block or delay a number of Guzmán's policy initiatives.[5]

During the Jorge administration the newfound strength of the legislature was in even greater evidence, despite the government's control of both houses. The Dominican legislature battled President Jorge on his negotiations with the IMF, in particular his move to create a unified currency exchange system, on the introduction of numerous tax proposals designed to raise needed revenue, and on the sanctioning of development loans from the Inter-American Development Bank, such as the controversial $150 million Madrigal dam project which the then Senate President Jacobo Majluta personally opposed.[6] In each of these instances the legislature was able to force the government to change its policy stance or accept defeat at the hands of an institutional adversary that was no longer lethargic. The Dominican legislature was especially effective in challenging the IMF austerity package and forcing the government to recognize the devastating effect of such measures on the lower classes. The delays in reaching agreement with the IMF were at least in part due to the concern of the Jorge administration over the legislative fallout.

Although the newfound strength of the Dominican Congress was seen best in its ability to challenge the Jorge administration on economic reform and fiscal policy, its status as an alternative source of public decision making was in evidence during debates over wage increases for disgruntled public and private sector employees. In response to a series of strikes by physicians, nurses, judges, teachers, and agricultural extension workers, the congress ignored administration concerns over the economic ramifications of pay increases on an already strained budget and passed new taxes on cigarettes and alcohol and enhanced the scope of the value-added tax. As each group presented its demands in public forums, it was the legislative branch that they looked to for relief rather than the government.[7] The Jorge administration accused the legislators of undermining its attempts to restructure the economy, but the PRD deputies and senators felt confident in their role as protectors of those who were being harmed by the government's policies.

What is perhaps most interesting about the formation of an active congressional check on Guzmán and Jorge was that the Dominican presidents faced their harshest criticism from legislators in the PRD. Angry over Guzmán's appointment of nonparty people to government positions and his refusal to take a more nationalist line toward United States economic interests in the country, PRD members in congress used the legislative forum to criticize the president and during the devastating hurricane of 1982 actually joined with the Balagueristas in an attempt to block Guzmán's appeal for emergency powers.

Salvador Jorge Blanco fared no better with the PRD. Opponents in his party, particularly Jacobo Majluta, harshly criticized the government and often joined with the Reformista and PLD (pro-Bosch) senators to obstruct government fiscal initiatives. When Jorge left office in August of 1986 he was an embattled president, not only because of the unpopularity of his economic polices, but four years of conflict with an active and vocal congress had forced him to recognize the difficulty of democratic decision making.

It is important, however, not to make too much of the renewal of legislative visibility and power in the Dominican Republic or to jump to any quick conclusions about the decline of centralized, personalistic rule. The Dominican president remains an enormously powerful national figure and despite Guzmán and Jorge's efforts to recognize the legislature as a partner in the policy process and to accept the limitations of a constitutional democracy, they were both presidents who did not hesitate to use the power of their office and to skirt around the constitution when necessary. Like Balaguer, who clearly ignored democratic institutions in favor of the personal approach, Guzmán and Jorge on numerous occasions became involved in local labor disputes and even entertained petty requests from concerned citizens. Using the broad executive powers granted by the constitution, Guzmán and Jorge ignored legislative entreaties and raised prices on fuel and food, declared national emergencies, and suspended personal liberties with little concern over the institutional ramifications. Their perceptions of the presidency were founded upon the belief that policy decisions should remain largely a matter of the executive branch, if not of the president alone. On issues of critical national importance the Dominican legislature was forced into a subsidiary role as a forum for dissent and as a body whose influence was felt more in terms of its ability to obstruct and amend rather than lead. Reinaugurated in 1986, Balaguer also sought to run a highly personalistic, centralized and patronage-oriented presidency.

If the legislative branch has been only intermittently successful in challenging the power of the executive, then the Dominican judicial branch can best be described as a severely weakened participant in the system of separation of powers. Although the Dominican high court has jurisdiction over matters concerned with the executive and legislative branches, it has developed over the years as a highly politicized body that is often unwilling or unable to exert an independent point of view. The source of the politicization is the fact that Dominican justices are not appointed for life and occupy the bench on removable four-year terms. The limited terms in office have forced justices to be ever conscious of national politics and the effect of court decisions on their tenure.

Despite the handicap of occupying a highly politicized position, the judges have not been averse at times to speaking out against government policy. Their most visible challenge to the political system was a three-month strike in 1985 over the failure of the Jorge administration to increase judicial salaries and provide the courts with a degree of autonomy. The strike called attention to the poor pay of Dominican judges and their institutional limitations, but did little to strengthen their position in government. In fact, the long-smoldering pay issue merely helped to accent the enormous level of corruption that had developed within the court system. It is now commonplace in the Dominican Republic to use money as a means of speeding up a trial date or filing legal documents. Although no sector of public life is immune from corruption, payoffs in the judicial system have further eroded confidence in an institution that is in desperate need of respect.

Fortunately for the judges, their strike was successful in that modest pay increases were provided and a greater internal autonomy was granted. It is unlikely, however, that the Dominican judicial system will be able to establish a more visible and influential position in the policy-making arena, since there is little call for depoliticizing the courts or providing them with more extensive powers such as judicial review. Where there has been some strengthening of the legislative branch in the Dominican Republic, the judiciary seems destined to remain a weak institution that is rife with patronage and corruption.[8]

The issue of the independence of the courts came to a head under

President Balaguer when former President Jorge faced embarrassing charges of corruption and malfeasance. Reacting strongly and protesting his innocence, Jorge appealed to President Balaguer to have the charges dropped. The appeal to the new president on a judicial matter was predictable, of course, given what we have said about the weakness and nonindependence of the courts, the correct route; but it got the former president in trouble for revealing his lack of faith in the judiciary. Meanwhile Balaguer showed little inclination to allow a political rival and adversary to get off the hook so easily.

But if the Dominican judiciary is a prime example of the difficulty of building governing institutions that mirror those found in the advanced industrial democracies, it is dwarfed by the problems besetting the Dominican civil service. Like many Latin American countries, the public sector in the Dominican Republic is enormous. Recent estimates place the public sector as generating nearly 40 percent of all investment, 20 percent of the gross national product, and 40 percent of all financial activities. More importantly, it is estimated that almost half of all Dominicans are employed by the government, primarily in 23 state enterprises such as the State Sugar Council or the consortium of public works and industrial enterprises called CORDE.[9] The fact that the government in the Dominican Republic acts as the employer of last resort and that presidents have traditionally used their office as the seat of patronage for loyal party activists, along with family and friends, has helped to create an ever-expanding bureaucratic payroll. In recent years, however, the need to cut back the large bureaucracy in order to relieve some of the economic pressures has created serious political dilemmas for presidents torn between efficiency and patronage.

The collapse of the economic "miracle" during the Balaguer years (which was achieved in part by holding the line on government salaries) placed enormous pressure on both Guzmán and Jorge to cut the public sector budget. Although both presidents paid lip service to the need for reductions in the government bureaucracy, and Guzmán even reintroduced a civil service reform bill designed to accent merit as a means of appointment and promotion, in the end political pressures and the attractiveness of the personal approach to staffing the government made them give up the efforts to move to a more modern system. In fact, as documented by Jan Knippers Black, Guzmán actually increased the number of government employees by some 50 to 60 percent and Jorge upped the numbers by an additional 40 percent.[10]

The problems within the public sector became so serious that the 1986 presidential campaign was played out against a backdrop of allegations related to bureaucratic overstaffing, mismanagement, and corruption. Both major presidential candidates pledged to address the problems in the public sector, but were vague on critical issues such as the closing of a number of unproductive sugar refineries, the selling of unprofitable government enterprises, and dismissing thousands of government workers who were creating bureaucratic delays and needless red tape.[11]

As the campaign progressed, rumors were rampant concerning high Jorge administration officials enriching themselves through their involvement in government enterprises. Although Jorge himself appeared to be an honest president, he seemed unable or unwilling to control the abuses of power of his underlings. Part of Jacobo Majluta's problem with the Dominican electorate was that as head of CORDE during the Guzmán administration, numerous allegations arose concerning his involvement in corruption. Majluta's past record as a public administrator certainly did not help the PRD in convincing the voters to bring them back to office, but it did set the tone for the election and took the PRD off a kind of leadership pedestal that had helped it avoid public criticism for so long. After eight years in office the aura of being a party dedicated to social change had disappeared from the PRD to be replaced by the cold realities of business as usual. Richard Kearney, in his study of the Dominican civil service, perhaps says it best when he describes the character of Dominican bureaucracy under the PRD:

As the political system has evolved into a legitimate democracy ... the administrative legacy has been transformed into an almost pure spoils system not dissimilar to that which prevailed in the United States prior to the Pendleton Act. The friends, family, and supporters of the newly elected president enjoy the advantages of government jobs and the self-enrichment that the appointments sometimes imply.[12]

The election once more of Joaquín Balaguer to the Dominican presidency in 1986 has disturbed many proponents of democracy and democratic practice. Balaguer, even though he is no swaggering "man on horseback," in the tradition of Trujillo, clearly operates in the personalistic mode of governance and can be expected to develop a highly centralized and to a certain degree secretive system of public policy decision making. Many Dominicans expect that whatever limited progress was made under Guzmán and Jorge toward accepting the role of the legislature and tolerating efforts at checking executive power will likely vanish or diminish considerably under Balaguer. Moreover, the explosion of public employment and party and family favoritism that occurred under the two PRD presidents is not likly to abate, simply because Balaguer can ill afford the social unrest that would follow massive layoffs or the development of an effective merit system within the bureacracy. During his earlier presidencies, in fact, Balaguer was a master of patronage politics.

To say, however, that the Dominican Republic will return to the old regime is premature since Balaguer enters his newest presidency in a different era. In the Dominican Republic of the 1980s, democratic government is now an accepted way of life, the rule of law has been strengthened, and public policy initiatives receive much closer scrutiny by a wide array of public participants. Balaguer will find it difficult to return to the days when he carefully avoided public debate, allowed himself to be intimidated by the military, and kept anxious ministers (as well as the U.S. Embassy) in the dark on critical policy issues.[13] But as a sign that Balaguer intends to operate differently this time around, the Dominican president supported an investigation of Jorge Blanco's alleged involvement in a RD $10 million military purchase scandal, purged officials in the armed forces and the national police connected to human rights abuse, and initially distanced himself from party regulars who began pressuring him for government appointments. The investigation of former president Jorge's involvement in the military purchase scandal revealed the extent to which Balaguer intended to crack down on government corruption (and also to discredit a potential presidential candidate in 1990). Pressure to go ahead with prosecution of Jorge by the Balaguer government became so intense that the former president and his family sought political asylum in the Venezuelan embassy in late April of 1987.

And yet, having said all this, it is important to remember that in a country like the Dominican Republic, where democracy is new and the old ways remain close to the surface, a leader like Balaguer may still be able to fashion popular government in ways that suit his temperament and values. If anyone has mastered the art of appearance over substance, it is Joaquín Balaguer. For all the progress democracy has made under PRD guidance, the Dominican Republic remains a country where the personalistic and caudillistic mode of governing still has considerable influence while the Western tradition is often used when convenient.

THE STATUS OF POLITICAL PARTY ORGANIZATION

Political parties have long been recognized as the substructures upon which modern democratic governments are built. With their capacity to mobilize the populace, identify issues of common concern, and offer candidates for local and national public office, political parties are fundamental for the creation of a democratic climate within a country. Without the parties' involvement in public affairs the democratic aspirations of the people would be undefined and disorganized. But besides acting as the chief agents of democratic practice in a political system, parties often reflect the quality and strength of democracy present in the country. Because they are so closely tied to the public and take the burden of initiating debate on public policy, political parties provide some of the most visible signs of either the maturation or degeneration of democratic practice.

In the Dominican Republic the role of political parties as this kind of bellweather institution for gauging the status of democracy is becoming increasingly obvious. Political party activity is firmly entrenched in the body politic and the general populace relies on these organizations not only to provide leaders for government, but to chart the future course of the nation. Although other institutions such as the military and the Catholic church occupy important positions in the socio-political framework of the country, democratic political parties have clearly emerged as the organizations that wield the most power and set the tone of internal political behavior. Despite serious economic dislocations, numerous instances of social disorder, and heightened criticism of administrative malfeasance, political parties continue to operate as the key source of leadership recruitment and policy formulation. The ability of the parties to survive and in many respects prosper amid such flux can be viewed as a sign of democratic maturity.

But, unfortunately, there are other ways of analyzing the condition of political parties in the Dominican Republic. By the onset of the 1986 presidential elections, political parties could best be described as organizations either torn asunder by factionalism or highly individualistic and opportunistic enterprises led by a cast of familiar faces. The Dominican multi-party system offered choices to the voters, but the choices were often more personalistic than programmatic and created a climate of democracy where the institutions of popular rule became secondary to the reputation of familiar caudillos. To date, Dominican political parties remain very weakly institutionalized and highly personalistic and fragmented.

The Partido Revolucionario Dominicano (PRD), unquestionably the dominant political organization in the Dominican Republic, spent most of the 1986 preelection period engaged in internal struggles over the choice of the presidential nominee and the future direction of the party. What was once a political organization that prided itself on its strong grassroots structure and firm commitment to social democracy (the PRD is a member of the Socialist International) and its ability to serve as the only true mass party in the country, had become in 1986 three or perhaps more subparties, each with its own leadership, policy priorities, and constituency. To many observers of Dominican politics, the PRD, after eight years in power, had lost much of its ideological commitment and compassion for the plight of the poor and was not so much a political party as a ruling clique concerned chiefly with remaining in power.[14]

The problems of the PRD are not merely the result of a transition from an opposition party with little power and influence to a governing party with responsibility for running the country. The central figures in the organization also failed to reach agreement on who would bear the mantle of the PRD in the most recent presidential campaign. For most of its history, dating back to its early work as the major exile organization opposed to Rafael Trujillo, the PRD was a party of ideas and ideals led by one man, Juan Bosch. But the 1965 revolution soured Bosch on social democracy and by 1973 he had left the PRD and founded his own party, the Partido de Liberación Dominicano (PLD). With Bosch gone, the PRD became a party with no central leader. In his place the PRD has been led by a number of individuals from different socio-economic backgrounds and with different perceptions of how the party should proceed in Dominican politics [15]

The most visible figure whom many felt was the heir-apparent to Bosch was José Francisco Peña Gómez. A fiery orator with definite leftist views and devoted support from the urban lower classes, Peña Gómez made no secret of his desire to run for the Dominican presidency, but he was hampered by his politics and the memory of many conservative Dominicans who heard the young PRD leader take to the airwaves in 1965 urging the populace to take up arms against the military. Moreover, Peña Gómez is the son of Haitian peasants who probably fled from the massacre ordered by Trujillo in the 1930s. His "Haitianness" has always been an issue within the party and indeed in the country where many view those with Haitian background as interlopers.

Although Peña Gómez had widespread support within the PRD, he never has been able to convince those more moderate members from the middle class that he would not radicalize the party or that he could hold on to the presidency in the face of a hostile military. It is because of this perception of Peña Gómez' deficiencies that more moderate and conservative members of the PRD have come forward and sought to place their mark on the organization. Antonio Guzmán, Salvador Jorge Blanco, and Jacobo Majluta can all be placed in the center or center-right section of the PRD. Guzmán, a millionaire rancher, and Jorge, a prominent lawyer (both from the Santiago area) presented themselves as responsible centrists who would bring reform, but also would have the ability to work with the conservative elites and the foreign community. Majluta, a businessman from Santo Domingo, also accented his center-right credentials in 1986, but stressed even more his ties to the commercial sector.[16]

With Jorge in the presidency and committed to seek only one term, the battle for the PRD nomination became a tug of war between Peña Gómez and Majluta. As an example of how divided the PRD has become, the party's nominating convention in November of 1985 is illustrative. Peña Gómez came to the convention confident that he had the necessary votes to be declared the nominee of his party. With the quiet support of Jorge and his reputation as a dedicated party man who had paid his dues, Peña Gmez felt that the PRD would once again accent ideology over practicality and cater to the interests of the urban poor. But in a tangled and violent party meeting in which one delegate was shot and killed, the forces of Jacobo Majluta prevailed over Peña Gómez. Majluta had most likely worked harder at convincing delegates that he could win the presidency than Peña Gómez, although Peña Gómez and his supporters alleged massive fraud on the part of the Majluta group.[17]

The squabbling within the PRD continued on after the convention with each group accusing the other of wrongdoing. President Jorge, for his part, stayed on the sidelines, but let it be known that he might consider accepting an offer to run as a compromise candidate. In January of 1986 a *pacto de unión* was signed that recognized Majluta as the presidential nominee and give the vice-presidential nomination to Peña Gómez. However, pressure from Peña Gómez' supporters forced him to reject the pact and drop out of the running. The internal dispute eventually quieted down with Majluta desperately trying to restore the image of the PRD, Peña Gómez leaving Dominican politics to accept the vice-presidency of the Socialist International, and Jorge laying the groundwork for another try at the nomination in 1990.

The internal divisions and petty disputes within the PRD are characterized by some party officials as merely a continuation of a tradition of vigorous debate and ideological separations within a basically cohesive political party organization. PRD leaders state firmly that their party, despite the personal antagonisms that surfaced during the 1986 campaign, will not disintegrate into a number of smaller organizations. Like their counterparts in North America and Europe, the PRD prefers to see itself as a modern political party that can hold together a number of different philosophies and leadership styles. Although the PRD did come together around the Majluta candidacy (albeit half-heartedly) and helped him to close the gap on Balaguer, there are some disturbing signs that suggest the factionalism in the party is more deep-rooted and troublesome than many would admit.

One of the more serious developments that could threaten the cohesiveness of the PRD is the formation of a number of electoral "tendencies" or parallel party organizations that sprang up during the campaign. These tendencies, such as Majluta's La Estructura (LE) and Peña Gómez' Bloque Institucional, signal perhaps the first step in the development of breakaway parties, should the PRD be unable to remain unified. Although both men relied upon these tendencies for support during the campaign, the real test of their viability will be in 1990 when most observers feel that the PRD will face a three-man race between Peña Gómez, Majluta, and Jorge. Also of concern is the heightened recognition within the party that the organization has lost its ideological base as a proponent of social-democratic change.[18] During the administrations of both Guzmán and Jorge, the PRD did little by way of addressing key social ills such as land reform and unemployment, even though these were presented as issues that had high priority within the party. Now with four years in an opposition role and little governing responsibility, a revitalization of ideology can be expected. But resuscitating old arguments about statism, foreign investment, income inequality and support for revolutionary change may only serve to further divide segments of the party.

In many respects the electoral defeat of the PRD in 1986 may be viewed as a blessing in disguise. The party now has time to get its house in order and revive a party organization that has consistently been viewed as one of the strongest and most professional in Latin America. With Balaguer's policies to focus on and a continuing large (but admittedly divided) reservoir of popular support, the PRD has an opportunity to rebound as a unified organization with a common purpose and a clear demarcation of leadership authority. The danger, however, is that the PRD may be entering a period of disintegration when personalities rather than the organization take precedence. Should the PRD see a continuation of the personalistic factionalism that surfaced in 1985 and 1986, the Dominican multi-party system may see an unfortunate growth in its numbers.

While the PRD has been hampered by internal factionalism, the other major political party in the Dominican Republic, Joaquín Balaguer's Partido Reformista, successfully completed negotiations with the Christian Social Revolutionary Party (PRSC) to form the Christian Social Reformist Party (with the same abbreviation). This combining of Balaguer's highly personalistic organization with a party that has a clearly defined program and extensive ties to party organizations in Latin America (Venezuela's COPEI) and Europe (West Germany's Christian Democrats) was perhaps the key to the former president's surprise electoral victory in 1986. Balaguer's Reformista organization was never held in high regard within the Dominican Republic. Its membership was much less than that of the PRD, party strength was confined primarily to the rural areas and among conservatives, and there was little in the way of an ideological base that could be used to show potential voters what they might expect should they choose to support the Reformista ticket. In the past, when democratic practice was weak and Balaguer had near complete control of the political system, a modern political party organization was not necessary, but with the victory of the PRD in 1978 and the new demands placed on presidential candidates, Balaguer was forced to revitalize the Reformista organization.

By joining forces with the Christian Democrats, Balaguer was able immediately to strengthen his organization and bring a sense of legitimacy to his candidacy. No longer just a personalistic former president,

Balaguer now became the standard-bearer of a party with strong ties to the church and to urban workers. Balaguer also gained access to financial and technical assistance that was provided by the Christian Democratic World Union and other organizations tied to the international Christian Democratic movement.[19]

For its part, the Social Christian party saw the alliance as an opportunity to play a much larger role in Dominican politics. Although it participated in the elections of 1978 and 1982, the Social Christians were never seriously viewed as challengers to the PRD or the Reformistas. The arrangement creating the Christian Social Reformist party thus benefited both Balaguer and the Social Christians and more importantly created a challenger to the PRD that was more than a loose assortment of cronies and would-be office seekers. Dominican politics now had two modern political parties with extensive organizational roots, an identifiable ideology, and ties to an international consortium.

In analyzing the alliance of the Reformistas and Christian Democrats it is important not to lose sight of the fact that this is a marriage of convenience actively sought after by a man who is without question one of the shrewdest politicians in the hemisphere. Joaquín Balaguer could not be expected to be wedded to the Christian Democratic program agenda after he assumed the presidency. Issues such as strengthening the social service systems in the rural areas, addressing the health and educational needs of the young, and bringing about social reform in a climate of strict adherence to nonviolence and respect for human rights have never been policy areas adequately addressed in previous Balaguer administrations. As a personalist caudillo figure, Balaguer prefers to go his own way regardless of any party or ideology.

What Balaguer has gained and the Christian Democratic leaders have agreed to is the pragmatic creation of a party network that can survive and prosper in the new democratic climate in the Dominican Republic. Balaguer and those around him, such as his vice-president, Carlos Morales Troncoso; Joaquín Ricardo, the secretary-general of the PRSC (and Balaguer's second cousin); and ex-President Donald Reid Cabral, who was the party's director of organization and was later appointed to the position of foreign minister, are looking past the 1986 victory and are in the process of building a party that can be a contender in 1990, when it is most likely that the PRSC will not be able to rely on the personalistic following and attractiveness of Joaquín Balaguer. In many respects what is happening in the PRSC is an exciting development for Dominican democracy, for it signals that even though the PRD may be in the process of serious decay and disintegration, the political system is vibrant enough to form new parties and perhaps revitalize existing electoral and governmental institutions.

The vibrancy of the Dominican party system can also be seen in the remarkable advances made by Juan Bosch's Dominican Liberation Party (PLD). From a party that received approximately 18,000 votes in the 1978 election (and in the process lost its legal status), the PLD garnered 18 percent of the electorate in the 1986 presidential contest and sent a clear message to the other two parties that the PLD is a force to contend with in the future. Much of the success of the PLD can be attributed to the continued popularity of Juan Bosch, coupled with the anger and frustration of the urban working class toward the PRD. Although Bosch has toned down some of his harsh leftist rhetoric, he remains an unabashed champion of the poor and a constant critic of Balaguer's toleration of repression during the 1970s and of the PRD's rape of the public treasury.[20] In fact, the slogan of the PLD during the 1986 campaign was "Neither a Murderer nor a Thief."

Although the PLD is Juan Bosch, the party has in the last few years picked up considerable support from Dominican intellectuals and college students who had become radicalized by the deficiencies of the Jorge administration. With new support to help mobilize the urban and rural poor and what some say is considerable financial assistance from Fidel Castro, the PLD has positioned itself to expand its support in the 1990 elections. As Rafael Herrera, the respected editor of the Dominican newspaper *Listin Diario* states, "If Bosch continues to live, don't think that this is his last opportunity. If the party grows during this last election, he will have another opportunity. A politician 80 years old is not so extraordinary here."[21]

Few Dominicans believe that Bosch and the PLD have a chance at winning the presidency in 1990, primarily because he is hated by the military and the business community (despite some attempts during the last campaign to assuage the fears of the Dominican Chamber of Commerce) and would be no favorite of Washington. But social forces in the Dominican Republic are highly volatile and should the Balaguer government fail to act upon the issues of unemployment, food prices, and housing, Bosch will have an attentive audience when he lashes out on his familiar themes of inequality and injustice. Much of the PLD support is from Dominicans below the age of 25. This also happens to be the segment of the population that feels the brunt of unemployment and dashed hopes. Bosch is a master at inciting the poor whether it be in his radio speeches, the party's newspaper, *Vanguardia del Pueblo*, or his informal talks in the barrios. He may never be permitted to enter the National Palace again as he did in 1963, but he and his party may be able to force both the PRSC and particularly the PRD to move from the center-right of the political spectrum and fashion policy issues from the leftist perspective.

At the present time political party activity in the Dominican Republic is dominated by the PRD, the PRSC, and the PLD. In the 1986 presidential elections four other parties participated, but received less than 1 percent of the popular vote and, more importantly, were viewed as personalistic organizations that more than likely will not be seen in 1990. Of the four, the conservative Progressive National Force of Mario Vinicio "Vincho" Castillo's followers may be able to develop into a party with a more substantial popular base. Vinicio, a former minister under Balaguer, is an articulate critic of the PRD with a strong advocacy for land reform which he hopes to translate into support in the rural areas where Balaguer and the PRSC are strong. Vinicio, like most politicians on the right, seems to be positioning himself for the time when Balaguer is no longer in the presidency or in control of the PRSC.[22] It is then that men such as Vinicio hope to become the spokesmen of the center-right in the Dominican Republic.

As to the far left, the candidacy of Bosch severely limited the visibility of parties like the Communist Party of the Dominican Republic (PACOREDO) and the Socialist Bloc (BS). These two parties chose not to run candidates in the 1986 election (in part because that would demonstrate their weakness), but nevertheless were quite active presenting their programmatic solutions and criticizing the major parties. The far left has never been a major force in Dominican politics and as long as Juan Bosch is able to rouse the masses with his Marxist-like rhetoric, the Communists and Socialists can be expected to languish.

In terms of numbers and ideological choices, the Dominican political party system can be described as quite vibrant. Voters in this country have come to expect a crowded field of candidates espousing a host of policy positions. But what is perhaps most interesting about Dominican party politics is that despite the numbers and choices, it is still the personalities—Balaguer, Bosch, Jorge, Peña, Majluta—that make a difference. With the onset of truly competitive democracy in 1978, political parties have been much more conscious of the need for developing effective organizations that inform the voters about issues and policies and then convince them to support the party's ticket. The convention victory of Jacobo Majluta and the decision by Balaguer to align with the Social Christians are but two examples of the importance now being placed on building a strong party organization.

Yet the emphasis on organization must share center stage of party strategy with the realization that Dominican voters continue to be attracted to leadership personality and style. Whether it be the quiet genius of Balaguer, the charismatic strength of men like Bosch and Peña Gómez, or the rather bland, but sincere administrative demeanor of Jorge and Majluta, appearance, reputation, stage presence, and, in Peña Gómez' case, ancestry, are critical variables in analyzing the character of Dominican electoral behavior. Lost, perhaps unfortunately, in this scramble to build organization strength and to play up leadership differences, is the decline of ideological commitment and programmatic emphasis. Dominican political parties are indeed becoming Westernized, but in the process seem more concerned with defeating party adversaries and building organizations that will ensure victory than presenting the people with workable solutions to an endless series of national problems.

DEMOCRATIC OUTPUT AND FEEDBACK: PUBLIC POLICY AND PROGRAMS

It is essential in a study of Dominican democracy to examine the public policy outputs of government in recent years and the reactions of the people toward those outputs. A study of democratic output and feedback, however, is not easily achieved in the Dominican Republic. There is little in the way of published reports that analyze in a rigorous way the performance of the Dominican government since the election of 1978, and only recently have the political parties developed reliable public opinion data.[23] In many instances one is able to find out more about how the Dominican government is doing and what the people think of their leaders from foreign sources, in particular, U.S. public and private officials who have developed their own studies and data bases.

What is available, from the Dominican perspective, on the issues of government output and popular feedback, is a rather extensive collection of information from public speeches and administrative pronouncements, newspaper accounts, and personal or street corner interviews. Such largely impressionistic data can at times be biased and concentrate too heavily on popular perceptions of a particular governing regime. But in a small country like the Dominican Republic with an open press and numerous personal interconnections between people in the private sector and relatives in the government, impressions can often provide a fairly accurate picture of what democratic governance has meant to the country and how it has been accepted by the people.

Public Policy under Guzmán, Jorge, and Balaguer

The onset of two-party democracy and a peaceful transition of power in the 1978 presidential election ushered in a what can only be called a honeymoon period for liberal democracy and social reform. Although the euphoria present after the departure of the Trujillos was missing, the inauguration of Antonio Guzmán and the months immediately after his ascension to the presidency were a time of great pride for the Dominican people. Even though Balaguer had attempted to squelch the democratic transition and placed limits on Guzmán's governing power, Dominicans were hopeful that democracy had matured to the point where power could be shared and alternative policy prescriptions could be implemented without fear of conservative backlash. To his credit, President Guzmán built on this era of good feeling by opening up the political system. His invitation to political exiles to return home, the legalization of the Communist party, and the immediate abrogation of repressive measures created an enormous amount of goodwill. Furthermore Guzmán's bold moves to de-politicize the military by transfers, retirements, and promotions of officers who support democratic practice quickly solidified his regime and gave democracy a reasonable chance of survival.

In the first real test of the new democratic government's ability to respond to crisis, the Guzmán administration received high marks for its performance during the devastating hurricane of 1982 which destroyed not only roads, bridges, powerlines, and left thousands homeless, but damaged valuable crops such as coffee, tobacco, and sugarcane. Although Guzmán relied heavily on U.S. military assistance provided from nearby Puerto Rico, international aid officials sent to the scene were impressed by the dedication of the government and the high level of efficiency in which it operated. Unfortunately the short-term success of the Guzmán government in responding to the hurricane was overshadowed by the long-term effects of crop damage, loss of internal infrastructure, and the inevitable need to borrow needed development funds.

The early successes of the Guzmán administration were quickly forgotten by the Dominican people as international indebtedness, skyrocketing prices for foreign oil, the collapse of the sugar and ferronickel markets, and the inevitable rise in unemployment, cast a pale over this new experiment in democratic reform. Praise for political toleration and internal peace gave way to increased criticism of government economic policy. Not surprisingly, Guzmán's popularity suffered, and with each new sign of economic decline and public corruption, Dominicans began to place less emphasis on the glories of their victory in 1978.[24]

The reputation of Dominican democracy was not helped any by the suicide of President Guzmán and the accompanying speculation that his death was connected to a trail of corruption that led to his immediate family. By the time of the inauguration of Salvador Jorge Blanco in 1982, confidence in Dominican democracy had been severely strained. Jorge promised new reforms, clean government, and a sound economy; but the new president enjoyed no honeymoon period and was unable to turn around a rapidly deteriorating internal economic situation. Throughout his four-year term, Jorge was saddled with a seemingly endless stream of strikes and protests from public workers demanding an increase in the minimum wage (eventually increased to 250 pesos a month after the threat of a general strike) to candlelight parades to show public outrage over the questionable death of a popular nightclub singer while in police custody. Although the harsh crackdown on food price protesters in April of 1984 received worldwide attention, this bloody outburst was but one of may incidents in a long chain of opposition actions against the PRD government.

But what was even more disturbing to those supporters of the PRD was the manner in which the government chose to handle protests. The Jorge administration gained a reputation as increasingly authoritarian. The arrest and detention of key labor leaders, the attempt to license journalists as a subtle means of control, and the disturbing claims of political repression against left-wing activists seriously eroded what was left of support for Jorge and led many Dominicans to wonder out loud what the difference was between PRD reform democracy and life under Balaguer's "showcase" democracy.[25]

The decline in public support for the Jorge administration was intensified by the onrush of corruption and mismanagement charges made against the government. Many in the Dominican Republic felt that the PRD would not succumb to the opportunities for enrichment and temptations of public office, as the authoritarian administrations of the past had done. When Dominicans realized that the PRD really had no different perception of government service than other political groups, the mantle of legitimacy vanished and so too did confidence in the reform democracy. By the time Jorge and the PRD left power in August of 1986, Dominicans had lost their idealism and had come to see that even though democratic practice is much different from authoritarian control, it does not guarantee domestic tranquility or erase the temptations of public life.

One interesting sidelight of the demise of the PRD democratic mystique is the generally positive reputation that the government, in particular the Jorge administration, developed within the international community. Officials at the International Monetary Fund (IMF), for example, were effusive in their praise of the courage that the Jorge administration showed in riding through the political storm that surrounded the austerity agreement. Most economists and bankers familiar with the Dominican situation agreed that reform of the currency exchange system, the tax code, the budget process, and import-export policies was long overdue and had been hindering the country's ability to compete in international markets.[26] The fact that Jorge refused to be influenced by internal political pressures and pushed forward with the changes that are now seen as responsible for a turnaround in the economy was characterized by IMF spokesmen as an example of one the most successful negotiations with a Third World nation.

State Department officials were also kind in their evaluation of the Jorge administration and the status of Dominican democracy. In light of the turmoil in neighboring Haiti and the continued ability of the Dominicans to pass the presidency on to political opponents with a minimum of internal disharmony, the United States continues to see the Dominican Republic as an example of a vigorous democracy that has been able to avoid the ravages of revolution (President Reagan, for example, called the Dominican Republic a "beacon of democracy"). As a sign of its confidence in Dominican democracy the United States increased aid for a time, both economic and military, and worked vigorously to arrange favorable agreements that smooth over outstanding bilateral debt problems with the international banking community (The Paris Club) and permit greater access of Dominican textiles products into this country. The United States was not able in 1986 under Gramm-Rudman budget restraints to avoid a cutback in aid to the Dominican Republic or a cut in the sugar quota. But the prevalent view among U.S. officials is that this country has done about all it can to show support for Dominican democracy.[27]

But while many U.S. government officials are quick to praise the determination of Dominican political leaders and tout the strength of Dominican democracy, they are also quick to point to the numerous deficiencies of the governing system. A common criticism made about Dominican government officials is their lack of administrative savvy, more specifically, their inability effectively to represent their government in negotiations with foreign banks or bureaucracies. Perhaps because of the low pay given public officials or the insidious nature of public corruption, Dominicans are often portrayed as novices with little talent for negotiating loan and trade agreements with foreign institutions. When attention is turned to domestic administration, the evaluation of Dominican policymakers and frontline bureaucrats becomes decidedly worse. Besides the numerous layers of unnecessary bureaucracy and the unending red tape, foreign visitors to the country are amazed at the fact that most public decisions are made by the same people—the technical secretary to the president, the president of the Central Bank, the minister of finance, and of course the president. The constant reappearance of these individuals in all decision areas suggests that there is little in the way of competent administration below the top ministerial level.[28]

The limitations of the Dominican administrative hierarchy are perhaps most visible when foreign investors seek to open up a new venture in the country. Interviews with corporate officials and lawyers reveal the frustrations that accompany dealing with the Dominican bureaucracy. Although the Jorge administration was responsible for eliminating unnecessary roadblocks, especially in the tourist industry and in the export of nontraditional exports, the efforts by foreign investors, anxious to develop agricultural exports such as melons and pineapples, have run

Table 4.1
Comparison of Key Social Economic Indicators in the Dominican Republic, 1978/1985

	1978	1985
Literacy	66%	68%
Unemployment	25%	30%
Life Expectancy	56 yrs.	61 yrs.
Percent increase in GDP	+4.4	-1.2
Infant Mortality	31/1,000	28/1,000
Inflation Rate	3.5%	38%
External Debt	$935 million	$2.6 billion
Percent of population with access to potable water	50%	55%
Exports (in US millions)	675	737
Imports (in US millions)	860	1,286
Trade Deficit	-185	-549

Source: Compiled by the authors.

up against a wall of bureaucracy that many times can only be broken by a bribe.[29] At a time when most outside observers of the Dominican economy agree that there is a crying need to decrease the state sector and enhance opportunities in the private sector, government policy appears wedded to public solutions and the inefficiency that seems to accompany those solutions.

So far we have approached the issue of governmental performance and popular support for that performance by concentrating on a number of internal and external evaluations of the two PRD recent presidencies. But in order to get a more complete picture of how successful PRD reform democracy was in its eight-year rule, it would be helpful to examine a few critical indices and compare their status in 1978 during the Balaguer administration with that of the last complete year of the Jorge administration. The above table compares ten areas of national life commonly used as standards for determining the status of economic and social progress and the quality of life.

As can be seen in Table 4.1, the record of the two PRD presidents in addressing key socioeconomic problem areas has been mixed and in many cases did not hold up well against the performance of the Balaguer administration. Although there has been some improvement over the Balaguer years in the important welfare areas such as literacy, life expectancy, infant mortality, and access to drinking water, the changes cannot be considered significant and have not had a positive impact on national life. The upward increase in life expectancy, which is the most dramatic positive improvement, can be partially attributed to Guzmán's program of developing better health care, especially in the rural areas.

The benefits achieved in the social welfare areas, however, are more than overshadowed by the failure of the government to control inflation, the foreign debt, and to make even a small dent in unemployment. These disappointing areas of government policy, coupled with the fact that GDP dropped in 1985 for the first time since 1965 and that the all-important imbalance between exports and imports has widened considerably since 1978, clearly suggests that the performance of PRD reform democracy was not impressive. It must be stated that these comparisons say nothing about special circumstances such as oil price increases, world market fluctuations, and changes in foreign trade policies that may have influenced the performance level, but they do show that despite a public commitment to bring reform to the lower classes and the political control of the administrative system, the PRD was unable to live up to its claim as a party that could change the life of the average Dominican.

Understanding the above comparison, one can better comprehend the electoral victory of Joaquín Balaguer in 1986 and the desire among many Dominicans, even those at the bottom of the social ladder, to bring back a leader, a style of governing, and a system of decision making that seemed to work better than the PRD's brand of reform democracy. Balaguer, in his inaugural address to the dignitaries gathered in the National Assembly, was vague on the specific policy program he intended to follow. But the Dominican president, always politically astute, stressed the twin goals of fighting corruption and relieving the plight of the poor.[30] Dominicans have heard this before from their governmental leaders and were faced with disappointment, but knowing the track record of Balaguer they seemed willing to give him and his brand of Dominican democracy another chance.

Balaguer began his new period in the presidency rather impressively. He cut back on the number of sinecures in the public service, put an end to some corrupt practices, brought a number of groups and factions into his cabinet, and promised to provide an honest and efficient government. But the economic crisis that he had inherited remained severe and, as we shall see in more detail in subsequent chapters, he was reluctant to continue the austerity measures that President Jorge had followed, faring their political consequences in the form of riots and even revolution. So Balaguer temporized and flip-flopped, leaving no one certain of his policies. The lack of determined action, particularly on economic policy, left the Dominican business sector confused and uncertain; it also produced confusion and some disillusionment with the president among other groups (the middle class, the U.S. Embassy) who could not be sure where the government was headed. Meanwhile President Balaguer continued to try to juggle the contending forces in the country and to provide the necessary leadership, a task not made any easier by his advanced age and the country's continuing economic difficulties.

THREE STYLES OF DOMINICAN DEMOCRACY

One of the more interesting and certainly significant facets of Dominican politics in the post-revolutionary period is the manner in which democracy has developed and been perceived within the country. It is safe to state that in the Dominican Republic there is not one commonly accepted version of democratic principle and practice, but rather three, which not surprisingly correspond to the philosophies and leadership styles of the primary political groupings and personalities currently active in public life. These can be defined as Balaguer's democracy of appearance, Guzmán and Jorge's compromise democracy, and Bosch's class-based participatory democracy.

The Balaguer regime, 1966–1978, despite its deficiencies in the area of human rights, popular participation, and institutional decision making, nevertheless avoided much of the harshness and repressive authoritarianism so often found in Latin America. Regular elections, a relatively open press, and toleration of political and social dissent, created a kind of quasi-democratic environment that allowed Balaguer to retain the support of the middle class and, more importantly, the United States.

The PRD era of Guzmán and Jorge was a time in which governmental leaders were conscious of forming politics along Western democratic lines, and to some extent they were successful. Both leaders vowed to avoid the excesses or omissions of Balaguer and to create a system of decision making that incorporated the principles of checks and balances and popular rule.

Finally, during both the Balaguer era and the PRD years Juan Bosch remained a vigilant opposition voice questioning both groups on their definition and application of democracy. In Bosch's view, Balaguer and the PRD severely compromised Dominican democracy by never making sincere efforts to represent the interests of the Dominican masses. Dominican democracy was either all form and no substance (Balaguer) or concentrated on macroeconomic policy at the expense of the social welfare of the people (the PRD).

The fact that the Dominicans have yet to agree on a proper definition and application of democracy is not remarkable considering that the country is new to democracy and had to build its democratic political system out of the ashes of Trujilloism. But what may be disturbing, particularly to those schooled in the Western democratic tradition, is the renewed popularity of Joaquín Balaguer, the internal struggles within the PRD, and the growing popularity of the Marxist left. Dominican democracy at the start of the fifth Balaguer presidency cannot be described as vital and stable, even though the system survived another election challenge and transferred power peacefully. A more accurate portrayal of Dominican democracy is that it is a system of governance that has become captive of very powerful social and political forces. Democracy is after all a form of government that exists because elites in society, either on their own or because of enormous social pressure, have determined that constructing a policy-making framework that incorporates popular participation is in the best interests of the country. As the Dominican Republic moves into the 1990s, both the elites and the masses seem divided over what kind of democracy they want and whom they want to benefit most from that democracy. The facts that the Dominicans are willing to forgive Balaguer for his years of quasi-democracy, that the PRD is back at the drawing board trying to determine why their reform democracy failed, and that Bosch's PLD increasingly represents the next generation of Dominicans, are clear signs that society is becoming polarized and that democracy is likely to be redefined.

One of the lessons learned by the advocates of democratic development in the 1960s is that the attainment of Western-style governance is not inevitable or unilinear. Rather, democratic development, if it occurs at all, is a kind of ragged process with numerous false starts and more than an occasional failure. The more optimistic projections of orderly democratic development have been replaced by the reality, oftentimes, of regression, disorder, and decay. The evolution of Dominican democracy since 1965 is an example of the difficulties that face a nation that wants to move away from its authoritarian past while avoiding the ever present temptations of revolution. The transition in 1978 from Balaguer's brand of democracy to that of the PRD was seen by many, especially in the United States, as proof that the Dominican Republic was indeed developing into a modern democratic state with a system of governance that mirrored what could be found in the more advanced industrial democracies. But while Guzmán and Jorge built on that tradition, they also allowed practices from the old regime to flourish, such as corruption, administrative inefficiency, centralized decision making, and an increased reliance on force. By the time Jorge left office and Balaguer returned to power in 1986, democratic government had become at least partially discredited and the champions of authoritarianism and revolution were heard more often.

A SUMMING UP

Dominicans have tried many forms of democracy. None of them have worked very well. Early in the 1960s they tried a quite pure (and some would say rarified and unrealistic) form of democracy under Juan Bosch. But he was overthrown after only seven months in office. In the Balaguer administration, from 1966 until 1978, the country experienced a form of authoritarian democracy; but his rule was eventually discredited because of its authoritarian practices. Under PRD presidents Guzmán and Jorge (1978–1986) the country returned to reform democracy but also incorporated some strong indigenous traditions (personalism, centralism, patronage). And in 1986 the country returned to the personalist, caudillistic, paternalistic leadership of an aging Balaguer who had his own understanding of democracy. But the indigenous formulas did not produce very happy results either. One reasonable conclusion about Dominican politics is that nothing—no political regime—has worked well. But on the other hand, democracy is now more firmly established than ever before. In its own groping, experimental, and often ad hoc way the Dominican Republic has begun to build a form of democracy that is in accord both with Western democratic precepts and its own historic traditions.

The victory of Joaquín Balaguer and the renewed popularity of Juan Bosch does not mean that Dominican democracy has reached its apogee and is now in full retreat. As stated earlier, there is present in the country now a more mature understanding of democracy and its limitations. Balaguer will not easily return the country to the days of his quasi-democracy. The parties, the unions, the media, the church, and a loose confederation of social and professional groups will certainly resist efforts to turn the clock back. Furthermore, now that the military has become more professionalized, Balaguer may be permitted to function in a more democratic mode, an opportunity that was denied him from 1966 until 1978. If there is any certainty about the future course of democratic development, it is that the presidential election of 1990 is already being viewed in the country as the real test of whether the Dominican Republic has matured as a nation and is capable of balancing its three versions of democracy. From the Western perspective, there is hope that in the next few years the Dominicans will be able to come to an agreement on their democracy, but it is more likely that there will be multiple interpretations of popular rule and more examples of regression, disorder, and decay.

NOTES

1. An example of the dissatisfaction with the possibilities of reform in Latin America can be found in Jerome Levinson and Juan de Onis, *The Alliance That Lost Its Way: A Critical Report on the Alliance for Progress* (Chicago: Quadrangle Books, 1970).

2. See Albert O. Hirschman, "The Turn to Authoritarianism in Latin America and the Search for Its Economic Determinants," in David Collier, et al., *The New*

Authoritarianism in Latin America (Princeton, N.J.: Princeton University Press, 1979), pp. 61–98.

3. Howard Wiarda, "Is Latin America Democratic and Does It Want to Be? The Crisis and Quest of Democracy in the Hemisphere," in Howard Wiarda, ed. *The Continuing Struggle for Democracy in Latin America* (Boulder, CO: Westview Press, 1980) pp. 3–26.

4. Howard Wiarda, "Democratic Development in the Dominican Republic: The Difficult Legacy," paper prepared for a conference on "Democracy in Developing Nations," Stanford University and the National Endowment for Democracy, Stanford, CA, December 19–21, 1985.

5. Michael Kryzanek, "The 1978 Election in the Dominican Republic: Opposition Politics, Intervention and the Carter Administration," *Caribbean Studies* 19, nos. 1 and 2, April–July 1979, pp. 61–64.

6. See Jan Knippers Black, *The Dominican Republic: Politics and Development in an Unsovereign State* (Boston: George Allen and Unwin, 1986), pp. 137–41.

7. Richard C. Kearney, "Dominican Update—Can Politics Contain the Economic Crisis?" *Caribbean Review*, December 1985, p. 14.

8. A recent crisis in the Dominican judiciary was the failure of the senate to name the country's justices some three months into the Balaguer administration. The problem stemmed from political battles in the senate between PRD senators and supporters of President Balaguer. See *Santo Domingo News*, December 4, 1986, p. 1.

9. Richard Kearney, "Spoils in the Caribbean: The Struggle for Merit-Based Civil Service in the Dominican Republic," *Public Administration Review*, March/April 1986, p. 146.

10. Jan Knippers Black, *The Dominican Republic*, op. cit., p. 141. See also José Maria Jacome-Martinez, *La evolución de la administratción pública en los paises en desarrolo y el caso de la República Dominicana* (Santiago: ONAP, 1981).

11. See Dennis Volman, "Dominicans Cry Out for Reform," *Christian Science Monitor*, April 28, 1986.

12. Richard Kearney, "Dominican Update," op. cit., p. 38.

13. See the Dominican newspaper *Ultima Hora*, December 27, 1986, p. 4. for a discussion of Balaguer's efforts to respond to alleged corruption in the Jorge administration.

14. The PRD's official ideology is outlined in *Tactica y estrategía* (Santo Domingo: PRD Departmento Nacional de Organizacion, 1980).

15. See "An Election Season Full of Color—and Sometimes Violence," Washington *Times*, May 19, 1986, pp. 22–25.

16. G. Pope Atkins, 1986 CSIS Latin American Election Studies Series, Dominican Republic Election Study Report, Report No. 1, May 1986, pp. 20–24.

17. G. Pope Atkins, CSIS Latin American Election Studies Series, Dominican Republic Election Study Report, Report No. 2, June 1986, pp. 9–13.

18. Ibid., pp. 17–18.

19. Jan Knippers Black, *The Dominican Republic*, op. cit., provides an excellent analysis of the ties between Balaguer and the Christian Democratic Party. See pp. 84–87.

20. G. Pope Atkins, Dominican Republic Election Study Report, Report No. 1, pp. 27–28.

21. As quoted in "An Election Season full of Color—and Sometimes Violence, Washington *Times*, May 19, 1986.

22. Jan Knippers Black, *The Dominican Republic*, op. cit., pp. 90–91.

23. See, for example, Bernardo Vega's election study "La campaña electoral del Dr. Salvador Jorge Blanco en 1982: Un caso de uso exitoso de encuestas políticas en La República Dominicana" (Santo Domingo, 1986).

24. See "Dominican Republic: The Launching of Democracy?," *Nacla Report on the Americas*, November–December 1982, pp. 13–20.

25. See Georgie Anne Geyer's analysis of the PRD and its problems in her syndicated column. *Brockton Enterprise*, August 15, 1986, p. 14.

26. Personal interviews, International Monetary Fund, Washington, DC, July 2, 1986.

27. Personal interviews, U.S. State Department Washington, DC, July 1, 1986.

28. Richard Kearney, "Spoils in the Caribbean," op. cit., pp. 147–48.

29. The American Chamber of Commerce for the Dominican Republic in its publication "Commercial News Dominican Republic" offers advice to potential U.S. investors on how to deal with the Dominican bureaucracy. See *Commercial News Dominican Republic*, July 1985, p. 7.

30. *El Caribe*, August 17, 1986.

5

GROUPS IN DOMINICAN SOCIETY: INTERNAL PRESSURES, FOREIGN INFLUENCES

A study of the Dominican Republic can easily place too much emphasis on charismatic and colorful personalities and the impact that key individuals have had on political development and the character of national life. Even though leaders such as Trujillo, Bosch, and Balaguer have personally changed the course of Dominican history, it is important not to forget that this country, like any other, is a mosaic of numerous social, economic, and professional groups that are clearly identifiable, compete openly for the attention of government, and in their own way effect the manner in which public policy is formulated and implemented.

As a nation that has evolved within the Latin American tradition, the relationship between societal groupings and politics in the Dominican Republic is critical for understanding power and authority, the process of decision making, and the dynamics of change.[1] Even though much attention is directed at the interaction of key national figures and governmental institutions, it is the social and interest groups that form the backdrop of politics. By representing Dominicans with similar backgrounds, articulating issues of common concern, and occasionally challenging government authority groups in the Dominican Republic force leaders to fashion policy with greater specificity and to recognize that democratic governance and pluralism go hand in hand.

Describing and analyzing Dominican groups and group behavior becomes a somewhat complicated task primarily because the divisions within society are not solely the result of economic differences, social standing, and cultural mores. Besides the traditional groups that are found in most Latin American and developing countries—the military, the landed oligarchy, the church, labor, peasants, and students—the Dominican political system must also deal with very visible and active external groups, such as the Haitian immigrants, the U.S. Embassy, the foreign business community, Dominican exiles, and the most recent addition to the group mosaic, international bankers and consultants. While the traditional groups are much larger, more active publicly, and are openly courted by political leaders anxious to strengthen their base of support, the external groups rely upon the fact that they represent a segment of Dominican society whose influence is not related to size or public display or vote getting, but rather comes from the fact that the nation needs their services, their money, or their support. Moreover, these external groupings frequently have close ties to, and are often intimately involved with the local groups and interests.

As we discuss the traditional and external groups that are active in Dominican society, it is important to keep in mind that the various participants in this mosaic contribute significantly to the nature and future direction of Dominican politics. Using the astute observations of Charles Anderson, they are all "power contenders" seeking to place their mark and influence on the body politic.[2] Some have been more successful than others, some are increasing in influence, while others are experiencing a decline. But since they are important power contenders, it is essential that these groups be presented not only as communities of individuals with similar backgrounds, interests, and functions, but as identifiable players in the game of Dominican politics. Who wins and who loses, what is accomplished and what is ignored are in large part the result of which power contenders are able to exert their influence on government.

THE CATHOLIC CHURCH

It may seem surprising to begin this discussion of Dominican interest groups by examining the Catholic church; but in recent years this institution, both at the parish level and in its hierarchy, has expanded its influence and assumed the task of ensuring that democratic politics and governance not only flourish, but also become permanent fixtures of national life. Because the church is without question the largest of the identifiable groups within Dominican society (Catholics make up 93 percent of the population) and one that has maintained its independence and integrity over the years, it has the capability to act as minister to the spiritual and personal needs of the people and to make a positive contribution to politics and public policy formulation.

The most recent example of the important political role that the church has assumed in Dominican national life is the involvement of the Archbishop of Santo Domingo in the election controversy in 1986. Archbishop Nicolás de Jésus López Rodríguez was appointed by outgoing president Jorge Blanco to head an independent Commission of Election Assessors (CAE) which acted as an advisory body to the official Central Electoral Board (JCE). Fortunately for Dominican democracy, the CAE, and particularly Archbishop López Rodríguez, played an active and critical role in the controversies surrounding the ballot count. With JCE members being accused by Jacobo Majluta of favoring Balaguer's candidacy, the

CAE stepped in and brought a sense of stability and fairness to what could easily have become a democratic nightmare. With the church-backed CAE lending its credibility to the election process, many Dominicans were convinced that Archbishop López Rodríguez provided a sense of legitimacy to the election and ensured that the political infighting did not create the kind of internal disorder that would stimulate a military response.[3]

Moreover, throughout the election campaign the Dominican archbishop constantly reminded the major electoral participants of their responsibilities as candidates and potential leaders of the Dominican Republic. In one important pastoral letter that revealed the increased involvement of the church in protecting democracy and creating a climate of justice and reform, the archbishop advised the three leading candidates of the importance of this election and the necessity of good government in the country. As the letter stated, "to govern is to serve, promote, and defend the common good and human rights; to distribute goods and services with justice and equity, to be concerned especially for the weak and needy; to protect natural resources; to respect legitimate liberties and to punish corruption."[4]

Although the involvement of the Catholic archbishop in the 1986 presidential election received a great deal of attention and revealed the church's desire to influence the course of national governance, it is at the local level, in the urban barrio parishes and the rural *comunidades de base* (grassroots church communities) that both the performance of the church and the conflicts within it can best be examined. In terms of its physical presence in the Dominican Republic, the church's involvement in the social and intellectual life of the country is considerable. In the health and welfare area the church currently operates some 25 hospitals and clinics, 21 dispensaries, six orphanages, and six homes for the elderly. In education the church runs over 180 schools at all levels and graduates some 15,000 students each year.

But despite this heavy involvement in tending to the personal needs of its people, the Catholic church, especially in the poorer regions of the country, has stepped up its social activism and translated the gospels into aggressive challenges to authority. Numerous recent incidents involving both parish priests and members of the hierarchy, in which traditional land ownership patterns and slow moving government agrarian reform programs were protested, point up the increased interest of church leaders in issues that effect the Dominican masses.

One agrarian issue that has caused an enormous amount of attention at the local level is the response of a number of parish priests and a few bishops to the tactics used by the large multinational corporations to acquire peasant-held land. On two occasions during the 1970s, church leaders tooks an active role in questioning the land acquisition policies of the Rosario Mining Company near the town of Pueblo Viejo and the unchecked power to control sugar production of the Gulf & Western Corporation in the eastern sector of the country.[5] In both cases local priests backed up by their bishop helped organize peasant protests and made public appeals to the Balaguer government to ensure that the interests of the farmers were being fairly represented. When the government clearly showed its pro-business colors, the church continued to press the issue and as a result became a target of police intimidation and repression. In the end, Rosario and Gulf & Western were able to continue their aggressive policies that either dislocated hundreds of peasants or forced them to work exclusively for a foreign enterprise, but the visibility and criticism of church leaders in these two regions pointed out the commitment of local priests and bishops to social justice and their unwillingness merely to rubber-stamp government policies.[6]

Despite the increased visibility of some radical priests challenging the status quo in the rural area, the Catholic church in the Dominican Republic remains a largely conservative institution with deep differences of opinion on the proper tactics to be used in dealing with injustice and the political role of local priests, many of whom ascribe to the so-called Liberation Theology. Fortunately for the church, it has as yet not been faced with the kind of outward expressions of dissension that have divided Catholic religious in other countries. Much of the church's energy has been directed at fighting both Balaguer and the PRD presidents on issues such as divorce liberalization and the introduction of family planning programs (encouraged and funded by the U.S. Agency for International Development). Where there have been disagreements on the proper role of parish priests in the rural area, the church in the Dominican Republic has in large part been unified in questioning policies that strike at the heart of family life and moral theology.

The failure of the church effectively to challenge the land system or to stop the liberal divorce and family planning policies of the government should not immediately lead one to the conclusion that the Catholic hierarchy and the religious in the field are powerless. If we are to understand the real power of the Catholic church in the Dominican Republic, it can be found in the pulpit where priests continue to command respect from their parishioners. Over the years the Dominican church has not hesitated to condemn political leaders and ideologies that it felt were a threat to civil and religious rights and to form alliances that would influence the future direction of politics.

Although the Catholic church was late getting on the bandwagon to depose Rafael Trujillo and cannot be credited with having an impact on the transition to popular rule, it was quite vigorous in its criticism of Juan Bosch and his leftward-leaning government in 1963. Bosch may have been his own worst enemy, but the branding of his policies as

"Communistic" by parish priests certainly made the coup against him easier and helped to marshal public opinion against the Dominican president.[7] During the administration of Joaquín Balaguer the church was at first supportive, but gradually spoke out forcefully against the paramilitary units that were terrorizing urban barrios and demanded that the president intercede to stop the bloodshed. The fact that Balaguer lost a good deal of middle class support in 1978 can be attributed in part to outspoken criticisms of church leaders. Even during the recent PRD rule local priests have joined with the people in criticizing the price increases and in demonstrating against the arbitrary arrests of political activists and union leaders. In fact due to the greater openness of the political system under Guzmán and Jorge, Catholic leaders are more visible than during the Balaguer era and more willing to take risks in challenging the government.[8]

As the Catholic church learns to function once again under Joaquín Balaguer, it faces a number of critical internal problems—a shortage of priests and other religious (there are only about 500 priests to serve the needs of nearly 5 million Catholics), a downturn in church attendance and vocations, an increase in Protestant sects and conversions, and a growing restiveness among Dominican youth, who are not convinced that peaceful protest and community organization are the answers to poverty, inequality, and unemployment. On the positive side, the alliance of Balaguer with the Christian Democratic party and his public support for its program can only strengthen the church's ability to influence government policy in the future. One can expect that chruch leaders will now pressure Balaguer to implement Christian Democratic programs, especially with respect to land reform and worker rights and to remind him of his obligation to continue the PRD record of upholding human rights.

But perhaps the greatest challenge to the Dominican Catholic church is to maintain its position as an institution that cannot be ignored by the people or the major political forces. The fact that the Dominican Republic is a predominantly Catholic country is no guarantee that church leaders will be able to influence policy. Despite its enhanced reputation in recent years and its continued commitment to meet the social welfare needs of the people, the Dominican church faces stiff competition from other power contenders who have their own agenda and other means of effecting public policy. Although the Catholic church remains the dominant religious institution in the country, Protestant sects have been growing vigorously. In fact, the Catholic church's new activism among the poor and in the cause of democracy is in part a response to the challenge it feels from the Protestant groups. Protestant churches, especially the Pentacostal and Evangelical movements, with roots in the United States, have shown remarkable growth. The appeal of the Protestant churches has been not only religious but also social and political. The Protestants have proselytized among Haitian immigrants and have also registered large number of converts among the lower and lower-middle classes. Protestantism has been associated with a stronger work ethic and with individual responsibility. Protestants in the Dominican Republic are thought to be honest, to be loyal family members, to be upright. They are not supposed to beat their wives or children or squander their earnings on liquor and prostitutes. For these reasons Protestantism is often very popular among wives, children, and employers; becoming Protestant is associated with middle-classness, which adds to its appeal.

THE MILITARY

While the Catholic church has become more visible in recent years and has participated more actively in Dominican politics, the military establishment has seemingly turned inward, away from public affairs and the burden of active involvement in national governance. Since the onset of the Guzmán administration and its policies of "depoliticization, institutionalization and professionalization" of the Dominican military, the armed forces no longer act as extra-legal guarantors of social order and backroom power brokers capable of intimidating presidents and shaping the details of public policy. Where Balaguer (and certainly Bosch and Reid Cabral before him) faced a military that viewed itself as a kind of guardian of the national patrimony with the responsibility of providing leadership and direction, the Dominican Republic today is witnessing its primary power contender being transformed into a partner in the democratic experiment and a supporter of a new status quo, one that is much different from that of a mere 15 years ago.

The term often used to describe the movement of an historically interventionist and praetorian military away from its political role is professionalization. In the Dominican Republic there has been a great deal of talk about the "new" professional military and the fact that it now functions in a more Western and modern manner by concentrating on issues such as defense of national borders, modernization of equipment, and training of staff officers and enlisted personnel. As a result of this new emphasis on professionalization, there are those in Dominican society who feel that the military of the 1980s has become more of a governmental bureaucracy and that the officer corps is now thinking as professional managers might, rather than as guardians of internal stability.[9] This view has gained credence because during crisis periods in both the Guzmán and Jorge administrations the military came forward and expressed its support of the government and the democratic process of decision making and change. Through devastating hurricanes, general strikes, street violence, and government inability to deal with numerous social and economic problems, the Dominican military showed itself to be remarkably restrained.

But what this view of the Dominican military lacks is an understanding of how public power is now being defined in the country. The military of the 1980s in the Dominican Republic is concentrating more on expanding its economic power, both individual and institutional. During the latter years of the Balaguer administration and continuing on through that of Guzmán and Jorge Blanco, the Dominican military officer corps gained a reputation as one of the most blatant participants in the use of governmental power for personal gain. Traveling through the wealthy neighborhoods of Santo Domingo, one is struck by the luxurious homes owned by high-ranking members of the armed forces. Stories abound in the country about military misuse of the armed forces budget and the involvement of military managers in corruption at state-run enterprise. Also distressing, but not surprising, are allegations of military complicity in the growing drug trade that is coming through the Dominican Republic. As Dominican military expert Pope Atkins states about the officer corps during the Balaguer era:

Most of Balaguer's generals were able to become multimillionaires through enterprises financed with government resources and through outright graft. More rich middle grade officers were found by the end of the Balaguer era than rich generals under Trujillo. Even junior officers were able to augment their incomes significantly with lower-level graft, such as skimming funds received to feed troops.[10]

Although there is no question that high level members of the military establishment have engaged in illegal acts and as a result have amassed enormous wealth, this may have been the price that had to be paid by recent presidents in order to gain the support of the armed forces and to ensure that they would remain "professional." During Joaquín Balaguer's 12 year tenure as president, he rewarded the military handsomely by increasing the number of generals in the high command, transferring budget funds earmarked for social programs to the various service branches, and permitting sizable pay increases for military personnel while other public servants experienced years of harsh austerity. Though many remember Balaguer's frequent shuffling of the military high command as a sign of his skillful ability to keep on top of the armed forces and dilute their ability to amass political power, this shuffling may also be interpreted as a way of spreading the opportunities for financial gain around to as many officers as possible.[11]

When the PRD presidents entered office the economic power of the military did not wane, although there was a greater sense of apprehension among officers about their ability to control the executive. Bolstered by a series of last-minute maneuvers by the departing president to insure a strong military presence in the new administration, the officer corps was confident that it could continue its domination of Dominican politics and the economic rewards that accompanied that domination.[12] President Guzmán, however, proved surprisingly resistant to these efforts at control. With the assistance of junior officers (commonly called the 19th of May Group), who not only were distressed at the corruption of the senior officers but secretly wanted their chance at enrichment, he began a full-scale replacement of the old regime. High on Guzmán's list were two military figures closely aligned with the reign of terror against the democratic left during the 1970s. General Neit Nivar Seíjas, chief of the National Police and General Enrique Pérez y Pérez, commander of the First Brigade of the army, were retired along with a score of other high-ranking officers. Because of the support among middle-level officers and also a strong revulsion among the Dominican populace against those members of the high command linked to the repression, Guzmán was able to revamp the officer corps and ensure a level of political security for both himself and Dominican democracy.[13]

Guzmán weathered the storm brought on by his campaign to reform the military hierarchy, but the new officer corps nevertheless continued in the tradition of its predecessors and turned its attention away from political intrigue and began a new round of personal enrichment and institutional advancement. Both Guzmán and, in particular, his successor Jorge Blanco found themselves providing the military with increased budget appropriations, new capital improvements, such as a general staff school and a military hospital, and generous pay increments. Helped in part by greater assistance from the United States (but certainly also prodded by the military high command), Guzmán and Jorge began a much needed modernization of the Dominican armed forces. Although primary attention was placed on support equipment such as radios, jeeps, and uniforms, the Dominicans began modernizing their aging air force and adding to their naval fleet.[14] The process of modernization is looked upon by the United States as a means not only of bolstering the defenses of a neighbor, but as another way of professionalizing the military. But from the perspective of the PRD presidents the fiscal outlays for the military serve as a kind of insurance policy against politically motivated intervention.[15]

The current relationship between the Dominican military and the U.S. government is a key one if we are to understand the influence that this institution has on national life. From the early days of the Trujillo regime (and even earlier), when U.S. presidents and secretaries of state saw this strategically located country as a key outpost helping guard the hemisphere from Nazi encroachment and, later, the Dominican dictator

Table 5.1
U.S. Military Assistance to the Dominican Republic, 1978–1986

FISCAL YEAR	MILITARY ASSISTANCE (in thousands of dollars)
1978	700
1979	1,000
1980	3,500
1981	3,430
1982	5,450
1983	10,250
1984	9,700
1985	8,750
1986	10,800

Source: U.S. State Department

as a bulwark against communism, to the 1965 revolution when the United States supported Trujillista officers in their struggle to survive against the constitutionalists, the Dominican military has been able to count on the United States to provide them not only with weapons, training, and advice, but also to recognize their role as participants in the process of governance. The Trujillo generation of military officers and the challenges that they faced are gone now, but the external and internal threats to Dominican security and stability that have concerned the United States have not disappeared. Rather they have reappeared in other forms providing the Dominican military with new incentives to modernize and the United States with new reasons to initiate more ambitious assistance programs.

After a period of time during the Balaguer era when the United States turned its attention to economic reconstruction rather than military modernization, the return to PRD rule in 1978 saw a renewed interest by the United States in the Dominican armed forces. With President Reagan increasingly conscious of the strategic importance of the Caribbean Basin region, neighboring Haiti in turmoil, and drug smugglers using the Dominican Republic as a transfer point into Miami and New York, the United States has worked successfully to convince Congress to provide the Dominican military with greater assistance. As can be seen by Table 5.1 the increases in U.S. military assistance have been steady and substantial during the PRD era.

Most of the assistance provided by the United States to the Dominican military has been in two categories—Foreign Military Sales (FMS), a program through which weapons and equipment are distributed, and the Military Assistance Program (MAP) which grants or lends defense articles, services, and training. A third category of assistance, the International Military Educational and Training Program (IMET), has not been funded extensively in the Dominican Republic, although an increasing number of Dominican officers are receiving training in Panama (along with all military cadets) and an elite unit specializing in counterinsurgency called the Cazadores de la Montana (Highland Rangers) has also been trained by U.S. experts. The combination of these three funding sources clearly has made the Dominican military a product of the United States and dependent on this country for its future modernization and professionalization.

But despite the close ties, the influence of the United States on the Dominican military cannot be characterized as substantial. The U.S. Military Assistance Advisory Group (MAAG) that is tied to the U.S. Embassy is quite small and there does not appear to be any compulsion on the part of U.S.-trained Dominican officers to rely solely on MAAG advice when making key policy decisions. Supporters of democratic governance hope that the U.S. connection will have a positive influence on the Dominican military and reenforce the importance of open elections and peaceful transfer of power. But as has been the case in a number of other Latin American countries where the United States is largely responsible for the development of the armed forces, training and aid do not necessarily lead to the unqualified support of democratic practice.

The key question concerning the Dominican military, despite its current interest in economic power and personal financial gain, is to what extent its interest in political power and governmental administration remains active. In the Dominican Republic, however, with its long history of military intervention, the question should more properly be phrased, under what circumstances would the military seek to control politics and what price would it pay for assuming national leaderhsip in terms of public respect, renewed factional disputes between the generals and middle range officers, and support from its patrons in the United States? The answers to such questions are of course highly speculative, but it is possible to comment on the mindset of the Dominican military and the consistency of their objectives as the premier power contender in the country.

It goes without saying that the Dominican military is a conservative institution interested in social stability, economic prosperity and political moderation. But it is also important to point out that the last few years in the Dominican Republic have not exactly been filled with stability, prosperity, and moderation. The riots, the debt crisis, and the rise of the left have certainly tried the patience of the military to the extent that new signs of unrest and displeasure with the civilian leaders are mounting in the ranks. Nevertheless, this is a military establishment with a degree of toleration and respect for democratic practice unheard of in the country's history. If one is to believe the public pronouncements of the generals, the military now fully supports the democratic system despite the problems that may arise from economic and social dislocations.

Amid all this optimism about the "new" military, one must not ignore the fact that support for democracy from the armed forces has come during a time when civilian presidents looked the other way while fortunes were being made by the generals, and enlisted men were enjoying the fruits of a modernized army, navy, and air force. Should President Balaguer make good on the promise to rid the country of corruption and address crying social welfare needs, and should Juan Bosch continue to attract young, vocal leftists, it is then that the allegiance of the military to democratic government will be truly tested. In many respects these have been good times for the Dominican military. While society suffered, its members have advanced. It is when the military itself is asked to make the sacrifices that their true colors as vital power contenders may be revealed.

THE WORKERS

Where the church's power is in its religious and cultural attachments to the people and the military has a monopoly of the means of force, the power of the Dominican working class resides in its sheer numbers and the fact that the urban and rural workers are the most frustrated, angry, and restive groups in the country. With a workforce estimated at 1,750,000, those Dominicans who labor in the industrial free zones, the ferronickel plants, the sugar refineries, and the tiny plots of overworked soil, have the potential to become a potent political force and a source of chronic social instability. Because of the size of the Dominican workforce, the wide differences in the manner in which they labor and the wide spectrum of complaints that they have registered over the years, this section will be divided into two parts, dealing first with urban workers, in particular the organized labor movement, and second with the rural farmers, the campesinos who continue to make up the largest segment of the working class.

The Urban Setting

As has been the trend in most less-developed countries, the Dominican Republic has experienced a massive exodus of its people from the rural areas into the cities. The promise of better jobs, better services, and of course better pay has lured thousands of Dominicans off the land.

The move to the cities, specifically to Santo Domingo, has, however, not necessarily meant a better life. With the Dominicans unable effectively to make the transition from a sugar-dominated economy to one that offers a broad base of employment, the urban worker has had to face unemployment, underemployment, or dependence on available and highly competitive public works jobs. Although the opening up of industrial free zones that cater to the so-called "screwdriver" assembly plants has provided thousands of jobs and a thriving tourist industry, with 50,000 new Dominicans entering the workforce each year, meeting the demand for jobs has become impossible. Despite the fact that Dominican factory workers are praised widely for their eagerness and ability to grasp manufacturing procedures by foreign business executives who have set up industries in the country, foreign investment capital plus local industrial development has not been enough to decrease even slightly the level of unemployment.[16]

But beside the ever-present problems in the employment market, the Dominican worker has had to contend with rising prices, shortages of basic necessities, and the uncertainties of living on the fringes of the economy. With a minimum wage that was only recently increased from 175 pesos a month to 250 pesos (after the threat of a national strike), most Dominican workers can barely get by. The April 1984 price riots (which were largely led by leftist labor leaders) were a sad reminder of the depth of the frustration experienced by the urban working class.

The severe employment situation in the Dominican Republic and the latent anger found among the urban workers has, surprisingly, not led to the formation of a strong labor union movement in the country. Only about 15 percent, or approximately 200,000 workers, are members of organized unions, and the union movement itself is currently in disarray and not a significant factor in the political arena. Due in large part to the anti-labor policies of the Trujillo era and to a restrictive Labor Code still in force from that era (public employees, which make up more than 50 percent of the workforce, are denied the right to strike), organized labor has found it difficult to establish a movement with sufficient clout to force government leaders to take it seriously. Furthermore, without a strong financial base from which to operate and to sustain a strike, unions in the Dominican Republic cannot employ with any effectiveness the primary means of challenging management or the government.[17]

What union organizations there are in the Dominican Republic are weak and divided with no respected leadership capable of unifying the working class or for that matter expanding the membership. At present there are eight national labor confederations, with the General Union of Dominican Workers (UGTD) leading the way in terms of active members. Labor confederations, like student organizations in the Dominican Republic, are often affliated with political parties and use their organizational strength as a means of furthering the ends of the party organization. The UGTD, for example, is tied to the PRD, while the Autonomous Confederation of the Working Class (CASC) is affiliated with the Social Christian Revolutionary party. Other confederations are affiliated with the Communist party or the Socialist bloc.

The disparate nature of union organization in the Dominican Republic has contributed to the ineffectiveness of labor as a pressure group in politics. For example on Labor Day, which is May first in the Dominican Republic, it is not uncommon to see three or more separate and competing celebrations or to have the confederations working at cross purposes on critical labor legislation, such as the demand for an increase in the minimum wage. With each confederation so closely tied to a political party, the objectives of labor oftentimes get caught up in ideological disputes or are sacrificed in the name of some other party priority. Left behind in this political battle are the interests of the general working man or woman who have had to endure the consequences of divisiveness.

Fortunately for the labor movement, there have been some signs of alliance. In March of 1985, through the sponsorship of the Catholic church, five major labor confederations met with representatives of management and the government in what was called a "tripartite dialogue." The meeting did lead to some basic agreements on the key problems facing labor and began the formation of an agenda of policies that need to be implemented to address the concerns of the working class.

Perhaps even more significant has been the formation in recent years of neighborhood strike committees, commonly called Comités de Lucha Popular (Committees of Popular Struggle) which have helped to coordinate strike activity and increase union membership. While the large confederations fight over turf and influence, the workers at the local level are building organizations that may enhance the power of the urban masses and serve to open new recruitment avenues for leftist political parties.[18]

Of particular interest in the discussion of Dominican workers and organized labor is their relationship to the growing presence of multinational corporations in the country. Contrary to the more common perceptions of labor-management relations in a foreign operated industry, the Dominican Republic has recently experienced a good record of collective bargaining and job satisfaction with firms from the United States and Canada. Central Romana (formerly the Gulf & Western sugar refineries and tourist complex) is the largest foreign investor in the Dominican Republic. Despite a long and bitter struggle with Gulf & Western during the late 1960s and 1970s in which union leaders became the targets of police repression, union relations in Central Romana are generally favorable. Workers are paid well, they receive benefits not provided other

Dominican workers, and, unlike during the Balaguer era, they have not felt the need to use the strike weapon. The 20,000-member United Union of Central Romana Workers is affiliated with the UGTD and has resisted efforts by some workers to join a union attached to Bosch's PLD. On the other hand, Codetel, the Dominican telephone company, which is owned by the Canadian affiliate of GTE (and is the only wholly owned U.S. public utility in Latin Amnerica) broke a telephone workers' union affiliated with a leftist confederation in 1983. Despite grumblings on the left, the Dominican telephone workers are the highest paid workers in the country and do not appear to be in a mood to jeopardize their salaries in a political challenge to their employer. Although these are but two examples of labor-management relations in the foreign sector, they are representative of the current situation. Unions have either formed a positive working arrangement with the multinationals or have accepted union-busting tactics as long as the price was right.

Favorable or at least tolerable labor-management relations in the foreign sector are an important part of the new employment environment in the Dominican Republic. But most of the men and women who make up the industrial workforce in this country are forced to settle for minimum wage, uncertain job security, few if any social or pension benefits, and little prospect of being able to enter a government-sponsored job-training program to improve their skills or their marketability. With prospects for significant job expansion in the future dim, there is little hope for the 30 percent unemployed and the additional 20 percent underemployed. And yet they still come to the barrios of Santo Domingo or to the industrial free zones near Santiago or San Pedro de Macorís. For some there is opportunity, but for most they become part of the vast army of the unemployed—angry, frustrated, and easily influenced by talk of revolution.

The Rural Setting

With increasing number of Dominicans leaving the land and moving to the cities and with the government placing greater emphasis on diversification of the economy instead of dependence on agricultural exportation as the prime source of foreign exchange, the rural workers (the campesinos) are experiencing a further erosion of their influence and a continuation of their position at the bottom of the social ladder in Dominican society. As one of the authors wrote earlier about the rural poor in the Dominican Republic,

The campesino has historically been the forgotten man in Dominican life. He has remained almost completely outside national affairs and has had no say in deciding matters that affect him most closely. The peasants produce little, consume little and continue to live in the manner to which they have always been accustomed.[19]

At the present time it is estimated that about 45 percent of the Dominican population live in rural areas and make their living off the land, usually as sharecroppers or owners of small farms (*finquitas*). Since land distribution in the Dominican Republic is thoroughly unequal with the top 10 percent of the rural population owning 62.7 percent of the available acreage, most of the campesinos are forced to live on unused private land or on land controlled by the state. Moreover, few peasants have clear title to their land and often find themselves the target of eviction by local landowners or the government, anxious to establish control of their property. If the peasants are permitted to maintain a residence and farm a small parcel of land, the quality of their life is usually quite abysmal. Most work is seasonal, leaving many campesinos unemployed for long periods of time (unemployment in the rural areas is upwards of 70 percent). Average yearly income is around $700. With such an unpredictable work schedule and a meager salary, the rural population is underfed, underclothed, and forced to live in thatch and mud shacks (*bohios*) with no running water and usually no electricity. Some campesinos in the more affluent farming regions in the Cibão may live somewhat better, but even there, life for the rural poor has not changed dramatically for generations.[20]

Despite the horrible conditions experienced by the rural workers in the Dominican Republic, they are perhaps the least well organized and the least political of the social and economic groups. Thirty years of Trujilloism, with its rape of the land and its enforced system of paternalism, created a rural population that was highly fatalistic and dependent on guidance from the local patron or the military *jefe*. Even though Trujillo is long gone and democratic governance has developed a foothold in the country, the peasant population has not responded as other groups have with aggressive participation in the political system. The Dominican campesinos have formed a number of local federations and cooperatives to assist them in modernizing their farming and building better community relations, but these organizations are primarily economic and social and rarely make a political statement.[21] It is only recently that rural peasants have developed a political organization to voice their concerns over land reform and government support of agriculture.

Currently the major group representing the Dominican peasant class is the Independent Peasant Movement (MCI), which has over 75,000 members. Although the MCI is a relatively young organization, founded in 1975, it has spoken out vigorously against the failure of the PRD reform presidents to address rural issues adequately. When the Guzmán administration's highly publicized "Year of the Farmer" turned out to be more form than substance, the MCI, along with radical labor, church, and student leaders, openly challenged the government and forced Guzmán to begin programs to settle landless peasants on privately owned land.[22] Yet despite the land distribution program and others to provide greater credit to poor farmers, organizations like the MCI grew increasingly disenchanted with the PRD. Cries of "Land or Death" were voiced by radical peasant leaders and instances of forced occupations of private and public lands increased during the Guzmán administration. By the end of Guzmán's highly touted Year of the Farmer, support for the PRD was waning in the rural areas as it became clear to the campesinos that the millionaire rancher was unwilling to take the necessary steps to alleviate the plight of the rural poor. As one farmer said during this time, "It's not true that the closer we are to the PRD the more we will cross our arms, seeing our families go hungry while the big shots get more land and do nothing with it."[23]

The anger building in the rural areas carried over into the Jorge administration, which did even less to meet the needs of the rural poor. With its attention directed toward the larger issues of debt and economic reform, and facing a number of instances of urban unrest from well organized groups, Jorge did little to move forward with land resettlement and easier farm credit policies. In fact, the Jorge administration developed more of a reputation for encouraging foreign investment in the agro-industrial sector and for continuing the semislave arrangements with Haiti that flooded the rural areas with cheap black labor. In both cases, President Jorge was viewed by the peasants as a leader who had turned his back on them and was more interested in productivity and profits than in social justice and the rightful demands of the rural poor.

The negative views of Dominican farmers toward Jorge and the PRD were in large part the source of Joaquín Balaguer's political rejuvenation in 1986. Many farmers had vivid memories of Balaguer's agricultural policies which helped modernize the rural sector after the civil war and initiated the first land resettlement program during the 1970s. Campesinos also remember Balaguer as a man who often visited the rural areas handing out pesos and listening to their personal concerns as a father figure who cared about their problems. Finally, Balaguer in recent years has taken some hard stands against the influx of Haitians in the rural areas and the competition for jobs that has been created between the Dominicans and their black visitors. Such a position plays well in the rural areas and can be seen as as contributing factor in Balaguer's newfound popularity.

Now that he has regained the presidency, there will be considerable pressure on Balaguer to meet the needs of the peasant population. Not only will there be pressure for land reform from better organized and more vocal peasant groups like the MCI, but there will be the expectation that the new government will address the high levels of corruption, favoritism, and mismanagment in the price support administration (INESPRE) and in the Agrarian Reform Institute (IAD). Although the rural campesinos can in no way be termed a power contender capable of forcing its will on government, a new generation of farm worker is emerging in the Dominican Republic. Balaguer can no longer count on passive farmers willing to listen to the local *patrón* or obey the local *commandante*. Despite the failures of the PRD presidents to reform Dominican agriculture, they have left the new president with a more active rural sector with higher expectations than at any time since the fall of Trujillo.

THE STUDENTS

Like many poor Third World countries, the number of young men and women attending college or university in the Dominican Republic is quite small. The most recent estimate of 80,000 students involved in higher education is only about 2 percent of the population. And yet despite the fact that most Dominican youth can neither afford a post-secondary education in nor have the proper background to enter or succeed in college, the role played by students in the political process has been and continues to be significant.

It was student leaders who in 1962 worked to ensure the victory of Juan Bosch and then joined his administration to further the democratic experiment. It was student radicals from organizations such as the 14th of June Movement and the Movement for Popular Democracy (MPD) who formed the core of the support for the "constitutionalists" and fought the loyalists and the U.S. Marines to a stalemate. And it was students who often challenged the repression and austerity policies of the Balaguer regime by initiating strikes and engaging the police in violent campus confrontations. In the case of the Dominican student movement, size has never been a barrier to participation in national politics.

Not unexpectedly, the student population in the Dominican Republic is stongly influenced by leftist, Marxist, and revolutionary ideologies and participates almost exclusively as critics of conservative government and of cooperative ties to the United States. Like the labor unions, student groups are usually aligned with a political party and pursue offices in the national Federation of Dominican Students (FED) or the local university councils in order to enhance the political position of the parent organization (and, one might add, to further their own careers as party functionaries). Also like the labor unions, student groups have been prone to divide and redivide into the smallest of factions as they espouse a particular dogma or cause.[24]

Most of the political activity in the student sector occurs on the campus of the Autonomous University of Santo Domingo (UASD). The largest of the Dominican universities with an estimated enrollment of 60,000, UASD is the only institution of higher learning that depends almost solely on budgetary appropriations from the government. Over the years, radical students have used the autonomous status of the university as a kind of shield behind which they could organize anti-government activities and in the process have angered government officials who responded by cutting budget appropriations. During the earlier 12-year regime of Joaquín Balaguer, for example, relations between the government and the students at UASD were especially strained primarily because the government consistently refused to provide the necessary funds to operate the facility. On a number of occasions Balaguer ignored the autonomous "sanctity" of the university and closed it down using National Police forces. In the ensuing confrontations some student leaders were killed and scores of others were imprisoned or detained.[25]

Although the UASD is the hotbed of political activity, other universities with less dependence on government funding have developed into quieter centers of higher learning. The Universidad Nacional Pedro Henríquez Ureña (UNPHU) in Santo Domingo has a relatively small enrollment of 10,000, and is funded largely through private contributions, although in the past it has received some subsidies from the government. UNPHU is not as strong academically as UASD, but it does cater to middle- and upper-middle-class youth and is viewed as a more "establishment" institution that has benefitted financially because of its conservative character.

If there is an emerging rival to the Autonomous University, it is the Universidad Católica Madre y Maestra in Santiago, and now with a prospering branch in the capital. Founded in 1962 by Catholic church leaders, UCMM has progressed rapidly into a first-rate institution of higher learning. It has attracted both excellent students and faculty (both of which are much less politically active than at the UASD) and has expanded its physical plant dramatically. Mixing government subsidies with private donations, loans from international agencies and other assistance from foreign governments, such as the United States and Britain, UCMM and its aggressive rector, Monsignor Agripino Núñez Collado, have gained a reputation for excellence. Thanks in large part to its benefactors and the distance of its main campus from the center of political activity in Santo Domingo, UCMM has not seen the educational process interrupted by constant strikes and police confrontations.[26]

Although most of the political activity at the university level in the

Dominican Republic occurred during the revolutionary era and in the Balaguer years, the PRD presidents were not immune to student criticism or protest. Student leaders were very active during the protests over price increases established by Guzmán and Jorge. In May of 1984 one student leader was killed and four others injured in violent protests at the Autonomous University over sharp increases in bus fares and the cost of textbooks. The protests were so extensive at this time that the government had to close the schools for a period of time. Granted that the stimulus for protest had shifted from political ideology to more mundane issues such as transportation and school supplies, still the students have shown that they cannot be taken for granted even though the government may be more reform minded.[27]

The fact that the student radicalism of the 14th of June Movement and the MPD has all but disappeared from Dominican politics points up a dilemma of student activism in this country. As with many aspects of national life, economic circumstances often define and drive political action. College students in the Dominican Republic are really no different from their counterparts in the United States—they want to use their college education to enhance their career opportunities. Politics remains a secondary facet of the college experience. Having said this, though, it is important to state that as the socio-economic divisions deepen in the Dominican Republic and unemployment touches even the middle classes, concern over jobs will undoubtedly spill into the political arena. Moreover, since many college students are heavily influenced by the Marxist interpretation of social organization and economic modernization, their participation both in the professional field and in politics can be expected to be heavily tinged with leftist and nationalistic viewpoints. Dominican conservatives and moderates can only hope that after leaving the college experience and entering the outside world, student radicalism will diminish in favor of more "responsible" attitudes. This perception may indeed be true, but the current generation of Dominican college students could easily follow in the footsteps of the generation of 1965 and take out their economic frustrations in radical political behavior.

THE ELITE

Describing Dominican social groups and their impact on politics and public policy, one is eventually drawn to a discussion of what can be called "quiet power," or the ability of some groups to affect national life in ways not as visible or controversial as others. The "quiet power" group in the Dominican Republic is actually an amalgam of the business, professional, and landowning elite that has consistently operated most effectively in the shadows of national politics. Occupying key positions in Dominican society as heads of local industrial enterprises, bank presidents, lawyers, cattle ranchers, and owners of large sugar, coffee, and tobacco estates, this elite is both the economic backbone and the leadership reservoir of the nation. But, more importantly, the Dominican elite forms the sounding board through which political and governmental officials gauge the appropriateness of public policy initiatives. While many of the groups discussed previously *react to* a major decision, it is the elite that often *initiates* decisions or has been consulted in advance to determine their views and seek their counsel.

Since the Dominican elite comes from such diverse economic and occupational backgrounds, there is no one organization that speaks for the entire group. In fact, because the Dominican Republic is a small country with a vast web of interfamily relationships that cross economic, social, and political lines, the opinions of elite members on public policy issues can easily reach the National Palace or the various governmental bureaucracies via the telephone or personal contact. Nevertheless, over the years a number of influential organizations have formed to present the positions of the elite membership in a more orderly manner and to a wider audience, both in the country and in the United States.

The most prominent of these organizations is the National Council of Businessmen (CNHE), an umbrella group representing all segments of the economic and business elite. Although CNHE presents itself as a nonpartisan group whose interest is in a sound economy, it nevertheless has been the most vocal of the organizations in the criticism of the economic policies of both Guzmán and Jorge. At one time during the Guzmán administration when public protest over price increases appeared out of control, the CNHE threatened to become more involved in the political affairs of the country, a signal of its willingness to intimidate, if not seek the replacement of, national leaders. Jorge fared no better with the businessmen, especially as a result of his implementation of tax reform and the unsettling nature of Dominican politics during the IMF negotiations. Not surprisingly, many in the businessmen's group came out in favor of Balaguer who developed a reputation during his 12 years in office as a friend of commerce and industry.[28]

Also of influence in the business community is the Dominican Chamber of Commerce, which brings together local entrepreneurs with foreign (particularly American) investors. The Chamber has been instrumental over the years in working with the government to create a better climate for foreign investment in the Dominican Republic by promoting legislation that allows for greater repatriation of profits and convincing wary bureaucrats of the importance of cutting away needless red tape faced by investors. During the 1986 campaign the Chamber of Commerce hosted a series of dinners in which presidential candidates could offer their views to the membership. It is in such settings that the elite often is able to judge the strengths and weaknesses of key political figures and forge personal alliances that may be useful in future dealings with the government.[29]

In the nonbusiness or professional sector the Dominican Republic has a number of organizations that represent the interests of its elite clients. The Dominican Association of Lawyers is perhaps the most influential organization. The legal profession in the Dominican Republic is highly respected and one that is most popular among those who see themselves as upwardly mobile in politics and governmental service (for example, both Jorge Blanco and Balaguer are lawyers). Of the elite associations, the Dominican Association of Lawyers has been the most outspoken in its criticism of governmental abuse of human rights and general disregard for the legal restraints placed on governmental power. During the controversial 1978 election many influential lawyers spoke out against the seizure of the ballot boxes by Balaguer's military and lent their support to Guzmán's call for a reopening of the voting process.[30]

In the agricultural sector the land-owning elite is organized into a series of associations that represent the primary commodities produced in the country. Since land remains a primary source of wealth and power, these associations can be considered the most influential in the Dominican Republic. The most visible these days is the Dominican Sugar Planters Federation. Its current president, Nicolás Casanova, is playing an important role in the political arena as a result of the cutback of the U.S. sugar quota and the rumored closing of five government sugar refineries by the Balaguer regime. The problems in the sugar fields have prompted layoffs of thousands of workers and complaints from medium-size cane growers that the State Sugar Council is not paying them for their production. With pressure from workers and growers Casanova and the Sugar Planters Federation will surely be a force to contend with as sugar continues to be phased out as the number one means of employment and an important source of foreign revenue.[31]

Like many of the other Dominican social groups that have been examined, the members of the business, professional, and landowning elite target their lobbying efforts not only internally toward government leaders, but also toward the United States, where U.S. presidents, secretaries of state, and corporate executives can prove helpful. Most of these organizations have good relations with the U.S. embassy in Santo Domingo and its leaders travel frequently to the United States, both for family reasons and for business. One important lesson that has been learned by the Dominican elite over the years is that the possessors of "quiet power" must recognize that they need access to two governments, their own and that of the United States—their own because that is where decisions are made, and the United States because that is where many of the economic decisions begin.

EXTERNAL PARTICIPANTS

A discussion of the social mosaic of the Dominican Republic would be incomplete without mentioning that the public sector and policies are also affected by a number of groups from outside the country. Because of the economic lure of the United States and Puerto Rico, the close proximity of neighboring Haiti, and the longstanding dependence of the country on foreign investment, the domestic groups mentioned above must vie for attention and influence with increasingly important external participants in the political life of the nation. As we shall see, despite the fact that groups such as the Dominican emigré community abroad, the Haitian immigrant laborers and the foreign investors, managers and technicians might not receive as much notoriety as perhaps the military, the church, or the elite, they nevertheless are a contributing factor in shaping politics and have in recent years heightened their visibility and their influence.

The Emigré Community

According to recent U.S. immigration studies, one out of every seven Dominicans now lives outside of the country. Translated into raw figures that means that around 900,000 Dominicans have left their country to seek work and a better life elsewhere. The largest percentage of this emigré community has settled in the United States, in particular in New York City where it is estimated that 500,000 legal and illegal Dominican aliens now reside. The remaining 400,000 Dominicans have either set up communities in other major United States cities such as Boston, Providence, and Hartford, or have opted to take a shorter route to the United States by flying or boarding a number of illegal ferries to nearby Puerto Rico where they may more easily blend in physically and culturally with the Spanish-speaking Americans.[32]

The exodus of such a large segment of the Dominican population is a reflection of the difficulties of maintaining a decent standard of living in the country, but the emigrés also provide benefits to those whom they leave behind. For example, it is estimated that Dominicans living in the United States send back to their loved ones approximately $500 million annually, which has now become the country's largest source of foreign exchange. One Dominican inteviewed said half seriously that the number one policy priority of the government should be the modernization of the postal system so that remittances from the United States could be distributed faster to the local populace than they are at present.[33]

But beside the flow of money from the United States to the Dominican Republic, the emigrés provide the country with a "safety valve," in that internal pressures for jobs, housing, and other governmental services have been lightened due to the regular and continuous exit of thousands of Dominicans. Although no public official has gone on record as favoring the exodus, the efforts of the government to close the door on illegal emigration have been quite weak. Also the United States has been a somewhat reluctant participant in this exodus as the embassy routinely processes visa applications which bring Dominicans to New York or San Juan. Once in the United States, most Dominicans stay beyond the visa expiration date and become another statistic in the growing illegal immigration problem.

One of the most interesting aspects of the Dominican emigrés is the manner in which they have created a distinct community in places like New York and built a base of influence that cannot be ignored in Santo Domingo. The Dominican community in New York City is a vibrant one with not only world-renowned figures such as Oscar de la Renta, but a substantial number of musicians, artists, professionals, and intellectuals. There are currently over 70 organizations in the city that seek to represent Dominicans. At the heart of the New York community is the Dominican Civic and Cultural Center, which frequently sponsors social and cultural events. The Center's major supporter is Enrique Onesimo Guerrero, who also is the founder of the New York Association of Dominican Professionals. The growth of such organizations and the determination of the Dominicans to carve out a life for themselves in the United States has not gone unrecognized. Mayor Ed Koch of New York has met regularly with Dominican leaders including a much celebrated meeting with his counterpart, Peña Gómez in 1984, (the then mayor of Santo Domingo) and the Catholic hierarchy has for over ten years celebrated the Feast of Our Lady of La Altagracia in St. Patrick's Cathedral as a sign of its acceptance of the Dominican presence in the city.[34]

Although most of the impact that the emigré community has on life back home is economic, political leaders recognize that the second largest Dominican city, New York, cannot be ignored come election time. New York has always been a kind of exile community for those Dominicans seeking to plan a political resurgence. Both Juan Bosch and Joaquín Balaguer settled in New York at various times in their long careers when they were out of the country and used the Dominican community there as a source of support and as a sounding board for their ideas. In recent years candidates for national office like Jorge Blanco reminded the Dominican community in New York that if they returned home they would be eligible to vote in the national elections and presumably help him secure his victory.[35] Most importantly though, New York has been the hub of financial assistance for political parties and political party leaders. New York Dominicans remain deeply interested in public life in their country and many continue to maintain strong partisan affiliations. For years the PRD and the PR had party offices in New York which not only served as a political link with home, but acted as fund-raising centers for party activities and for costly campaigns. Candidates for office in Santo Domingo now regularly campaign in New York City.

For most Dominicans, however, life in the United States does not revolve around partisan politics or the formation of a network of social organizations. The United States is quite simply a country that is accessible and affords much larger economic opportunities than are found in the Dominican Republic. But despite the wages and the chance for social mobility, Dominicans in the United States have not really been assimilated. As one Dominican describes the emigré community in New York, "they end up half here and half there, feeling that they really don't belong in either place." Interestingly, Dominicans in New York probably have had a better time adjusting to their new home than those who have travelled the short distance to Puerto Rico where they face a much more competitive job market and a local population that has not welcomed them with open arms.

And yet despite the uncertainty and the loneliness, Dominicans continue to line up at the U.S. consulate in Santo Domingo (which is now the third largest in the world, due to the exodus of Dominicans) and board the planes to Kennedy Airport. The growth of the emigré community in the United States is a clear signal that the Dominican Republic may be permanently split into two nations, one in the Caribbean, poor and underdeveloped, and one in cities like New York, more prosperous and hopeful but sadly detached from its roots.

The Haitians

While Dominican emigrés continue to leave the country for the opportunities of the United States, the influx of Haitians to the Dominican Republic has been growing steadily forming a new social and racial group that has profoundly influenced Dominican national life. Since 1915, when the United States occupied an unstable Haiti and the internal agricultural system failed, Haitian laborers have regularly crossed the shared border with the Dominican Republic to participate in the yearly sugarcane harvest (zafra). Although many of these Haitians returned to their homes with some meager earnings, an increasing number have stayed in the Dominican Republic as illegal aliens hoping to meld into the population and benefit from the higher standard of living that the Dominicans enjoy. At present it is estimated that as many as 500,000 Haitians now live in the Dominican Republic creating a clear racial distinction in the country between the local Dominicans who think of themselves as "white" mestizos and the blacks from the western end of the island.[36]

Life for the Haitians in the Dominican Republic has never been a happy one. Despite their growing numbers and the important fuction they serve in the economy (Dominicans generally refuse to cut sugarcane, thinking it is beneath them), Haitians continue to face discrimination, exploitation, and numerous incidents of repression at the hands of police officials and greedy plantation owners (including the Dominican government itself). The most serious problem surrounding the Haitian influx into the Dominican Republic is the yearly roundup of the black laborers (commonly called "Kongos") and the contractual arrangements that have been developed between the two governments.

For years going back to the previous Balaguer administration and continuing on during the supposedly human rights-sensitive regimes of Guzmán and Jorge, upwards of 20,000 Haitians were brought into the Dominican Republic by the Duvalier government, which had an agreement with Dominican sugar officials. In 1982–1983, for example, the Haitian recruitment fee paid to the Duvalier regime was US$ 2,225,000 for the services of 19,000 sugarcane laborers. Once in the Dominican Republic, the Haitians were paid below the official minimum wage of 3.50 pesos a day and required to work a backbreaking 12-hour day. While in the Dominican Republic, they are forced to live in the most inhumane conditions. The sugar plantations provide barracks-like housing (*bateys*), but most are without light, water, or toilet facilities. The food is terrible and the local boses are often abusive and corrupt.[37]

The Haitian situation became so bad that in 1983 the International Labor Office (ILO), upon the request of the British-based Anti-Slavery Society, sent an investigative mission to the Dominican Republic to explore the charges of inhumane treatment and near slave-like control of the workers. Later, in 1983, the ILO released findings which embarrassed the Jorge government, but did little to alleviate the plight of the Haitians.[38] The Catholic church has also attempted to make public officials sensitive to the inhumane treatment of the Haitians and even began airing radio programs in creole, but in 1982 the government demanded that they be taken off and that the church concentrate on programming that accented Dominican culture.

Dominican governmental leaders, much like the majority of the "white" population, have little sympathy for the Haitians and see them as inferiors who are destined by their heritage and cultural background to harvest the sugarcane of their neighbors. In fact, Joaquín Balaguer, in a book published in 1984 entitled *La isla al revés: Haiti y el destino dominicano*, reenforces the prejudices of his countrymen by praising the Dominican culture, while ignoring the accomplishments of the Haitians. As stated earlier, Balaguer's fears of Haitianization of the Dominican Republic and his refusal to endorse an opening of the frontier between the two countries contributed to his electoral popularity. Now that Balaguer is again in the presidency, it may be safe to assume that there will be little done to address the concerns of the Haitian laborers or to move forward toward the creation of a working bi-racial society—although by now the border between the countries has once more been reopened.[39]

But what political leaders like Joaquín Balaguer are reluctant to do may be forced upon them as a result of changing political circumstances. In early 1986, with the fall of Bébé Doc Duvalier, many Haitians refused to return to the Dominican Republic for the zafra. The attempts by Haitian militiamen to begin the yearly roundup (or *embauchage*) were largely unsuccessful as many "Kongos" fought back. In the Haitian town of Leogane eight men were killed and 20 others were injured in the protest over the continuation of this neoslavery arrangement. The impact of the protests was devastating on the Dominicans who were now left without the labor to harvest a crop that they themselves felt was a demeaning task. The Dominican government pleaded with the Dominican peasants to harvest the sugar and even President Jorge spent an afternoon cutting cane (before the television cameras) to entice his reluctant countrymen to go out into the fields.[40] In the end the government forcefully rounded up local Haitians from poor neighborhoods and used raw military recruits to cut the cane. Although most of the sugar was harvested, the uncertainty of Haitian labor may force Dominican officials to make the yearly trek eastward more attractive by increasing the pay and creating a more humane work environment.

The critical issue for the future with the Haitian community in the Dominican Republic is their assimilation into Dominican society. Despite the change in government in Haiti, the illegal emigration to the Dominican side of the island is constant. But with generations of prejudicial attitudes and the Haitians occupying the bottom rung of the socio-economic ladder, inevitable tensions have developed. Racial incidents and racially motivated crime are now more common in a country which has a tradition of orderliness. Public attacks by political leaders like Joaquín Balaguer against the Haitians can be heard with greater frequency and diplomatic efforts to normalize relations with the new government in Port-au-Prince have not moved very far along.

And yet even though there are serious problems in the areas of the sugar harvest, crime, and negative world image, the Dominicans appear unwilling to face up to the fact of the Haitianization of their society or, for that matter, take measures to alleviate the sources of tension. A large part of the problem is that the Haitians are the weakest and least organized of the groups active in Dominican society, and therefore unable to mount a campaign to have government recognize their needs. But unfortunately there is more to this Haitian problem than organization and leadership. The 500,000 Dominican-Haitians live in a country that needs them but does not want them and feels no obligation to accept them. This contradiction of economic need versus socio-cultural acceptance is at the heart of the Haitian problem in the Dominican Republic and is not likely to be overcome in the near future.

The Foreigners

The Dominican Republic has often been described as a country that is not completely in control of its destiny. Outside agents and outside forces, particularly from the United States, are viewed as having an inordinately large influence on the political, economic, and cultural life of the country. In most instances such dependency is presented in historical and institutional terms accenting the manner in which foreign nations have effected public policy decisions and contributed to the Dominican Republic's underdevelopment and instability over the years.

What such analyses fail to do, however, is to make the foreign influence on the Dominican Republic more "real" by identifing the individuals and groups that have a marked impact on Dominican affairs and describing the ways in which they operate. The foreign community in the Dominican Republic is a highly visible and active participant in the national life. Whether representing governments, corporations, lending institutions, or nonprofit entities, it is this corps of diplomats, investors, bankers, technicians, missionaries, and tourists that is responsible for developing a relationship with the Dominican government and the Dominican people that has been both beneficial and troublesome.

In approaching the study of the foreign community in the Dominican Republic, it is best to concentrate first on the governmental and institutional presence in the country since this is what most Dominicans view as the core of the outside influence. At present there are representatives from 22 foreign countries in the Dominican Republic with the majority of the diplomats coming from Latin America and Central America, although Spain, France, Germany, Italy, Japan, Israel, Korea, and Jordan have also established offices in the country. The United States, of course, with its embassy and its affiliated agencies, commands the largest diplomatic presence in the Dominican Republic. Although by U.S. standards the embassy, on a quiet residential street in Santo Domingo, is modest, in terms of numbers of political, military, and commercial attachés, the large consular section and the considerable commitment of the United States in the area of foreign assistance projects (the Agency for International Development) and the Peace Corps combine to create a substantial and complex governmental presence that overshadows the other foreign embassy operations.

While many embassy operations, including the United States, have cut back their presence in the Dominican Republic, or, in the case of the Belgians and British, have shut down their offices completely, the foreign business and banking community has grown dramatically in recent years. Spurred on in part by the development of eleven duty-free zones, interest in setting up a small assembly plant or a textile manufacturing outlet by foreign investors has mushroomed. For example, recent estimates place the number of U.S. firms with operations in the Dominican Republic at over 160. Although many U.S. companies operating in the Dominican Republic are familiar multinationals such as Bristol-Myers, The Chase Manhattan Bank, Xerox, Singer Sewing Machine, and 3M, the bulk of the United States corporate presence is in the small assembly and textile plants such as Delta Brush Manufacturing Co., Taino Leather Products, and Dominican Shoes and Parts Corp.[41]

Together the multinationals and the small independent firms have made a $175 million investment in the Dominican Republic which is not only important in terms of revenue generated, but also because of the thousands of semi-skilled and skilled jobs (11,000 in the duty-free zones alone) that are created. Moreover, the presence of U.S. executives, plant managers, technicians, salespeople, and their families has had a major social and cultural impact on smaller free-zone cities, such as San Pedro de Macóris, where the foreign community is more visible and has more opportunity to interact with the local population.

Added to the considerable corporate presence in the Dominican Republic is the large number of private organizations that operate in the country for religious, humanitarian, developmental, or educational purposes. A recent accounting of these private organizations put their number at over 80 and growing, particularly as a result of the economic hardship experienced by the Dominican people. A small sampling of these private organizations will give a sense of the assistance, orientation, and nonprofit character of this foreign presence.

American Bible Society

Boy Scouts of America

Catholic Relief Services

Family Planning International Assistance

Ford Foundation

Goodwill Industries

Heifer Project International

Lions Club

Mennonite Central Committee

Salvation Army

Save the Children Federation

Young Men's Christian Association[42]

The above groups and the other nonprofit organizations that operate in the Dominican Republic often do not get the attention that corporate or banking institutions receive since much of their work is of a charitable nature and free of controversies that may arise over issues of profit remittances, nationalization, and worker-management relations. Yet the private groups often have more direct influence on national life in the Dominican Republic than the powerful institutions, since they work directly with the people and are involved in tasks that assist those Dominicans most in need. It is these organizations that most often create the favorable image of U.S. citizens that is so prevalent in the Dominican Republic.

But the foreign-based group that consistently dwarfs the representative of governments, corporations, banks, and nonprofit organizations is the tourists who come in increasing numbers to Santo Domingo, the resort complex at La Romana, and now on the North Coast in and around Puerto Plata. In 1985, nearly 600,000 foreign tourists came to the Dominican Republic, an increase of over 100,000 from 1983. The increase in tourism has had a favorable impact on the internal economy generating over $320 million in receipts in 1984 and helping to fuel a building boom in resort areas. There are now 8000 tourist hotel rooms in the Dominican Republic compared to 6000 in 1983, and more are planned in newer areas such as along the underdeveloped east coast.[43] What is most important about the arrival of the foreign visitors is that the tourist industry has now replaced sugar as the prime generator of foreign revenue and key source of employment. The tourists may stay shorter periods than the diplomats, businessmen, and missionaries, but they may have greater financial impact on Dominican life.

Cataloging a list of foreign institutions, organizations, and groups active in the Dominican Republic certainly provides a sense of the extent to which the foreign community participates in Dominican affairs. But what is perhaps even more helpful, if we are to understand the impact of the foreigners on Dominican national life, is to examine the status and role of some key individuals who work within the political, financial, and commercial systems. In recent years there have been a number of individuals who clearly have left their mark on the Dominican Republic and have helped to reenforce the view that the foreign community indeed wields considerable influence in Dominican affairs.

U.S. Ambassadors

The most influential foreigner in the Dominican Republic is the U.S. ambassador. Whether it was John Bartlow Martin or Tapley Bennett during the crisis-ridden 1960s, or Charles Yost during the critical election of 1978, or Robert Anderson during the uprisings connected with the

IMF dispute, the U.S. ambassador is a person with enormous status and leverage in the Dominican Republic. Some ambassadors such as Martin became personal advisers to the Dominican president seeking to shape the country in a U.S. image, while others, such as Yost and Anderson, acted primarily as diplomatic lobbyists informing, cajoling, and on occasion pleading with Dominican officials about a particular point of view or policy position. But whatever the style employed, the U.S. ambassador occupies a unique position in Dominican society. As a representative of the country that is the Dominican Republic's major trading partner, source of aid, source of tourists and foreign revenue as well (not to mention the sometimes unwelcome guardian of internal political stability), the U.S. ambassador has access to national decision makers and in most instances is listened to respectfully by political, governmental, and business leaders, no matter what their feelings may be toward the "Colossus of the North."

A key point that must be stressed concerning the U.S. ambassador and his influence is that this country does not automatically get what it wants from the Dominican government nor is it always able to use its considerable power to coerce political leaders. This is not to say that on numerous occasions the U.S. ambassador does not utilize foreign aid cutbacks, trade restrictions, or the possibility of military intervention in order to influence Dominican decision-making. But in the modern era, especially during the administration of the two PRD presidents, U.S. ambassadors have found themselves spending most of their time explaining U.S. policy, relaying Dominican concerns and frustrations, and encouraging the government to adopt policies that were in the interest of both countries. The relationship has always been friendly, but there have been increasing signs of tension and impatience with the United States as U.S. diplomats found the Dominicans more independent and more willing to criticize policy preferences that came from Washington. As a result, the modern U.S. ambassador to the Dominican Republic has been transformed from a kind of minister without portfolio in charge of democratization and modernization to a kind of information conduit and, when permitted, a practitioner of pressure group politics for U.S. interests.

The Bluhdorns and the Fanjuls

The Gulf & Western properties in the Dominican Republic have been a source of pride and controversy. After 1967, when Gulf & Western acquired the South Puerto Rico Sugar company, the U.S. multinational invested over $200 million in some 90 businesses in the Dominican Republic.[44] Besides sugar, Gulf & Western was involved in tourism, cattle ranching, real estate, and other small businesses. Although the enormous presence of Gulf & Western was often focused on charges of political corruption, anti-union repression, and tax evasion, there is a personal side to the involvement of this corporate giant in the Dominican Republic. Charles Bluhdorn, the Austrian-born, former president of Gulf & Western, became personally involved in the Dominican operation. Bluhdorn traveled to the Dominican Republic often and his daughter took a deep interest in a number of cultural and restoration projects. Bluhdorn also was instrumental in trying to change the image of Gulf & Western as a brutish corporate entity by initiating a number of social welfare programs around the major sugar city of La Romana. But to many on the left in the Dominican Republic, Charles Bluhdorn remained the quintessential multinational president who reaped enormous profits, cheated the government out of tax revenues, bought off politicians and military commanders, and used his power to maintain and expand his company's holdings in the Dominican Republic.

When Bluhdorn died in 1983, the new president at Gulf & Western had none of the attachment to the Dominican Republic of his predecessor. With sugar prices down and synthetic sweeteners reaching the marketplace, Gulf & Western put the company up for sale. In January of 1985 the Gulf & Western holdings in the Dominican Republic were sold to a Miami-based group headed by the Fanjul brothers, Alfonso and José. The Fanjuls are Cuban-born U.S. citizens who have prospered in Florida producing sugar, and saw the Gulf & Western properties as an opportunity to enlarge their operations.

To date, the Fanjuls have kept a lower profile than Bluhdorn, but already there are those who express concern over the conservative politics of the two brothers and their ties to right-wing groups both in the United States and in the Dominican Republic. Many leftists like Juan Bosch fear that the Fanjuls will use their base in the sugar industry to pressure the Balaguer government to adopt policies favorable to their interest. The fact that Vice-President Carlos Morales Troncoso is a close friend of the Fanjuls lends some credence to this concern. Although the Fanjuls have been able to remain in the background and avoid controversy, the outcome of the rumored closing of refineries and the laying off of sugar workers will allow Dominicans to make judgments on whether the replacements for Charles Bluhdorn and Gulf & Western at La Romana have a different corporate vision.

José González and the IMF

The International Monetary Fund (IMF) is best described as an austere and faceless lending organization headquartered in Washington. But with many nations like the Dominican Republic hard hit by trade deficits and debt payments, the IMF has moved to the forefront of public attention. The IMF has become the primary provider of emergency loans and credit arrangements to Third World governments in desperate need of monetary resources. But any institution, no matter how austere and faceless, cannot avoid the conflict and the personal and institutional attacks that economic and financial reform necessitates. Perhaps nowhere has the judgment and operation of the IMF been challenged so vigorously as in the Dominican Republic, and no IMF official has had to endure the personal and political attacks of a nation fearful of change as the chief negotiator for the Fund, José González.

José González, a Colombian with years of experience in debt renegotiation and financial reform, is a highly respected member of the IMF team that worked with the Dominican government during the Jorge administration. A quiet and likable man with a sincere concern for the social implications of debt reduction policies, González became the point man in charge of convincing the Dominican government to adopt policies that were sure to create a social backlash. At one time during the negotiations, when the IMF was planning to open an office in Santo Domingo, a violent demonstration occurred in which crowds shouted down the IMF and demanded that González not be permitted to enter the country to negotiate any future agreements with the government. During 1984 and 1985 it is safe to state that other than president Jorge, José González was the most unpopular man in the Dominican Republic and the subject of unceasing criticism.

With the successful completion of a standby agreement in 1985 and an upturn in the Dominican economy in 1986, the troubled days of April 1984 and the name José González have receded into the background. It is only infrequently that a bureaucrat in a large institution like the IMF can occupy center stage in a critical situation, but the tenure of José González in the Dominican Republic reveals the impact that a foreign (in this case international) institution can have on the country. When González left the Dominican Republic, there was no question that he had made a permanent impression on such key policy issues as trade laws, budget formulation, tax collection, and currency exchange. Although Dominicans made the final decisions, it was González and the IMF that set the paremeters of change.

Wilson Rood and the U.S. Chamber of Commerce

The U.S. ambassador may be the most influential foreign official in the Dominican Republic, but if one were to name the individual who is best known and connected it would have to be Wilson Rood, the executive director of the U.S. Chamber of Commerce of the Dominican Republic. Rood has been involved with the Chamber for over 20 years and from his office in the Hotel Santo Domingo has helped build the

Chamber from 200 members to over 1300 (only 75 of which are U.S.-owned firms) and in the process has received widespread acclaim from the business community and from President Reagan, who recognized Rood and his efforts with a special presidential commendation.

Rood's success has been achieved because of his ability to bring together Dominican and U.S. business leaders and to convince Dominicans of the benefits of creating a favorable climate for commerce and industry. The Chamber under Rood's direction has developed a number of services which have enhanced the relationship between the United States and the Dominican Republic. Among these services are: frequent consultation on laws, decrees, and regulations that may adversely effect both foreign and domestic enterprises, protection of Dominican exporters from measures contrary to their interests in the American market, immediate action to deal with measures adopted in the United States which may harmfully effect the Dominican private sector, and access to current information on the Caribbean Basin Initiative and its implications for Dominican trade.

The Dominican Republic is currently viewed as one of the countries that has benefited most from the Caribbean Basin Initiative and other tax laws that are directed toward investment in the Caribbean. Although the laws and bureaucratic framework are in place and a steady stream of new investors are arriving in the Dominican Republic, it is individuals like Wilson Rood who are responsible for bringing the complex of laws, agencies, political leaders, corporations, and entrepreneurs together. In the Dominican Republic Wilson Rood is one of the most successful practitioners of this interweaving of public and private, Dominican and U.S., participants in commercial development.

WHO RUNS THE DOMINICAN REPUBLIC?

These four short sketches of influential foreigners in the Dominican Republic raise an important question concerning not just the externally based groups active in Dominican society, but those that clearly derive their composition from internal circumstances, such as the military, the business elite, labor, landed interests, and those politicos in the higher levels of government bureaucracy. Simply put, who runs the Dominican Republic, the Dominicans or key foreign agents representing powerful economic and political interests? A question such as this is designed to zero in on the issue of whether the foreign sector controls domestic decision making or whether it is just another interest group in the crowded arena of public policy determination.

There is no doubt that the traditional power contenders—the military, business, landowners, and governmental ministers—are central factors in the Dominican power equation. They make decisions, invest money, choose other leaders, and plan for the future. In a real sense, they run the Dominican Republic. Individuals such as the president of the country, his technical secretary and minister of finance, the president of the Central Bank, the head of the armed forces, the chief of the National Police, the officials in charge of the sugar and electric enterprises, and the leaders of the major business and landowning operations are clearly in the front ranks of powerholders in the Dominican Republic.

And yet when listing these Dominicans who run their country, one is immediately drawn to the fact that each individual is inextricably tied to or dependent on factors outside the Dominican Republic. There are few positions of power in the Dominican Republic that are not connected to events or conditions outside the country. The Dominican president is forced to revamp the economy based on IMF guidelines; the president of the Central Bank is constantly worried about foreign exchange reserves; the head of the Armed Forces and the chief of the National Police depend on arms, assistance, and training from the United States in order to maintain defense and internal security; sugar officials bemoan the U.S. quota cutbacks and electric power officials constantly look at the price of foreign oil; and industrialists and landowners are ever nervous about trade policies and investment potential from abroad. At every important position of power in the Dominican Republic one can find a "parallel power" from the outside that acts as either a controling agent or is an essential contributor to the internal power equation.

Who runs the Dominican Republic thus becomes a much more complex question, since the foreign sources of power have become an integral part of public policy formulation and implementation. In the end perhaps the best that can be said in answer to this question is that yes, Dominicans run their country, but, in the new more modern world of both dependence and interdependence, it is the foreigners that often determine the direction, the speed, and the quality of Dominican development.

NOTES

1. The most complete analysis of Dominican groups, although written in the 1970s, is Howard Wiarda's *Dictatorship, Development and Disintegration: Politics and Social Change in the Dominican Republic* (Ann Arbor, MI: Xerox University Microfilm Monograph Series, 1975).

2. Charles Anderson, *Politics and Economic Change in Latin America* (Princeton, NJ: D. Van Nostrand, 1967); see especially Chapter 4.

3. See Jonathan Hartley, "The Dominican Republic 1985–1986," in *Latin America and Carribean Contemporary Record*, ed. Abraham Lowenthal (New York: Holmes and Meier, in press).

4. As reported in the *Times of the Americas*, May 28, 1986.

5. See Penny Lernoux, *Cry of the People* (New York: Penguin Books, 1982), pp. 233–36.

6. "Bad Land Distribution Brings Hunger to Dominicans, Study Shows" (Santo Domingo: National Catholic News Service, September, 1975).

7. John Bartlow Martin, *Overtaken by Events: The Dominican Crisis from the fall of Trujillo the the Civil War* (New York: Doubleday, 1966), pp. 283–90.

8. Black, Jan Knippers, *The Dominican Republic: Politics and Development in an Unsovereign State* (Boston: George Allen and Unwin, 1986), pp. 98–101.

9. An excellent and contemporary discussion of the Dominican military can be found in G. Pope Atkins, *Arms and Politics in the Dominican Republic* (Boulder, CO: Westview Press, 1981).

10. Ibid., p. 55.

11. Now back in the presidency, Balaguer wasted little time in reshuffling the higher levels of the military and national police. Twenty-four military officers and 33 police officials were either dismissed or retired in the first two months of the new Balaguer administration. See *Times of the Americas,* October 29, 1986.

12. Michael Kryzanek, "The 1978 Election in the Dominican Republic: Opposition Politics, Intervention and the Carter Administration," *Caribbean Studies* 19, nos. 1 and 2, April-July 1979, pp. 62–63.

13. Atkins, op. cit., pp. 118–19.

14. See "Bilateral Assistance for Latin America and the Caribbean, FY, 1984," United States Department of State, Washington DC, p. 7.

15. Balaguer has recently instituted a new system for awarding military contracts that is designed to lessen the opportunity for corruption in the armed forces, but may also create unrest among those in the military who have benefited from a lack of administrative control of budgets and purchasing polices. See Santo Domingo *Times,* December 11, 1986, p. 6.

16. *Commercial News Dominican Republic,* in its March 1986 edition describes the Dominican labor force as "ample and trainable" and cites the Dominican government for its vocational training program through its National Institute of Technical Professional Development (INFOTEP). See "Offshore Manufacturing Opportunities" *Commercial News Dominican Republic,* March 1986.

17. The best source of analysis of the Dominican labor movement can be found in the annual labor report of the American Embassy in Santo Domingo. The most recent report, entitled "Labor Trends in the Dominican Republic," is dated March 14, 1986.

18. Jonathan Hartley, "The Dominican Republic, 1985–1986," op. cit., pp. 10–11.

19. Howard Wiarda, *The Dominican Republic: Nation in Transition* (New York: Praeger, 1968), p. 91.

20. A good description of the plight of the Dominican campesino can be found in Robert W. Mashek and Stephen G. Vetter, *The Inter-American Foundation in the Dominican Republic, A Decade of Support for Local Development Organizations* (Rosslyn, VA: Inter-American Foundation, 1983), pp. 13–14.

21. See Stephen Vetter, "Portrait of a Peasant Leader: Ramon Aybar," in *Grassroots Development,* 8, No. 1, 1984, pp. 2–11.

22. "Dominican Republic—The Launching of Democracy?", *Nacla Report on the Americas,* November-December 1982, pp. 22–24.

23. Ibid.

24. Jan Knippers Black, *The Dominican Republic*, op. cit., pp. 101–02.

25. Michael Kryzanek, "Diversion, Subversion and Repression: The Strategies of Anti-Opposition Politics in Balaguer's Dominican Republic," *Caribbean Studies*, 17, nos. 1 and 2, April-July 1979, pp. 95–96.

26. Ian Bell, *The Dominican Republic*, (Boulder, CO: Westview Press, 1981), pp. 177–82.

27. Michael Kryzanek, "The Dominican Republic 1984–1985," in *Latin American and Caribbean Contemporary Record*, ed. Jack Hopkins (New York: Holmes and Meier, 1986) pp. 696–97.

28. See *Nacla Report on the Americas*, "Dominican Republic—The Launching of Democracy?," op. cit., p. 26.

29. Washington Times, May 14, 1986.

30. The Dominican Association of Lawyers took out full-page newspaper advertisements during the "ballot theft" controversy, urging the Balaguer regime to resume the election. See *El Caribe* from May 22 to May 26, 1978.

31. See Tom Wicker's analysis of the decline of Dominican sugar in his column entitled "Disastrous sugar diplomacy in the Caribbean," New York *Times*, March 14, 1987, p. 27.

32. Aaron Segal, "The Half-Open Door," *The Wilson Quarterly*, New Year's 1983, p. 121.

33. Personal interview with Ramon B. Martínez-Portorreal, Washington DC, July 3, 1986.

34. *Dateline: Dominican Republic* II, no. 4, July/August 1980, pp. 66–67.

35. New York *Times*, February 22, 1982, B3.

36. See Pamela Constable, "A yearly harvest of shame in Hispaniola," Boston *Globe*, May 18, 1986, pp. A1, A4.

37. Paul R. Latortue, "Neoslavery in the Cane Fields—Haitians in the Dominican Republic," *Caribbean Review*, December 1985, pp. 18–20.

38. Jonathan Hartley, "The Dominican Republic, 1985–1986," op. cit., pp. 27–28.

39. Pamela Constable, "A yearly harvest of shame in Hispaniola," op. cit.

40. Ibid.

41. A list of American businesses and private aid organizations in the Dominican Republic can be found in Caribbean/Central American Action's resource document entitled *Caribbean Datebook*, Washington, DC, 1983.

42. Ibid.

43. "Foreign Economic Trends and Their Implications for the United States," American Embassy, Santo Domingo, June 1986.

44. See Hank Frundt, *Gulf & Western in the Dominican Republic: An Evaluation* (New York: Interfaith Center on Corporate Responsibility, 1980).

6

THE DOMINICAN ECONOMY: THE CONSTANT STRUGGLE FOR GROWTH AND INDEPENDENCE

Economically, the Dominican Republic has over the years developed strong ties to the outside world. From the days of the Spanish conquest to the current period of democratization, Dominicans have become used to the fact that both the prosperity and poverty they have experienced over the years are in large part the result of circumstances beyond their control. Whether it be the near destruction of the Dominican economy by the machinations of the Spanish, French, and Haitians at the outset of national history or the more recent domination of economic policy-making and agenda-setting by international lending organizations, private banks, and foreign cartels and governments, the Dominican Republic has had to accept the reality of enormous external influence on its trade relations, capital investment, budget formulation, modernization priorities, foreign exchange liquidity, tax initiatives, and credit policies—indeed, on all areas of the Dominican economy.[1]

As we shall see, the Dominican Republic fits neatly into the traditional parameters of a dependent economy, especially when one examines the impact of U.S. trade, aid, and investment on such critical areas as available public revenues, debt management, and industrial diversification.[2] But while the evidence points clearly to the dependent status of the Dominican Republic, it is important also to accent the ways in which the Dominicans are working to achieve a modicum of independence from external economic influence. In the Dominican Republic today the economy is best presented as struggling against underdevelopment and in the midst of a struggle for independence from its historic reliance on the outside world. Dominican leaders in all sectors of national life are working not only to improve and strengthen the economy, but to build institutions and introduce policy measures that lessen their country's dependence and allow them to take back control.[3]

There are a number of ways to approach the discussion of the Dominican economy and to describe the struggle that is occurring as the country seeks to attain a higher level of economic growth and independence. Although it is tempting to present a kind of laundry list of economic woes faced by the Dominican Republic, it is more helpful in terms of understanding the Dominican response to their difficulties to review the current economic scene through a series of brief issue or policy vignettes that outline the challenges faced by governmental and business leaders as they deal with their economy. To accomplish this review, six economic vignettes will be presented that describe both the sources of the economic malaise faced by the Dominicans and the policy initiatives being taken as the country strives for independence.

THE IMF DEBATE—FROM CRISIS TO REFORM

Although the period of intense International Monetary Fund (IMF) involvement in Dominican economic affairs has been discussed earlier, it is important to examine the impact of the IMF guidelines and the U.S.$78.5 million standby agreement of April 1985 on government re-form policies. The key reform that led to the standby agreement was the decision in January of 1985 by the Dominican government to unify the exchange system at free market rates, a move which ended the multi-tiered system whereby certain transactions were conducted at rates of RD$1.00 equals U.S.$1.00. The decision to let the Dominican peso float freely was in the view of financial experts the most significant reform since the formation of the modern Dominican monetary system after World War II and one that many felt would have long-term positive implications for the Dominican economy.[4]

Along with the unification of the exchange rate the Dominicans also agreed not to use Central Bank funds to finance the public deficit, to eliminate foreign debts over a number of years, and to improve the Central Bank's net foreign reserve position. Although these reforms did not receive as much attention as the devaluation of the Dominican peso and its impact on the buying power of the average citizen, the decision by the government, for example, to adopt a tight monetary policy led to severe restrictions on credit and a fierce competition among companies seeking to acquire whatever monies were available. Those who found themselves without access to the traditional sources of credit used a number of unregulated financing houses which provided loans with rates ranging from 30 to 60 percent.[5]

The tight monetary policies along with renewed efforts by the gov-ernment to trim government expenditures contributed to a number of short-run problems in the Dominican economy. The construction and manufacturing industries were especially hard hit and experienced sig-nificant declines in housing starts and productive output. Although in-flation dropped down considerably from 38 to 15 percent, the unemployment rate continued to inch upward as the country remained in a deep recession. To counteract the ill effects of the IMF reforms the government froze prices and increased food subsidies along with granting a 40 percent in the minimum wage.[6] But despite these measures, the Dominican people experienced the negative effects of economic and financial reform during most of 1985. Although the IMF praised the Dominican government for meeting all performance criteria and in some cases for exceeding targets (particularly in the area of credit availability), this was small consolation to those who saw reform as only causing them more economic and financial distress.

In March of 1986 the IMF ordered the final disbursement of the special drawing rights which signaled that the Dominican economy had reformed sufficiently and was no longer in need of the kind of financial intervention that had characterized its role in much of 1984 and 1985. The Dominican Republic is in no way free of the debt and dependency that first brought the IMF into the sphere of internal Dominican economic and financial policy-making, but the reform stimulated by the Fund's guidelines and pressure has had a generally positive effect on the internal economy. Most often pointed to as a sign of the economic rejuvenation of the Dominican economy was the strengthening of the peso from a high of RD$3.32 to U.S.$1.00 in early 1986 to around RD$2.80 to U.S.$1.00 by mid–1986. Although other factors, such as lower fuel costs and higher prices for staple commodities contributed to the stronger peso, many experts are convinced that the unification of the exchange rate which was the cornerstone of the IMF agreement (and the source of political and social disorder) will have only a positive long-term impact on the Dominican economy.[7]

When Balaguer came into office again in 1986, he took some needed but potentially politically risky steps by reducing the size of the public sector and insisting on honesty and probity in the administration of the public accounts. But Balaguer had problems with the standby arrangement of his predecessor. His advisers were fearful that adherence to the IMF guidelines would again produce riots that might topple the regime. As a traditional statist, furthermore, Balaguer was reluctant to give up very many of the economic and political strings that he held in his hands. He was also fearful that an agreement with the IMF would restrict his capacity to act as a patronage politician with discretion to dole out support-building public works projects. The result by 1987 was considerable economic uncertainty. Businessmen who had initially supported Balaguer's earlier economic steps became unsure as to where he was heading. The peso weakened against the dollar. Pressure was put on the government to negotiate a new agreement with the IMF that could actually be favorable to the Dominican Republic, but for political reasons the Balaguer administration was reluctant. Eventually, some such agreement would have to be reached.

THE PARIS CLUB NEGOTIATIONS

The IMF agreement of January 1985 not only addressed a series of glaring deficiencies in the Dominican economic and financial sectors, but paved the way for the renegotiation of $ 280 million in debts with a number of bilateral country lenders, more commonly known as the Paris Club. With a total external debt of U.S.$3.5 billion and the ratio of external debt service to merchandise exports at a staggering 183 percent, it was incumbent upon the Dominican government to act on the debt problem or else face default and the prospect of seeing its traditional lines of credit dry up. By proving to Paris Club members that its economic and financial house was in order, the renegotiation of the bilateral debt moved along smoothly and also opened the way for a similar renegotiation of a substantial commercial debt. Later in 1985 the Dominican government successfully rescheduled nearly $800 million in private bank debt which allowed the Dominicans to repay their outstanding arrears over a 13-year period.[8]

Together, the Paris Club agreement and the commercial renegotiation had a marked effect on the Dominican economy. Not only have the rescheduling agreements lowered the debt service incurred by the country, but more importantly the Dominican Republic has in a real sense regained its respectability as a Third World borrower. It is interesting to note, however, that even though the negotiating of credit arrangements with foreign countries and commercial banks has normalized, the Dominican Republic remains a debtor nation dependent upon the strength of its export economy and the price of foreign oil. Fortunately for the Dominican Republic, the debt rescheduling achieved in 1985 helped to create a balance of payments surplus of U.S.$110 million and the anticipation of another surplus in 1986. Moreover, higher coffee prices, increased tourism, and lower oil costs along with better markets for Dominican gold, tobacco, and cocoa are helping to offset the decline in sugar revenue to create a healthier balance of payments situation.[9]

The somewhat positive outlook for the Dominican economy achieved as a result of the IMF agreement and the debt renegotiations should not tempt one to be overly optimistic about the ability of this country to avoid a replay of its earlier debt problems. The Dominican economy continues to rely heavily on revenue from commodities—primarily sugar—that are prisoner to world demand and from a tourist sector that is heavily influenced by the strength of the economy in the United States and the fickle tastes of the Caribbean vacationer.[10] It is a virtual certainty that the Dominican Republic will have to again reschedule its bilateral and commercial debts since there is little evidence that the economy is making significant strides to diversify and lessen its reliance on its traditional crops of coffee, cocoa, and tobacco in addition to sugar. Even though 1985 and 1986 were years in which prices for Dominican staples rebounded somewhat, these advances are largely cyclical and can be expected to experience a downturn. When this downturn period of low commodity prices returns, public and private indebtedness will likely increase and the Dominican Republic may again be faced with the prospect of restructuring its economy and rescheduling its debt. Meanwhile, under Balaguer, the economic outlook remained quite uncertain.

THE U.S. SUGAR QUOTA

The day may have now passed when the word sugar and the Dominican Republic were thought of as synonymous. In recent years the Dominican Republic has seen its position as one of the largest exporters of sugar to the world diminish as the introduction of corn sweeteners, protectionist legislation for sugar beet producers, and a cutback in the traditional quota relationship with the United States severely weakened the Dominican sugar industry and forced the government to think the impossible—a phase out of sugar as a dependable source of foreign revenue.[11] The crushing blow to the Dominican sugar industry was the decision by the United States to cut drastically (by 48 percent) its sugar quota. The decision grew out of the fact that the United States is virtually self-sufficient in sugar, from the pressures exerted by U.S. sugar beet growers, from the glut of sugar on the world market, from the desire on the part of the Reagan administration to end these kinds of subsidies, and from a desire to force the Dominicans to further diversify their historically one-crop economy.

The decrease in the quota caused a decline in output in the Dominican Republic in 1985 of nearly 20,000 tons and further stimulated calls for the closing of government-owned sugar refineries, even though this would pose an enormous hardship on rural workers who have no other source of employment. Perhaps more importantly for the overall economy, raw sugar export proceeds dropped by a third to $111 million in 1985 and were largely responsible for an increase in the trade deficit from $389 million in 1984 to $547 million in 1985.[12]

The decision by the United States to cut the sugar quota and the resulting decline in sugar exports has put a strain on relations between Santo Domingo and Washington. For years, going back to the Trujillo era, the Dominicans enjoyed the largest sugar quota granted a U.S. trading partner and reaped the benefits of a ready market for their primary export commodity (at its highpoint the United States was importing nearly 70 percent of Dominican sugar). The quota cutback not only reversed this long-standing relationship but angered Dominican leaders who saw the decision as one that would severely weaken the economy and threaten the social base upon which a thriving democracy had been built.[13] President Balaguer, for example, encouraged a highly publicized flirtation with Cuba in part because of bitterness over the U.S. sugar quota reduction. To soften the blow caused by the cut in the sugar quota the U.S. Department of Agriculture is promoting a program in which surplus foodstuffs are provided to sugar-producing countries like the Dominican Republic in order to help exporting nations make what are termed "short-term economic adjustments."[14] But it will still be up to the Dominicans to adjust by further diversifying their exports.

Even though the U.S. share of Dominican exports has remained stable at about 56 percent, due in large part to the growth in nontraditional exports, the Dominicans see the quota issue as the beginning of an internal struggle that will have a marked effect on productive efficiency, industrial diversification, refinery closings, unemployment, and social order. From a corporate and market economy perspective, the transition from a sugar-based economy to one that is much more diversified is long overdue. But from the Dominican standpoint, the quota cutback strikes at the heart of Dominicanness and creates not only economic problems, but social and political ones as well. In today's Dominican Republic the sugar quota cutback has been grudgingly accepted as another example of how dependency serves to perpetuate economic weakness. The attention now has shifted to the more serious ramifications of the cutback as the Balaguer government deals with the horribly inefficient State Sugar Council and the thousands of rural workers who would be added to the rolls of the unemployed should the government choose to deemphasize sugar as the engine of the Dominican economy.

PUBLIC ENTERPRISES, PUBLIC DEBT

One of the legacies of the Trujillo regime are the vast public enterprises that were once the base of the dictator's enormous wealth but now, as state-owned enterprises, are one of the major sources of the government's financial difficulties. In 1985, for example, the Dominican government ran a public deficit of RD$267 million which was an increase of RD$90 million over that of 1984. The deficit was largely the result of payments made to the corrupt, patronage-bloated, ailing, and inefficient public enterprises, in particular the sugar company (CEA), the electric company (CDE), the public works company (CORDE), and the food price stabilization institute (INESPRE).[15] As the U.S. Commerce Department said in its yearly review of the Dominican economy, "All these companies (CEA, CDE, and INESPRE) have suffered from poor management, excess payroll and government-set low prices in the domestic market."[16]

The CDE and INESPRE, in particular, are often the targets of criticism. As documented by Jonathan Hartley, the CDE is thought to be losing some 40 percent of its generating capacity due to "inefficient generation, poor maintenance, transmission losses, theft or underbilling of energy and non-payment of bills."[17] The failure of CDE to provide efficient electrical transmission has forced some private commercial and industrial enterprises to purchase emergency generating plants. As for INESPRE, the food stabilization institute has been criticized for a number of years for its high level of corruption and its inability to pay farmers for crops sold to the government. In 1985 INESPRE came under fire for its inability to pay rice growers over RD$80 million and for opening up storefront food shops which undercut private establishments.[18]

The harsh criticism leveled at the public enterprises as a drain on the budget and the epitome of bureaucratic inefficiency and corruption must, however, be balanced against the fact that these institutions do not operate on their own, but are influenced by outside forces. Although the featherbedding, corruption, and inefficient management are political and organizational problems, the drain on the public budget attributed to the CEA, CDE, and INESPRE, is primarily the result of low world commodity prices, the high cost of foreign oil and the stark realities of feeding a population of angry poor people who cannot afford basic staples due to inflation and the devaluation of the Dominican peso. The public enterprises are thus hampered not only by personnel deficiencies, but by the critical connection between internal bureaucracy and external market forces.

The criticism of the public enterprises in the areas of budget deficits and mismanagement is right on target, but the revitalization and reform of these huge bureaucracies will require bold governmental initiatives that will certainly challenge the administration of President Joaquín Balaguer. Not only are the enterprises the source of government patronage and an accepted means by which employees supplement poor governmental salaries, but they are part of a long-standing statist approach to economic development in the Dominican Republic. Dominican leaders, whether Trujillo, Balaguer, or the PRD reform presidents, have been reluctant to relinquish their commitment to state control of vital natural resources or essential services and opt for privatization in these areas.[19]

Despite numerous calls for the government to remove itself, especially from sugar production and electricity (calls that often have come from foreign consultants and governments), the Dominicans have dragged their feet on public enterprise reform and as a result have had to accept the harsh results of this policy at budget time. The reason they do this is that politicians will lose patronage opportunities, sources of job appointments, and votes if they ever seriously move toward privatization. But due to IMF pressure, the Jorge government did attempt to generate more revenue by passing new taxes, strengthening tax collection procedures and decreasing Central Bank credit to the public sector. These measures did provide a modicum of fiscal relief, but not enough to erase a deficit tied to export revenue, oil costs and the constant demands of affordable food. Balaguer must move toward such an accommodation as well.

AGROINDUSTRY AND THE PUSH FOR NONTRADITIONAL EXPORTS

Strengthening the Dominican economy will ultimately be tied to diversification in the agricultural sector, which in a phrase means moving away from dependence on sugarcane and sugar-generated revenue and accenting what has come to be called nontraditional exports. The Dominican government in recent years has encouraged foreign investors, particularly from the United States, to grow a variety of agricultural commodities for the export market that previously have not been traditional trade items.[20] Through a series of complex bureaucratic procedures Dominican agricultural land, owned either by the State Sugar Council or by private sugar growers represented by the Dominican Federation of Sugarcane Growers, can be leased or a joint venture relationship established. With import restrictions on many agricultural commodities relaxed as a result of the 1983 Caribbean Basin Initiative, Dominican farmers and their U.S. partners are quickly moving to fill the void created by the precipitous decline in sugar prices and sugar exports.[21]

The creation of these nontraditional export enterprises, or as they are more commonly called, agroindustries, has been quite successful. From 1984 to 1985 an estimated $U.S.30 million has been invested in agroindustry creating 12,000 new jobs and transforming former sugarcane land into areas where melons, citrus fruits, cashews, oranges, olives, and other vegetables are grown. Dominican governmental and business leaders are now firmly committed to transforming the sugar lands into diversified agroindustry and seem less apprehensive than before about forming joint ventures with U.S. investors. As evidence of this support the Dominican legislature has passed the Agroindustrial Incentive Law # 409 which grants income tax exoneration that can reach 100 percent of net taxable income and allows duty-free entrance of machinery and raw materials.[22] Recently the Dole Fruit Company signed a lease agreement to grow pineapples on state-owned lands; and despite the cries of opposition politicians that it involves giving away the national patrimony, it is likely that some of the former Trujillo properties including some sugar lands will be sold to the private sector.

Yet despite the growing commitment to nontraditional exports and the expansion of agroindustry, all is not well in this promising new economic sector. One of the major stumbling blocks to continued growth is Foreign Investment Law # 861 which limits foreign participation in agroindustries to a maximum of 49 percent of equity. This restriction has posed a problem to many U.S. investors who feel that the law is retarding the growth of these export industries.[23] Also of concern is the process required to lease sugar lands in the Dominican Republic. Companies such as Castle and Cook have been negotiating with the government for years over acquisition of lands that they wish to use for the production of new crops. Seemingly endless bureaucratic delays, fears of expanded foreign influence, and the pervasive nature of government corruption (payoffs to speed up the administrative process) have all contributed to frustrating delays and apprehension among potential investors.

The problems in the agroindustrial sector, however, are not insurmountable as evidenced by a 10 percent growth rate in 1985 (a figure that was viewed as low by experts considering the depreciation of the Dominican peso). That sector is expected to grow substantially over the next years, especially since the overall economy has been strengthened and, as the Inter-American Development Bank states, "accelerated growth and employment (in the agroindustrial sector) may be forseen now that the export surcharge has been abolished, more goods are allowed quota and duty-free access to the United States market under the Caribbean Basin Initiative, and new marketing opportunities have been explored."[24] The favorable outlook for the agroindustrial sector in the Dominican Republic is a welcome sign, especially since sugar cane production seems no longer capable of supporting the economy. The question that remains is whether growth in agroindustry will be sufficient to replace adequately the dropoff in sugar revenue. If such replacements are not found, the Dominican Republic may once again be thrust into another round of economic crisis.

THE DUTY-FREE ZONES

From the Dominican perspective, the future of their economy can be seen by traveling to the cities of Santiago, La Romana, San Pedro de Macorís, and Puerto Plata, where the country's four industrial-free zones are located. A diversified economy with an ever-expanding industrial base has long been a dream of the Dominicans, particularly when sugar prices and revenues were following a rollercoaster ride in the 1970s and 1980s. With the establishment of the zones by the Balaguer administration in 1970 and their steady growth since then, Dominican business leaders and government officials are convinced that their country can transform itself from an agricultural-export economy to one modeled after the assembly and light industrial economies of the Pacific Basin.[25]

In many respects, the confidence of the Dominicans in the prospect of transforming their country into a Caribbean version of Taiwan is not without foundation. The four industrial free zones contain 130 manufacturing and assembly plants, employ over 30,000 people, and are currently stretched to capacity causing a backlog of requests for space by foreign investors. Although 85 percent of the companies operating in the zones are U.S., the Dominicans seem unfazed by this new form of intervention and concentrate on the economic benefits that the U.S. presence has created and the transformation of the country from agriculture to industry that the zones represent. Both conservative and liberal Dominican governments have championed this policy.[26] The success of the zones and the commitment of the Dominicans to continue the process of industrialization have spurred the development of seven more areas in Barahona, Azua, San Francisco de Macorís, El Seibo, Higüey, Baní, and La Vega, although financial restrictions tied to the IMF agreement have slowed the completion of these zones. Because of the public-financing restrictions, one of the new zones will be privately developed, anchored by an electronics complex built by Westinghouse.

The lure of the industrial zones and their enormous growth in recent years is the result of favorable tax laws, wage and operating conditions, and import duties. Assembly and manufacturing firms in the zones are exempt from limitation on profits earned outside the country and are not required to report profits to the Dominican Foreign Investment Commission. Furthermore, companies in the zones are granted exemptions of anywhere from 75 percent to 100 percent on income, municipal, and patent taxes. What is even more tantalizing to foreign investors is the fact that space rented in the zones is available at around $U.S.0.14 per square foot, per month, and the minimum hourly wage is $U.S.0.37 (plus the added advantage of almost nonexistent unions). Finally, custom and other duties on goods brought into the zones for assembly are quite favorable. At present there are no custom duties for the installation of machinery, office equipment, construction materials, semi-finished products, spare parts, and other essential components of the production process.[27]

In return for these substantial exemptions and favorable conditions, the Dominican government has enjoyed a considerable foreign exchange return on local expenses incurred by the foreign companies in the zones. Under existing Dominican law, companies are required to pay for local expenses (wages, plant leases, local supplies) in U.S. dollars exchanged for local currency at the Central Bank. These transactions brought the Dominican government $U.S.55.6 million in 1983, $U.S.56.8 million in 1984, and an estimated $U.S.30 million in 1985 (the dropoff due to the currency devaluation).[28] It is because of the foreign exchange earning capacity of the industrial free zones that the Dominican government has placed a high priority on the future development of the zones and has

expanded its efforts to attract foreign investment. The Jorge administration, for example, developed the Investment Promotion Council
which is responsible for attracting new foreign investment and for as-
sisting foreign investors with the cumbersome application process. As
Jorge stated in his state visit to the United States in 1984, "evidence of
our desire to stimulate foreign investment is the fact that we have created
the Dominican Foreign Investment Promotion Center to assist any investor interested in learning more about the Dominican Republic."[29]

Fulfilling the dream of transforming the economy from agriculture to
industry has begun in the Dominican Republic, but it is important not
to lose sight of the fact that the industrial free zones contribute only a
small share to the overall productive output of the country and have
had little effect on the unemployment crisis. And yet, as with agroindustry, there is a sense of movement and excitement about the possibilities that industrialization can bring to the Dominican Republic. The
Dominicans are the first to realize that they are a long way from becoming
the Taiwan, Singapore, Hong Kong, or South Korea of the Caribbean,
but there is a consensus in the country that the zones are a vision of
the future, a progressive and growth-oriented vision that is not beyond
their reach.

SUGAR AND OIL DEPENDENCY—THE CRITICAL CHALLENGE

When examining a poor and struggling Third World nation like the
Dominican Republic, one is naturally drawn to the task of finding villains—the source or sources of the poverty and economic malaise that
has created enormous debt, unemployment, inflation, and an inevitable
bout with social and perhaps even political disorder. In the Dominican
Republic it is not difficult to target the villains that helped initiate the
economic and financial crisis during the administrations of Guzmán and
Jorge, and most likely contributed to the resurgence of Joaquín Balaguer
in 1986. To recast a familiar phase so as to apply it to the Dominican
situation, "oil and sugar do not mix." As a country with a long history
of dependence on foreign trade to generate revenue and provide for its
modernizing needs, the Dominican Republic has literally been built on
sugar income and has enjoyed a level of prosperity when sugar prices
were high and foreign oil costs were manageable. Without a diversified
industrial base to complement the sugar sector and with few internal
sources of energy, the Dominican Republic has been forced to endure
the effects of an economy that operates much like a rollercoaster with
growth "highs" stimulated by favorable world prices for sugar combined
with fuel bills that could be met by sugar revenues followed by stagnating

"lows" caused by precipitous drops in sugar prices and the resulting inability to pay for imported oil.

The oil-and-sugar crisis in the Dominican Republic is so critical for the future of the economy and indeed the country that it is important to examine the impact of this key export-import axis. The best place to begin is to return to the last administration of Joaquín Balaguer, from 1974 until 1978 during the so-called "miracle" period, when favorable sugar prices generated significant internal growth, and follow the Dominican economic rollercoaster through the presidencies of Guzmán and Jorge, when the country hit bottom as both falling sugar and rising oil prices combined to bring the country to the brink of bankruptcy. By examining this 12-year period from 1974 to 1986, it will be possible to see the enormous influence that sugar and oil have had on the Dominican economy and most likely will have in the future.

As Joaquín Balaguer began his third term as president in August of 1974, the Dominican Republic was being touted as a mini-Brazil, since its growth rates of 5 percent in the early 1970s were approaching 9 percent in 1974 and heading for double digits in 1975. Despite the devastating civil war period (1965–1966), per capita income increased from $513 to $1,050 between 1960 and 1980 and gross domestic product rose from $1.8 billion to $5.7 billion from 1960 until 1980. Many of these increases came after the civil war and are attributed to the immense amounts of money the United States (seeking to prevent another Cuba) pumped into the economy and the return to "normalcy" that occurred during the Balaguer years. But Balaguer and normalcy were not the only reasons for this enormous growth spurt. In 1975 sugar prices on the world market were at an all-time high of $.76 a pound, creating a situation where the petroleum bill absorbed only 60 percent of the sugar revenue, thereby allowing the government greater leeway in spending for public works projects such as housing and road construction. With sugar revenue high and the government able to meet its import bills, Dominicans, particularly those in the middle class, enjoyed a period of prosperity as witnessed by the increase in imported consumer goods, the expansion of private business enterprises, and the greater concern with style, leisure, travel, and consumption.[30]

With an economy so tied to foreign demand and supply, it was not long before the miracle period came to an end and sent the rollercoaster down toward stagnation and recession. That turnaround came in the period from 1977 to 1981, when prices on sugar and other agricultural commodities declined by 30 percent while oil costs increased fourfold. This turnaround in sugar revenue and oil costs fostered a significant change in the terms of trade for the Dominican Republic. Where petroleum costs in 1977 absorbed 60 percent of sugar export earnings, in 1982, during the Guzmán administration, the petroleum bill absorbed 133 percent of the sugar revenue. The oil bill for the Dominican Republic in 1981, for example, was $U.S.574 million, which when added to other import costs created a trade deficit of over $U.S.400 million. As one Dominican put the oil and sugar dilemma, "1,000 pounds of sugar in 1974 bought 12 barrels of oil, now in 1981 the same 1,000 pounds of sugar barely buys three barrels."[31]

Besides the drop in sugar prices and the jump in oil costs, the Dominican economy was also affected by a third external factor. Due to the recession in the industrialized countries, in particular the United States, export volume declined considerably. According to data from the World Bank, by 1982 the volume index of exports had declined one fifth below its 1978 value. On the import side, however, the demand for capital goods and raw materials continued to grow at a rate of 8 percent a year from 1975 until 1980. This import binge, although necessary from the Dominican perspective in order to keep the economy afloat and respond to the needs of the people, forced the government to increase its external borrowing. Unfortunately the borrowing by the Guzmán government occurred at a time when interest rates in the advanced countries were rising significantly causing service payments on public foreign debt to rise from $U.S.87 million in 1978 to $U.S.250 million in 1982.[32]

With the Dominican economy hit by unfavorable terms of trade, declining export volume and high interest rates, the miracle of the mid–1970s came to an abrupt halt by 1977 and by 1981–1982 the Dominican Republic was in the midst of a severe economic crisis. Not only had growth rates dropped to around 4 percent in the Guzmán years, but public sectors deficits and external debt obligations continued to rise. By the time of Guzmán's death in July 1982, the Dominican economy was a shambles. Sugar prices had dropped to single digits, ($.05–.06 per pound from the high of $.75), there was scant relief from other commodities such as coffee, cocoa, and tobacco, and the ferronickel industry, which earlier held out hope of diversifying the economic base, suffered from low world demand. Moreover, the foreign oil bill for 1982 was over $600 million, while export volume declined by 25 percent. Publicly, Dominican officials saw hope for oil prices and the economy as OPEC seemed less able to agree on pricing and production, but privately those in the middle class worried over rising inflation, slow growth and dramatic increases in bankruptcies. As for the vast majority of the poor who understood little about balance of trade, debt servicing, and world price fluctuations, their only concern was over the price of rice, the availability of gasoline and the growing level of unemployment.[33]

Much has been made of President Jorge's measures to revitalize and reform the Dominican economy. His austerity policies, such as cutting government salaries, banning the importation of foreign cars, and placing new taxes on imported goods and capital gains helped to ease the pressure on the national budget and the balance of payments. Also his controversial negotiations with the International Monetary Fund and eventual acceptance of their recommendations on exchange rates, taxation, and public sector spending are often credited as responsible for a strengthened economy in the last year of his administration (they also produced strikes, food riots, and widespread protest demonstrations). Although one cannot deny the importance of the actions taken by Jorge, particularly the currency devaluation, it is important not to lose sight of the fact that part of the resurgence in the Dominican economy can be traced to changes in the sugar trade and the plummeting price of foreign oil.

As mentioned earlier, the cutback in the U.S. quota combined with only modest increases in the world price has prompted Dominican leaders to take more aggressive measures to deemphasize the country's reliance on sugar cane as a key source of export revenue. The continued development of nontraditional exports along with the beginning of a national debate over the wisdom of maintaining large, publicly owned sugar refineries may be looked upon by future generations as the real legacy of the Jorge administration. Although the Dominican Republic continues to rely too heavily on the sugar trade (sugar accounts for over 30 percent of Dominican exports, down from 60 percent 25 years ago) for foreign revenue, the economic crisis of the early 1980s has awakened the Dominicans to the dangers of a sugar-driven economy. Making the transition away from sugar will not be easy, for political as well as economic reasons, but the memory of Balaguer's miracle collapsing as sugar prices dropped is just as vivid as the harsh measures taken by Jorge to correct its economic and financial system. All recent Dominican governments have been convinced of the need to diversify away from sugar; the key concerns are the best means to do so and the political costs that will be incurred.

While much of the attention on trade reform has centered on sugar, the Dominicans have begun to benefit from the near collapse of OPEC in the mid-1980s and the resulting drop in the world price of oil. United States government projections for 1986 show that the oil bill for the Dominican Republic will drop to $U.S. 272 million from $U.S. 427 million in 1985.[34] Although no one can predict with certainty how oil prices will change over the next years, the Dominican economy once again is benefiting from a situation where export revenue is sufficient to pay for imported oil. The Dominicans remain vulnerable in the area of oil importation and have not been able to initiate the kind of transition that is apparently occurring in the sugar sector. There has been some oil exploration in the country and the development of a small ethanol industry using the by-products of sugarcane, but for the near future the price of oil may be the deciding factor as to whether the economic rollercoaster is riding upward or heading for a new low.

THE POLITICIZED ECONOMY

As in most countries, every economic action has a political reaction. But in the Dominican Republic the economic actions taken have often been so drastic and controversial that the political reaction has caused serious dislocations in terms of internal unrest and successful challenges to existing governmental authority. As we shall see, the general weakness and uncertainty of the Dominican economy has forced governmental leaders to make some hard choices in recent years not only because its dependent status offers few avenues toward sustained growth, but because the policy options available in many instances create unacceptable social and political problems that may be more troublesome than the original economic malaise.

In order to better comprehend this interconnection between economic problem, policy, and outcome, it may be helpful to consider Table 6.1, which describes in a more orderly fashion the hard political choices that have faced Dominican leaders and more than likely will face them again in the future. The table first lists the problem, then describes the government's policy response, and last shows the often negative outcomes of the policies chosen.

As Table 6.1 indicates, the Dominicans are not without solutions to the considerable economic challenges that face them, and in many instances have instituted programs and policies to address their deficiencies. The critical issue for the future, however, is whether governmental officials possess the courage and foresight to deal with the inevitable political fallout from their actions. This is particularly difficult for a democratic government. Moreover, it is not merely the politicians who will require the special talents for responding to the effects of public policy, but the democratic system must be resilient enough to survive the inevitable threats from those who will be adversely affected by reform or restriction or revitalization.

In each of the problem areas mentioned in the chart, the solution or solutions are not mysterious or unachievable. The Dominicans know exactly what has to be done with respect to their economy and in most instances are familiar with the policy options. Austerity measures, for example, are not new in the Dominican Republic, since Balaguer at the end of the miracle period placed harsh restrictions on wage increases and governmental expenditures. A similar public familiarity with what should be done exists in the areas of import restrictions to correct trade imbalances, conservation measures to limit foreign oil consumption, and numerous training and job creation programs to alleviate the unem-

Table 6.1
The Public Policy Dilemma in the Dominican Republic

PROBLEM	POLICY	OUTCOME
Large public deficit	Austerity measures - decline in public works projects and credit crunch	Sluggish growth, clamor for housing, jobs and local capital
Inefficient public enterprise	Preliminary discussions on consolidation and privatization	Predictions of worker unrest and political infighting over lost sinecures
Low world prices for agricultural products	Diversification through agro-industry and non-traditional exports	Greater influence of foreign business; streamlining of entrenched bureaucracy (if possible)
Regular trade imbalances	Currency devaluation, import restrictions, export enhancement programs, greater stress on tourism	Lower purchasing power, unavailability of some consumer products, heightened social unrest, transition to new and unfamiliar economic system
High Foreign Debt	Rescheduling based on IMF guidelines, limits on size of state sector	More favorable financial position in banking circles, but greater restrictions at home, including higher taxes. Possibility civil disorder.
Fluctuating foreign oil costs	Conservation measures, greater efficiency at Dominican Electric Company new efforts to develop local sources of energy	High energy costs, disgruntled consumers, continued dependence on foreign oil despite conservation efficiency and development programs
Consistently high unemployment	Job training, expansion of free zones, tourism and light industry, continued reliance on public works projects	Some success, but economy unable to match birth rate Inherent contradiction between job creation and cuts in public sector

Source: Compiled by the authors.

ployment problem. What is new, of course, are the IMF reforms that have changed traditional currency, credit, and tax practices and the growing emphasis on diversification, privatization, and cooperation with foreign investors. But even here the newness of these initiatives and the threats they pose to established practices and beliefs has been overshadowed by the positive results they have achieved in strengthening the economy and enhancing the reputation of the Dominican Republic as a country that has met its problems head on.

The critical problem in the Dominican Republic, however, is not a shortage of solutions, but the outcome, implementation, and most especially the political consequences of the policy chosen. As can be seen from the chart, with each one of these economic policy initiatives, there will be a serious social and political price to pay. Austerity, privatization, currency devaluation, debt rescheduling, diversification, conservation, and job creation—all necessary if the Dominican Republic is to develop—will inevitably cause hardship, dislocation, and anger. Workers will most likely have to be dismissed to attain greater efficiency in key industries, credit lines will dry up as government attempts to control public spending, consumer products may be harder to find as import restrictions continue, household incomes and general standards of living may decrease as prices inch upward and staple commodities become scarce. In general the Dominican people will be asked to shoulder larger financial sacrifices for the good of the nation's economy. Already such sacrifices have caused a series of violent outbursts by the poor, grumblings among the middle class, and the demise of the governing party in the last election. Since each one of these policy initiatives has the potential to create a negative social and political backlash, it is a virtual certainty that in the future actions taken by the government may on the one hand solve (or at least ease) a serious economic or financial problem, while at the same time foster or exacerbate an unstable internal political climate.

Of critical importance in the area of public policy outcomes is what the government does to offset the reductions in public sector expenditures and the accompanying move to attain greater efficiency in the state enterprises such as sugar and electricity. The enormous drain on the Dominican economy caused by the bloated state budget and the ever-growing bureaucracy coupled with the realization that inefficiency in the state sugar centrals and in the Dominican Electric Company is retarding growth has forced governmental officials, both Jorge and now Balaguer, to take forceful measures and propose controversial changes in the way the public sector operates. Should the public sector budget continue to be cut back and the state enterprises experience real internal reorganization, the end result will certainly be the creation of a stronger and more efficiently operated economic base. But at the same time these admirable economic goals will undoubtedly lead to higher unemployment, increased financial distress for a large segment of the working population, and a likely return to a period of unrest and harsh criticism of the government.

The Dominican economy has gone through a number of changes in the last decade and has experienced the rollercoaster ride of success and failure. What is most interesting about this period of ups and downs is that not only have the Dominicans begun the process of a major transformation of their economy, but they have also become unwilling experts on the outcomes of economic policy. One can only hope that in the future this experience in both economic policy and economic outcomes will serve Dominican leaders well should the rollercoaster ride continue.

THE FUTURE OF THE DOMINICAN ECONOMY

Speculating on the direction that the economy of any country will follow is risky business since there are so many internal and external factors that can contribute to an upturn or a period of decline. In the case of the Dominican Republic, all that one can state with a degree of certainty is that the future strength or weakness of the economy will be largely determined by external forces. For example, the Inter-American Development Bank in its year-end report on the Dominican economy stated that for the future, "world prices of certain Dominican commodities such as coffee, sugar, ferro-nickel and gold are either stabilizing or improving, while recent oil price decreases may improve the trade balance, reduce inflation and contribute to the economic recovery. . . . the Dominican Republic seems to be in a good position to capitalize on its favorable resource endowment, its closeness to the United States market and its ample supply of low-cost labor."[35] The U.S. Embassy in Santo Domingo echoed the Inter-American Development Bank prediction when it described the outlook for the Dominican economy as "brighter."[36] Its reasons were lower prices for imported diesel fuel and gasoline which will aid consumer purchasing power and manufacturing costs, the continued growth of the tourist industry and nontraditional exports, and the loosening of rural credit and some price controls.

In both of these analyses the accent was on how external circumstances and conditions would benefit the internal Dominican economy. Although the Dominican public and private sectors are actively involved in modernizing and reforming their economic base, the prospects for sustained growth remain closely tied to the level of imports by the United States, the world price of export commodities and resources, the price of foreign oil and the availability of external investment. While both the Inter-American Development Bank and the U.S. Embassy seem confi-

Table 6.2
Key Economic Indicators (in millions of U.S. dollars)

	1984	1985	1986	1987
GDP in current dollars (millions)	2,966	4,694	5,491	-
Real GDP growth	0	-1.2	2	-
Consumer Price Index % change	24	38	15	-
Industrial production % change	-1.0	-4.0	0	1.0
Government deficit as % of GDP	2.7	2.0	3.0	
Exports (F.O.B.)	868	737	811	820
Imports (F.O.B.)	1,257	1,286	1,232	1,250
Trade Balance	-389	-549	-421	**-430**
Foreign Investment				
Total	270	260	280	290
U.S.	170	175	190	198
U.S. share (%)	63	67	68	68
U.S. exports to D.R.	630	726	696	
U.S. imports to D.R.	488	429	450	
Trade Balance	142	297	246	
U.S. share of D.R. exports %	50	56	56	
U.S. share of D.R. imports %	56	58	55	

Sources: National Statistics Office of the Dominican Republic, Central Bank of the Dominican Republic, U.S. Commerce Department, U.S. Embassy estimates.

dent that in the short run economic growth will be modest (the U.S. Embassy feels in the neighborhood of 2 percent), there is an underlying uncertainty in their predictions as they often hedge their bets by constant reference to foreign markets, world prices, oil costs, and investment potential.

To predict more accurately where the Dominican economy may be headed in the future, Table 6.2 shows key indicators for the three-year period from 1984 until 1987 and may provide some insight regarding what challenges and opportunities may await the Dominicans.

Perhaps the two most encouraging statistics in the table are the real GDP growth figure for 1986 and the projection of industrial production for 1987. In both areas there are signs that the Dominican economy has weathered the financial and public policy adjustments brought on by the IMF guidelines and is now in a position to achieve modest levels of growth. Although the projection for 1987 was only made with respect to industrial production, Dominican and foreign analysts believe that positive economic growth should continue because of encouraging world prices for basic commodities, a substantial decline in the inflation rate, and a steady stream of foreign investment into the country.

On the negative side, of course, is the ongoing deficit in the trade balance and the continued growth in the public sector. In these areas there does not seem to be any major relief in sight, even though the Dominicans are making efforts to rejuvenate the export economy and limit governmental spending. As Table 6.2 suggests, it appears that the Dominican Republic will continue to be an "export poor" nation that requires a large public sector to prop up a weak economy in the context of an increasingly restive social climate. Moreover, the export nature of the Dominican economy remains closely tied to the United States. Very little has changed in the last few years in terms of the U.S. share of Dominican exports and imports. The future development of the Dominican economy will thus still depend in large part on decisions made in governmental circles in Washington and corporate headquarters in New York.

As with any country, the future of the Dominican economy rests also with the policies adopted by the Balaguer government. In the days immediately after taking the presidency, Balaguer sent a clear signal to the country and to foreign investors that he was going to rely more on private sector development and the economic forces of the marketplace. In statements made by Balaguer upon naming Luís Julián Pérez as governor of the Central Bank, Roberto Saladín as minister of finance, and Roberto Martínez as minister of industry and commerce, the new president let it be known that the Dominican government would encourage business expansion and begin to take steps to lessen the influence of the large state sector.[37] The domestic and foreign business sectors were cheered by these pronouncements.

As proof of Balaguer's resolve, he ordered that social programs supported by funds from the national lottery be suspended and that monies from the lottery be deposited directly in the state treasury. Although no mention was made of how the redirected monies will be used, it is thought that Balaguer's public promise to revive the sagging construction industry, especially in the area of public housing, may benefit from this new transfer of funds. Balaguer also instructed his vice-president, Carlos Morales Troncoso, to take over the administration of the 12 state-owned sugar refineries for what is expected to be a major reconstitution of this bloated and inefficient public enterprise. As stated previously, any reconstitution process will inevitably lead to layoffs, closings, consolidations, and privatization.

Already there are some signs that Balaguer does not intend to sit idly by and ignore the high level of unemployment that is potentially a social time bomb. Preliminary figures for the first 90 days of the Balaguer presidency revealed that the government had created over 31,000 new jobs in the construction sector and spent $40 million to build low-income housing, roads, bridges, and city streets. The government was also planning large public works projects in the tourist areas, building new hotels, and enlarging existing airport facilities. Even though the 31,000 new jobs have had little affect on the overall unemployment problem, the gesture did signal the strategy that Balaguer intended to follow in the coming years.[38] Because of these initiatives, some Dominicans began calling the generally conservative Balaguer a "populist."

In many respects no one should be surprised by the initial policies of the Balaguer regime since in his first three administrations the crafty Dominican leader relied heavily on a mixture of support for private enterprise and large labor-intensive public works projects. What is disturbing to many critics of the new government's initiatives is that they may serve to further overextend the government budget and precipitate a new round of foreign borrowing. Balaguer has in fact admitted that over $500 million in foreign debts may not be met by the conclusion of 1986. Furthermore, there are those both in the International Monetary Fund and the State Department who privately lament that all the work of 1984 and 1985 may be wasted because Balaguer has never really embraced the reform program of the Jorge administration and has let it be known that he is not necessarily committed to continuing reforms, such as the currency devaluation.[39]

It is still too early to make judgments on the wisdom or the ultimate direction of the Balaguer economic program. All that can be said with certainty is that the Dominican economy will not only respond to the initiatives of the governing authorities, but will be shaped by forces outside of the country—in commodity trading centers, in international lending agencies, in foreign banks, and in corporate boardrooms. Besides being a shrewd politician, Balaguer has in the past also been an enormously lucky national leader who has benefited from favorable external economic influences. As he maneuvers through his fifth term as president there are signs that he may once again benefit from such influences. The key for the future, however, remains what Balaguer does with these favorable trends and how he implements public policy so as to avoid a return to the years after his "miracle" became an economic nightmare.

NOTES

1. A useful discussion of Dominican dependency can be found in Ruben Berrios Martínez, "Dependent Capitalism and the Prospects for Democracy in Puerto Rico and the Dominican Republic," in Paget Henry and Carl Stone, eds., *The Newer Caribbean: Decolonization, Democracy and Development* (Philadelphia: Institute for the Study of Human Issues, 1983), pp. 327–39.

2. For a recent discussion of the impact that the United States has on the Dominican economy, see "Foreign Economic Trends and Their Implications for the United States," United States Embassy, Santo Domingo, June 1986.

3. One of the authors was most impressed with an interview of the then Dominican Ambassador to the United States, Eulogio Santaella, who was quite forceful in his views on the need for the Dominicans to establish new trade relationships with the external sector, in particular the United States. Personal interview, Washington, DC, July 1, 1986.

4. Personal interviews, World Bank and International Monetary Fund, Washington, DC, July 2, 1986.

5. "Foreign Economic Trends and Their Implications for the United States," op. cit., p. 7.

6. *Economic and Social Progress in Latin America, 1986 Report*. Inter-American Development Bank, pp. 253–54.

7. The Balaguer government, in an effort to create new jobs and to acquire imports of capital goods, is considering a new program which converts the Dominican Republic's foreign ($U.S.) debts into local currency, then considering those monies as foreign investments. Similar plans have been adopted in other countries and Balaguer seems intent on continuing the recovery started by the Jorge administration, but he insists on handling the nearly $4 billion debt in a manner different from that suggested by the IMF. Santo Domingo *News*, December 4, 1986.

8. See Jonathan Hartley, "The Dominican Republic, 1985–1986," in *Latin American and Carribean Contemporary Record*, ed. Abraham Lowenthal (New York: Holmes and Meier, in press).

9. *Economic and Social Progress in Latin America, 1986 Report*, op. cit., p. 255.

10. See Aaron Segal, "King Sugar Is Ending Reign," *The Times of the Americas*, September 12, 1984. See also a speech by President Balaguer's minister of tourism, Fernando Rainieri at the Plaza Hotel in New York, designed to set off a new campaign to bring United States tourists to the Dominican Republic. As reported in the Santo Domingo *News*, December 11, 1986.

11. The issues connected to the sugar crisis between the United States and the Dominican Republic are discussed by Scott B. MacDonald in *The Times of the Americas*, January 28, 1987.

12. These figures are provided by the Central Bank of the Dominican Republic and the U.S. Commerce Department.

13. This theme was first forwarded by former President Salvador Jorge Blanco in a speech at the Smithsonian Institution. At that time he stated, "Only through improvement in our terms of trade will our country be attractive to foreign investment. Neo-protectionism, if carried out, would not only represent an economic stumbling block for us, but also a psychological shock which might inhibit those Dominicans with less perseverance. Since we propose to create new agro-industries in our country, it would be very difficult for us to execute these plans if the production of our traditional agro-industry, sugarcane, did not find doors totally open in that country from which we Dominicans expect the biggest collaboration." Speech given by Salvador Jorge Blanco at the Woodrow Wilson International Center for Scholars, Smithsonian Institution, Washington, DC, February 23, 1982.

14. Washington *Post*, December 16, 1986.

15. See Frank Moya Pons, ed., *Causas y manejo de la crisis económica dominicana 1974–1984*, Santo Domingo: Forum No. 18, 1986.

16. "Foreign Economic Trends and Their Implications for the United States," op. cit., p. 7.

17. Jonathan Hartley, "The Dominican Republic, 1985–1986," op. cit., pp. 9–10.

18. Ibid., p. 10.

19. Richard Kearney, "Spoils in the Caribbean: The Struggle for Merit-Based Cival Service in the Dominican Republic," *Public Administraion Review*, March/April 1986, pp. 144–45.

20. See "Products Investment and Trade Promotion," *Commercial News Dominican Republic*, July 1985, p. 4.

21. See "The Dominican Republic Investment Climate Report," December 1984, Paper prepared by the United States Embassy, Santo Domingo.

22. *Summary of Investment Laws*, United States Embassy, Santo Domingo, January 1985.

23. The Balaguer government moved quickly to correct the problems with Law # 861. The Central Bank announced on November 27, 1986 that it was drafting a bill to amend the law and would liberalize the restrictions that have been placed on foreign investors. *El Caribe*, November 28, 1986.

24. *Economic and Social Progress in Latin America, 1986 Report*, op. cit., pp. 255–56.

25. See, for example, an article by Wilson Rood, "CBI is a Resounding Success," *The Times of the Americas*, September 11, 1985, in which he and others familiar with the Dominican economy hold out great hope for the transformation of the country from one of agriculture to one of assembly and light industry.

26. Balaguer continued the support of the duty free zones. After only one month in office Balaguer, through his National Council on Industrial Free Zones, authorized nine new firms to begin operations in the zones. The government estimated that the nine new firms will hire over 4000 employees and invest some RD 28 million. The Santo Domingo *News*, December 4, 1986.

27. *Summary of Investment Laws*, op. cit., p. 2.

28. "Offshore Manufacturing Opportunities," *Commercial News Dominican Republic*, March 1986, pp. 1–3.

29. Washington *Post*, April 11, 1984.

30. Jan Knippers Black, *The Dominican Republic* (Boulder, CO: Westview Press, 1981), pp. 63–64.

31. Michael Kryzanek, "The Dominican Republic 1981–1982" in Jack Hopkins, ed., *Latin America and Caribbean Contemporary Record, 1981–1982* (New York: Holmes and Meier, 1982), p. 550.

32. *Dominican Republic: Economic Prospects and Policies to Renew Growth*, Washington, DC: World Bank Country Study, 1985), pp. xi-xvii.

33. Michael Kryzanek, "The Dominican Republic 1982–1983," in Jack Hopkins, ed., *Latin American and Caribbean Contemporary Record, 1982–1983* (New York: Holmes and Meier, 1983), pp. 673–75.

34. "Foreign Economic Trends and Their Implications for the United States," op. cit., p. 6.

35. *Economic and Social Progress in Latin America, 1986 Report*, op. cit., p. 256.

36. Foreign Economic Trends and Their Implications for the United States," op. cit., p. 5.

37. *Times of the Americas*, September 3, 1986.

38. *Times of the Americas*, November 26, 1986.

39. Personal interviews, International Monetary Fund and United States State Department, July 1 and 2, 1986.

7

THE POLITICS OF INTERNATIONAL RELATIONS IN THE DOMINICAN REPUBLIC

The theme of this book has been that the Dominican Republic is a country whose identity, development, and direction is in considerable measure the result of external influences. Although the impact of the outside world on the Dominican Republic has been examined from an historical perspective and in terms of political institutions, social groupings and economic conditions, the study would be incomplete without exploring the broader involvement of the Dominicans in the international community of nations. Because of its unique position in the Caribbean Basin, its increasing interdependence with the outside world both politically and economically, its increasing contact with a broad range of international institutions and agencies, and its desire to be recognized and respected by neighbors, allies, and adversaries, the Dominican Republic must be examined as an active, and in many instances an independent participant in regional and international affairs.

The Dominican Republic, despite its size and its traditional preoccupation with matters of internal political and economic stability, has in recent years broadened its ties to its immediate neighbors and to those countries in the industrialized world who can be of assistance in the process of modernization.[1] Instead of remaining as a near "vassal state" of the United States, Dominican leaders have made serious attempts to become more a part of the Caribbean region and to spread out or diversify their dependence to Europe and the Far East. The Dominicans of the 1980s are much more attuned to the impact that events or conditions outside their borders have on the character of national life. As a result, Dominican leaders have become more visible participants in regional and international affairs. Leadership roles in international organizations have been actively sought after, new diplomatic and economic ties have been established, and issues of foreign policy and strategic relations have been widely debated in the country.

To see the manner in which the Dominican Republic has fashioned a foreign policy in the 1980s and expanded its visibility in the international community of nations, a discussion of the challenges faced by the Dominicans as they engage in external relations is in order. Identifying and analyzing these challenges is critical as they often define the issues of foreign and strategic policy and set the limits of governmental action and reaction. By examining how Dominican leaders have responded to these challenges, it will be possible to understand why international politics is increasingly becoming a crucial element of internal politics in the Dominican Republic.

COPING WITH THE EFFECTS OF GEOGRAPHY

Just as the position of the Dominican Republic at the center of the Caribbean chain of islands contributed greatly in the colonial era to the seemingly endless series of invasions and disputes over control, the specter of leftist revolution and superpower jockeying for influence in the 1980s has once again made Hispaniola, and in particular the Dominican side of the island, an important piece of real estate. As former U.S. ambassador to the Dominican Republic, Robert Anderson has stated, "the location of the country on one of the most important strategic and commercial arteries of the United States speaks for itself."[2] Specifically, Anderson was alluding to the fact that one-half of the U.S. trade, two-thirds of imported oil, and 70 percent of the troop reenforcements in the event of a NATO conflict with the Soviet Union or Eastern bloc countries pass through the Caribbean Sea by the Dominican Republic.[3]

Categorizing the Dominican Republic as a kind of strategic and commercial crossroads in what is now an important geopolitical region of the world is the result of a serious U.S. concern (and not just a figment of the Reagan administration's imagination) that the Caribbean Basin may become the next flashpoint as the United States seeks to contain the spread of revolution and Soviet enchroachment into our traditional sphere of influence. To the Dominicans, however, this new interest in their country is unsettling since quotes like that of Ambassador Anderson suggest that should the region erupt as a result of guerrilla warfare or a superpower confrontation, the Dominican Republic might well become involved simply because of where it is situated on the map. As a result of their reluctance to become too closely identified as a strategic and commercial crossroads, the Dominicans have been careful not to appear overly interested in calling attention to their geographic location.

Although the Dominicans have accepted increased U.S. aid for modernization of their military and have cooperated with U.S. military officials, they have shown little eagerness to assume a larger geopolitical role. In fact, when a U.S. naval vessel sought to make a courtesy call in the port of Santo Domingo during the Jorge administration, there were major demonstrations as the Dominicans let it be known that they did not want their country openly identified with U.S. strategic interests or involved in negotiations that would link their country to a network of Caribbean defense arrangements.[4] The concern of many Dominicans is not only generated from the memory of the 1965 invasion and the extensive military agreements initiated by Rafael Trujillo, but also by the long-held view among U.S. military planners that the Samaná Bay region is the best natural water port in the Caribbean and an excellent prospect for the establishment of an agreement providing for docking privileges. Although it is doubtful that Samaná Bay has the same strategic value to the United States now that it had in earlier decades, Dominicans continue to believe that it does.[5]

Of much greater concern to the Dominicans, in terms of geographic placement and external relations, is the unrest in neighboring Haiti. The ouster of the Duvalier regime and the movement toward democracy has not brought a sense of relief to the Dominicans. In fact the change of power in Haiti has created great unease in the Dominican Republic as many Dominicans feel the struggle for power is not over and that future political instability may spill across the border. Rumors abound in the Dominican Republic about *Duvalieristas* using Dominican bases as they prepare a comeback or an assault on the new government. On a number of occasions the border between the two countries has been closed and the Dominican military has been put on alert.

Since the much-heralded agreements between Antonio Guzmán and Jean Claude 'Bébé Doc' Duvalier in 1979, which expanded contact between the two countries in the areas of trade and irrigation, relations between the Dominican Republic and Haiti have deteriorated steadily.[6] Despite the fact that after almost 20 years the Dominican Congress ratified in 1983 the U.S.-sponsored International Convention on the Elimination of all Forms of Racial Discrimination, the scandal of the working conditions of Haitian sugarcane cutters, the racist attitudes of the Dominicans toward those blacks who have immigrated to the eastern end of the island, and now the political upheaval in Haiti, have combined to heighten tensions and return the relationship to the days when both nations made little effort to develop ties.[7] Joaquín Balaguer may have initiated a series of commercial agreements with the Haitians in the early 1970s, but his recent harsh criticism of the "Haitianization" of Dominican society makes it unlikely that much effort will be made to open up new channels in the coming years.

An even more serious result of the renewed tensions between Haiti and the Dominican Republic is the prospect that the Balaguer government may hold to its promise of repatriating thousands of Haitians who have illegally settled on Dominican soil. Heretofore most of the transit of Haitians to and from the Dominican Republic has been as a result of an economic arrangement between the two governments. But the heightened level of anti-Haitian feeling in the Dominican Republic may spur

Balaguer and his supporters to develop an accompanying political arrangement that places a ceiling on Haitians in the country and results in a policy that speeds up and expands the process of sending illegal aliens back across the border. Should such a political arrangement become reality, it is certain to fuel the already bad feelings between these close but distant neighbors.

One final foreign policy issue that has arisen as a result of the geographic location of the Dominican Republic is the increase in drug trafficking in the country. As mentioned earlier, the use of the Dominican Republic as a transshipment point for drugs from South America, in particular from Colombia, to the United States has been tied to a number of elements within the Dominican armed forces and is one of the major sources of public corruption. But because of the international implications of drug smuggling, the Dominicans are now working closely with foreign governments to limit the impact of the drug trade on their country.

U.S. customs and drug enforcement officials have stepped up their contacts with the Dominican government in an effort to try to curb the transit of drugs from Santo Domingo to the emigré community in New York. Besides providing assistance to modernize the Dominican Navy, which is now primarily involved in the detection of drug smuggling, police officials in both countries are cooperating to break up a number of drug organizations working in the United States. In what was termed a major development by U.S. officials, two Dominican diplomats working in New York were arrested by the police and charged with conspiracy to smuggle millions of dollars of heroin into the country. Dante Sánchez, Dominican vice consul in New York, and Rafael Peña, a Dominican working at the United Nations, along with two U.S. citizens of Dominican descent, were the principals in a smuggling operation that used customs and other diplomatic privileges to bring the heroin into the country.[8] The Dominican government is also working with the supplier countries to halt the drug trade. In 1986 the Jorge administration signed an extradition treaty with the Colombian government which was designed to send a message to smugglers that both countries are serious about prosecuting the practitioners of the drug trade.

The Dominican Republic thus remains a country that cannot avoid the fact that geographic placement and strategic location have had a profound impact on its relations with the outside world. The Dominicans have tried mightily to direct their attention to matters of internal modernization and democratization, but as in the days of *conquistadores* and pirates, it has been difficult to avoid the effects of geography.

DEVELOPING CLOSER TIES TO THE REGION

The most significant developments in the external relations of the Dominican Republic have occurred in the area of regional ties. Under the administrations of Antonio Guzmán and Jorge Blanco the Dominican Republic sought to become more a part of the Caribbean Basin either out of economic necessity or a growing desire to become involved in the future direction of this vital region. Starting with the oil-for-sugar arrangement between the Dominican Republic and the governments of Venezuela and Mexico during Guzmán's presidency (often termed the San José agreement), Dominican governmental leaders have gradually moved away from the position that economic and political relations with regional neighbors diminished the opportunities for furthering their ties with the United States, Europe, and the Far East. The position today in the Dominican Republic in both governmental and business circles is that efforts should be made to expand contacts with other countries in the region and to participate where appropriate in trade and monetary associations and in peacekeeping organizations. Although the Dominicans continue their very close and considerable relations with the advanced industrial nations (and in particular the United States), integration into the Caribbean region appears to be a high priority.

The most widely debated action of the Dominican government concerning regionalization was the decision to seek observer status in the Caribbean Economic Community (CARICOM). At the urging of Prime Minister Edward Seaga of Jamaica, who has consistently sought wider ties with the Dominicans and the incorporation of the Dominican Republic and Haiti in CARICOM, the member countries of the Caribbean Economic Community placed the issue on their agenda in 1984. After a heated controversy between Seaga and leftists in CARICOM, such as the late Forbes Burnham of Guyana and Maurice Bishop of Greneda, the Dominicans were granted observer status.[9] The concerns among CARICOM members were not only over Seaga's free market approach running up against the socialist ideology of Burnham and Bishop, but the fact that the Dominican economy was so much larger than any of the island mini-states that make up the economic community. Despite the disappointment over not gaining full entry into CARICOM, the Dominicans made a first step and in the process acquired a staunch supporter in Seaga of Jamaica. In fact, ties between the two countries have grown considerably over the last few years. The attainment of full membership in CARICOM has been put on hold as the smaller members of the community continue to be concerned about the impact that the Dominican membership will have on their economies.

While the Dominican Republic was successful to a certain extent in expanding its regioonal ties by gaining observer status in CARICOM, it was rebuffed in its attempts to join the Contadora peace-keeping process. Although the four original Contadora countries—Colombia, Mexico, Panama, and Venezuela—have been at the forefront of the efforts to reach an agreement on the hostilities in Central America, a subsidiary group of Latin American countries—Brazil, Peru, and Uruguay—has formed the Contadora Support Group. The Jorge administration worked vigorously to convince Latin American leaders that the Dominican Republic should be asked to be a member of the Support Group. But despite backing from such countries as Honduras, the Dominican Republic was not included.[10] Despite the Contadora setback, and the unsuccessful bid to gain the Latin American seat in the United Nations Security Council in 1983, Dominican political leaders continued to seek a larger diplomatic role in regional and international affairs. In late 1987, for example, the Dominican Republic hosted a series of meetings between representatives of the Sandinistas government and the Contra rebels.

Perhaps the most promising regional relationship for the Dominican Republic has been developed with neighboring Puerto Rico. Cultural and tourist ties have long been the mainstay of the relationship between the Dominican Republic and Puerto Rico, but in recent years the Dominican and Puerto Rican governments have been expanding their economic ties and building upon the intent of the Reagan administration's Caribbean Basin Initiative. Utilizing over $700 million in funds created by the tax-free earnings of U. S. corporations operating in Puerto Rico (often referred to as 936 funds, after Internal Revenue Code 936 that applies to U.S. corporate earnings in Puerto Rico), the Puerto Ricans, working through their own Government Development Bank, assist in financing existing or new operations in Puerto Rico. The firms receiving the 936 monies then invest their own funds in what are called complementary operations elsewhere in the Caribbean. This "twin-plant" arrangement has met with success as over eleven 936 operations have been started in the Dominican Republic with more planned. Although the base of operations for these "twin-plants" remains in Puerto Rico, Dominican governmental and business leaders seem pleased with the opportunity for expanding their industrial capacity.[11]

But while the regional approach seems to be working in terms of the 936 program, the proximity between the Dominican Republic and Puerto Rico has created problems that may limit future expansion of favorable relations. At the crux of the problem is the increasing number of Dominicans who are entering Puerto Rico illegally, seeking work and a life away from the enormous unemployment back home. Despite language, religious, and other cultural ties, a Puerto Rican backlash has emerged much like that of Dominicans toward the onrush of Haitians immigrants. There have been a number of violent incidents involving Dominicans and Puerto Ricans and high-level meetings between officials of both governments to address the issue of illegal migration.

The Dominican Republic's attempt at becoming more a part of the Caribbean region must at this time be described as only a partial success. New relationships have been developed and some successes recorded. Moreover, the Dominicans are now recognized as a people who want to break away from their image as an extension of the United States. Yet integration with the region will not be easy. In many respects the Dominicans are loners in the region. They have little in common with many of the neighboring countries, except perhaps Puerto Rico, and the Spanish culture that is at the heart of Mexico and Central America is hundreds of miles away. Nevertheless the Dominicans seem anxious to pursue regionalization in order to reduce reliance on the United States.

RESPONDING TO REVOLUTION IN THE REGION

The Dominican Republic has been cautious about aligning itself closely with leftist or Marxist governments in the region. Rather, the foreign policy image that the Dominicans have chosen to accent is that of a moderate, social reform-oriented democracy willing to talk with and even recognize revolutionary regimes, but more comfortable dealing with governments that reflect the Western, liberal tradition. As a result, Dominican governments in the period since the 1965 revolution attempted to walk a fine line between showing support for movements of social change and avoiding overt ties that would detract from its democratic image and cause concern with its major benefactor, the United States.

The best evidence of this foreign policy balancing act is seen in the limited relationship that the Dominicans have developed with neighboring Cuba. Despite frequent calls from the Dominican left to normalize diplomatic relations with communist Cuba, a succession of governments have been unwilling to recognize the Castro government formally. But in lieu of formal ties the Dominicans have been quite willing to develop a number of informal ties to Cuba. Athletic, scholarly, and cultural exchanges have been quite numerous in recent years and there has been an increase of visiting commercial delegations from both countries.[12] There has also been a number of unofficial visits by leftist leaders to Cuba allegedly for educational purposes, but more likely for training in Marxist-Leninist organization and subversion.

These contacts have raised very few eyebrows as they are not seen as an official recognition of the Castro regime, but rather as normal relations between neighbors. The only real controversy over contact with Cuba came during the devastating hurricane of 1979 when President Guzmán refused to allow Cuban relief supplies into the country. Although the issue was the acceptance of Cuban assistance, the underlying motive of Guzmán's actions was his ongoing dispute with leftists in his own party who, in the president's opinion, were using the destruction caused by the hurricane as a means of expanding Cuban influence in the Dominican Republic.

In 1986–1987 President Balaguer continued the opening to Cuba. There were numerous cultural, sports, and other exchanges; the Dominicans and the Cubans emphasized their common historical and social ties; and Fidel Castro actively wooed Dominican leaders. Balaguer, however, has already put limits on the opening: exchanges of various kinds but no formal diplomatic relations. Moreover, with its weak economy, Cuba has little to offer the Dominican Republic; and since both are primarily sugar producers, they are competitors for world markets. There is some suspicion that Balaguer is using the Cuba opening to put pressure on the United States and as a way of getting even for the reduced sugar quota, the drop in foreign aid, and for interfering in the ballot counting in the 1978 election that resulted in Balaguer's defeat by Guzmán.

While there has been a semblance of consistency in successive Dominican regimes, in wishing to open up new relations with Cuba, the Dominicans have shown less agreement on how to deal with the Sandinista government in Nicaragua. Early on in the Nicaraguan revolution, President Guzmán and his PRD followers were openly supportive of the Sandinistas and took positions commending the goals and policies of the revolution, despite the fact that such support was looked on with disfavor in Washington. But during the Jorge administration, when the Dominicans were desperately in need of financial assistance from the United States and were being hailed by President Reagan as the "beacon of democracy" in the Caribbean, it seemed unwise to publicly take positions that could jeopardize relations with Washington. Besides remaining silent during the U.S. invasion of Grenada, while many other Latin American countries decried the intervention, President Jorge and even prominent leftists in the ruling party toned down their support of the Sandinistas. Thus, when Daniel Ortega was inaugurated in 1985, President Jorge was not in attendance, although he did find the time to travel to the inauguration of Peru's democratic president, Alan García.

Although there is no doubt that Dominican foreign policy in large part gets its cues from Washington, it is too simplistic to suggest that governmental leaders are reluctant to support revolutionary movements because of their fear of the reactions from the United States. The Dominican Republic has been a country where support for Marxist revolution is minimal and where political leaders pride themselves on being able to meet the needs of the people without resorting to radical ideology.[13] It would be wrong to describe the Dominicans as a nonrevolutionary people, especially in light of the 1965 struggle. But at the same time it is important to stress that during that struggle the "constitutionalists" carefully avoided contact with Castro's Cuba and constantly emphasized the democratic nature of the revolution. Marxist revolution has recently become an integral part of the geopolitics of the Caribbean Basin and the foreign policy concerns of the Dominican Republic, but Dominican politics and the political culture of the country are steeped in a tradition that seems content to keep the proponents of radical change at arms length.

REDEFINING RELATIONS WITH THE UNITED STATES

It seems safe to state that the Dominican Republic will remain closely aligned with the United States, its major benefactor, primary trading partner, and occasional nemesis. But what is important in describing and analyzing this critical relationship is that it is never constant. Rather it evolves through various stages and accents different aspects of the numerous ties that have developed between these two countries over the years.

During the Trujillo era, for example, relations between the Dominican Republic and the United States were defined in terms of the sugar trade and later on in a more strategic mode as the United States used its ties to the Dominican dictator to advance its anti-communist policies in the region. After Trujillo's assassination the relationship changed as both the Dominicans and the United States turned their attention to the institutionalization of democracy and the implementation of much-needed social reforms. When this experiment in democracy collapsed in 1963 and the Dominican Republic was caught in the web of revolution two years later, the United States lost much of its leverage and had to rely upon military intervention and later on extensive economic assistance in the post-revolution period in order to regain its traditional dominance. The ascension to power of Joaquín Balaguer returned the Dominican Republic to normalcy and also redefined the relationship between the two countries, as political and military considerations gave way to economic development and an expansion of the U.S. corporate presence. Although the election controversy of 1978 and President Carter's aid cutoff threat to the Balaguer government brought the United States back into a political relationship with the Dominican Republic, the ability of the Dominicans to insure peaceful transfers of power since 1978 has helped to stave off any further blatant U.S. involvement in internal political affairs.

The relative success that the Dominican Republic has achieved in the institutionalization of democracy in recent years, along with the increased influence of other foreign governments in the country, has contributed to a new approach toward the United States. Dominican leaders appear more confident in their dealings with the U.S. embassy in Santo Domingo and policymakers in Washington. They speak their mind more often, especially on matters relating to trade barriers and sugar quotas, and exhibit a new-found resolve as they negotiate with United States governmental and business leaders.[14] To some, this may seem as heightened nationalism or a spirit of independence, but it also can be looked upon as a maturing of the relationship, a pragmatic recognition on the part of the Dominicans that even though the United States possesses considerable economic control, the Dominican Republic has much to offer them and therefore possesses its own degree of leverage. Rich agricultural lands, beautiful beaches, low wage and tax rates, cooperative workers, close proximity to the mainland, and now a stable political system, are attractive features that can be used to put forward a favorable image of the country in discussions with governmental and corporate officials from the United States.

The Dominicans therefore are increasingly becoming aware that even though the United States holds most of the economic and political cards, they have the ability to use their vast human, geographic, natural and environmental resources in order to redefine this critical relationship. There may be serious defeats on issues like the cutback on the sugar quota or declining foreign aid, but in the face of these devastating circumstances the Dominicans have developed a reputation as cooperative partners with the United States willing to expand programs that invite new industries into the duty-free zones, liberalize investment laws, and transform the country into the fastest growing tourist center in the Caribbean. Moreover, after Joaquín Balaguer returned to the presidency, there was an even greater spirit of business cooperation in the Dominican Republic. Once in office Balaguer moved quickly to send a signal to the United States that policy changes beneficial to foreign corporate investment would become reality. In particular the issues of profit remittances of foreign businesses, opportunities to expand external involvement in the extractive sector of the economy and a greater accent on joint cooperation in agroindustry were being addressed by the government in ways that will further encourage foreign investment.

This new emphasis on cooperation and openness to foreign interests has not gone unnoticed in the United States. Not only has the business sector intensified its involvement in the Dominican economy, but governmental officials from the State Department to the Commerce Department view the country with less concern. There is widespread disppointment that protectionist legislation and budget restrictions may cause havoc with a fragile Dominican economy, but at the same time there is more confidence that the problems in the country will not pose a danger to the security interests of the United States. In many respects the Dominican Republic under Balaguer is again returning, at least from the perspective of policy-makers in Washington, to that era of normalcy in which the relationship between the United States and the Dominican Republic was defined almost exclusively in economic terms.[15] The key for the future of this relationship will be the strength of the democratic political system should social unrest recur or if Balaguer fails to pay attention to human rights. It is at that point that Washington will again have to determine to what extent it is willing to redefine the relationship and become politically involved in the course of Dominican internal development.

In this way, both sides to the U.S.-Dominican relationship have changed, with change on the one side feeding upon the other. The Dominicans, after two decades of stable growth both economic and political, are more confident, more mature, more pragmatic in their relations with the United States. And the United States, reflecting this greater maturity, moderation, and strengthening of Dominican institutions, has moved away from its earlier pro-consular role toward a relationship that is almost, in diplomatic terms, normal. The Embassy is still an important actor in Dominican internal affairs, and for the Dominican Republic the United States is by far the most critical external force; but the relations have matured to the point where the U.S. Embassy no longer de facto dictates government policy, nor does the prospect of a U.S. Marine occupation seem even remotely possible. Given the earlier history, that represents considerable progress in Dominican-U.S. relations.

INTERNATIONAL ASSISTANCE: THE IMPACT OF THE DEVELOPMENT PIPELINE

Analyzing the ties that the Dominican Republic has to the outside world would be incomplete without a discussion of the numerous development projects that are funded by foreign governments and international agencies. In many respects these projects are the most visible examples of the extent to which the external sector influences the course of Dominican modernization. Moreover, the assistance provided by the more advanced countries or by multilateral lending banks has become a critical component of the policy process as the Dominicans try to balance increased development pressures with the reality of scarce budgetary resources. By providing the financial backing to build hydroelectric facilities or construct a major highway or install an agricultural irrigation system, the agents of international assistance serve to fill a void that, if left neglected, would not only retard economic growth, but would more than likely create potentially destabilizing internal social and political pressures.

Tables 7.1–7.2 provide a general outline of the total dollar transfers to the country from foreign governments and international agencies in recent years.

As can be seen from these two tables, development assistance is provided the Dominican Republic from two primary sources—the United States and the InterAmerican Development Bank. From 1946 until 1984

Table 7.1
Bilateral Official Development Assistance

	Advanced industrial countries calendar years 1978-83 (millions of dollars)
UNITED STATES	266.0
GERMANY, FED. REP.	38.8
JAPAN	18.9
NETHERLANDS	11.6
CANADA	7.0
OTHER	17.9
TOTAL	360.2

Source: U.S. Agency for International Development

Table 7.2
Assistance from International Agencies – Committments

	Fiscal Years 1983-1985 (millions of dollars)		
	1983	1984	1985
IBRD - WORLD BANK	7.1	3.8	5.8
IFC - INTERNATIONAL FINANCE CORPORATION	10.5	0.0	0.0
IDB - INTERAMERICAN DEVELOPMENT BANK	150.0	113.7	187.0
UNDP - UNITED NATIONS DEVELOPMENT PROGRAM	.8	.3	0.0
OTHER UN		1.4	
TOTAL	168.4	119.2	192.8

Source: U.S. Agency for International Development

the United States provided the Dominicans with over $929 million in nonmilitary loans and grants. This assistance has been channeled to the Dominican Republic in policy areas such as agriculture, rural development and nutrition, population planning, health, education and human resource development, and to offset the ravages of declining revenue from agricultural exportation.

Despite cutbacks in foreign aid allocations worldwide, the United States continues to be committed to providing the Dominican Republic with assistance, although the emphasis has changed somewhat as the Agency for International Development (AID) is more concerned with

Table 7.3
Program Summary (in thousands of dollars)

Fiscal Year	Total	Agriculture, Rural Development and Nutrition	Population Planning	Health	Education and Human Resources Development	Selected Development Activities	Other Programs	
							ESF	Other
1985								
Loans	13,946	12,370	-	-	1,036	540	-	-
Grants	111,132	4,640	263	1,448	6,402	3,379	95,000	-
Total	125,078	17,010	263	1,448	7,438	3,919	95,000	
1986								
Loans	11,240	7,540	-	-	-	3,700	-	-
Grants	53,260	1,560	2,450	1,300	4,531	3,419	40,000	-
Total	64,500	9,100	2,450	1,300	4,531	7,119	40,000	
1987								
Loans	16,000	11,000	-	-	-	5,000	-	-
Grants	62,658	4,000	1,650	3,200	1,100	2,708	50,000	-
Total	78,658	15,000	1,650	3,200	1,100	7,708	50,000	

Source: U.S. Agency for International Development

financing projects in the areas of balance of payments support, agricultural diversification, development of light industries, and training of mid-level entrepreneurs.[16] There continues to be a commitment to social welfare programs by the United States, particularly family planning, health care, and education; but these three policy areas have been overshadowed by the Reagan administration's accent on private sector development. To consider the current AID program (Fiscal years 1985–1987), see Table 7.3.

While the United States has cut back somewhat its aid operation in the Dominican Republic due in large part to domestic budget restraints, the InterAmerican Development Bank has attempted to maintain a consistent level of assistance despite its own financial restrictions. In fact, Dominican public officials are relying more heavily on the IDB in order to move forward on many of its key projects, especially in the areas of water resources (irrigation and water purification) and public works (harbor construction and road building). Recently, however, the Dominicans have begun to negotiate loans with the IDB in such areas as tourism, agroindustrial development, and the enhancement of agricultural production. For example, in 1986 the IDB provided the Dominican Central Bank with a $50 million loan to help finance tourism credit programs, a $90 million loan to support the acquisition of equipment

Table 7.4
A Comparison of Externally Financed Projects in the Dominican Republic, 1983/ 1986

AGENCY	NUMBER OF PROJECTS	
	1983	1986
Dominican Electricity Corp	6	11
INDIRI (Water Resources)	8	10
Public Works	7	8
Central Bank	6	1
Agriculture	4	4
Public Health	3	4
Education, Art and Culture	3	3
Technical Secretary of President	2	
State Sugar Council	1	1
Housing Institute	1	1
Water and Sewage - Santo Domingo	1	1
Dominican Agrarian Institute	1	1
Agriculture Bank	1	2
National Drinking Water and Sewer Institute	1	1
Others	4	6
TOTAL	49	55

Source: World Bank

for the growing agro-industrial sector, and $500,000 to foster the continued growth in livestock and marketable fish.[17]

The heavy reliance of the Dominican government on development assistance from the United States or international agencies like the InterAmerican Development Bank is best seen not only by presenting the dollar contribution of the donor and the areas where assistance was provided, but by comparing the number of externally financed projects over time. In order to bring these various factors of external development assistance together, Table 7.4 compares the externally financed projects in the Dominican Republic in 1983 with those in 1986.

As can be seen from the comparison of the 1983 and 1986 externally supported assistance programs, the Dominican Republic has been placing increased emphasis on developing key elements of its internal infrastructure. Water purification, hydroelectric power, and public works projects such as road building are at the forefront of the domestic priorities of the Dominican government. Although there appears to be more attention paid in 1986 to areas such as public health, vocational training and planning issues (a catch-all category that includes everything from Food for Peace programs to projects that strengthen the administrative corps), the bulk of the revenue allocated from the external sector (which in some cases is matched by Dominican expenditures) is targeted to basic societal needs, such as water, electricity, and transportation.

The fact that the financial contributions and project areas of foreign governments and international institutions providing assistance to the Dominican Republic are primarily in critical sectors of national life points up the importance of the external development pipeline. Despite the fact that the Dominicans continue to make efforts to disengage their country from dependent relationships, through greater regionalization and diversification and establishing a more independent stance toward the United States, other forms of external influence develop and begin to play a prominent role in the process of modernization and reform. Granted that loans from foreign governments and international agencies are financial arrangements and cannot be equated with political decisions involving sugar import quotas or other protectionist legislation, they nevertheless reenforce the view that the Dominican Republic is a country that would find it very difficult to provide its people with basic human necessities without significant and continuous external development assistance.

DOMINICAN EXTERNAL RELATIONS AND THE FUTURE

If it is possible to present an underlying theme of the external relations of the Dominican Republic over the years, it is that governments, whether conservative or reformist, have been very cautious about moving the country in new directions. There has indeed been evidence of change and the development of ties to governments heretofore ignored or feared, but Dominican political leaders have seemed reluctant to make major commitments that depart from familiar relationships. There are indeed constants in Dominican foreign policy—a continued willingness to cooperate with the United States, a deepseated fear of neighboring Haiti, a willingness to expand ties to Europe and the Pacific Basin, and a small-state mentality that leads to an avoidance of assuming leadership positions or entangling alliances. Yet although there is a foundation of values and perceptions from which the Dominicans look at the outside world and make decisions on foreign policy matters, it is possible to point out some emerging trends or future areas of controversy that may challenge these established values and perceptions and force governmental leaders to rethink external relations.

One of the most interesting developments in the foreign policy sector is the sale of Dominican sugar to the Soviet Union in 1987. As Miguel Guerrero, director of the Dominican Sugar Institute stated, the sale to the Russians was, "on terms incredibly beneficial for the country.... The operation was carried through because we needed new markets due to the reduction of our quota in the U.S. markets."[18] Although representatives of previous governments have occasionally visited communists countries, the Dominican Republic has not developed formal diplomatic or economic ties to the Eastern bloc or the Soviet Union. Talk of such ties may be designed primarily to cause concern in the State Department, but considering the loss of a considerable part of the U.S. market, the Dominicans have to take their sugar somewhere and the communist countries may be a logical destination. The key elements in this possible new approach is not that the Dominicans may be changing their basic ideology or forsaking their longstanding ties to the United States, but rather that they are continuing their pursuit of expanded ties to the outside world and expressing increased independence from the United States.

While the future may see the Dominican Republic look to Eastern Europe for a new sugar market (the same area, of course, where Cuba is trying to expand its sales), governmental leaders like Joaquín Balaguer can be expected to utilize to the maximum the investment possibilities that are connected to the Reagan administration's Caribbean Basin Initiative. Speaking at a conference of business leaders in Miami in November of 1986, Balaguer reiterated his belief that the Caribbean Basin Initiative would be critical in the development of his country and that the investment opportunities stimulated by the CBI could transform the region into one similar to that found in the Far East. In fact, Balaguer went so far as to describe the CBI as the greatest achievement in the history of relations between the United States and the countries of the Caribbean.[19] If the signal of an overture to the Eastern bloc countries is taken then in tandem with the glowing embrace of the Caribbean Basin Initiative, one can expect that President Balaguer will be attempting to take the Dominican Republic in a new foreign policy direction while maintaining his traditional base of support in the United States.

As has always been the case in the Dominican Republic, the future direction of foreign policy depends upon the course of internal politics. Joaquín Balaguer may not seek another presidential term, and José Francisco Peña Gómez, the leftist former mayor of Santo Domingo and currently the vice-president of the Socialist International, firmly believes that it is his "turn" to gain the nomination of his party.[20] Should the popular Peña Gómez get the nod as the PRD'S candidate, it can be expected that positions in favor of normalization of ties to Cuba, support for revolutionary movements in Central America and heightened criticism of the United States will be advanced. Many observers, however, think Peña's time may have already passed.

But discussing with any accuracy the future of Dominican external relations may in the end be foolhardy since foreign policy initiatives often are the result of domestic crisis or decisions made in Washington. Try as they may, the Dominicans are well aware of the fact that foreign policy and the development of external relations have also become part of its status as a dependent nation-state. There may be opportunities to exert a degree of independence or to follow a new course of action, but after years of dependency in so many other areas of national life one can expect that the Dominicans will continue to develop their external relations with an eye toward the United States, even though in their heart they may want to begin to diversify further their external ties.

NOTES

1. Jan Knippers Black, *The Dominican Republic: Politics and Development in an Unsovereign State* (Boston: George Allen and Unwin), pp. 122–128.

2. As quoted in the *Wall Street Journal*, January 7, 1983, p. 1.

3. See a further discussion of the strategic value of the region in and around the Dominican Republic in "The Soviet-Cuban Connection in Central America and the Caribbean," U.S. Department of State and Department of Defense, Washington, DC, March 1985, pp. 3–5.

4. Michael Kryzanek, "The Dominican Republic 1981–1982," in Jack Hopkins, ed., *Latin America and Caribbean Contemporary Review*, 1981–1982, (New York: Holmes and Meier, 1982), p. 547.

5. In 1982 Admiral Harry D. Train, commander of the U.S. Atlantic fleet, began talks with the Dominicans to try to convince them to lease a U.S. naval base in the country and also enter into a mutual assistance agreement with the government of Puerto Rico.

6. For background on Dominican-Haitian relations, see Georges A. Fauriol, "The Dominican Republic and Haiti: The Limitations of Foreign Policies," in Richard Millett and W. Marvin Will, eds., *The Restless Caribbean: Changing Patterns of International Relations* (New York: Praeger, 1979), pp. 182–92.

7. For a more recent discussion of Dominican-Haitian relations, see Michael Kryzanek, "Hispaniola in Ferment: Contrasting Responses to Regional and International Issues," in Richard Millet and W. Marvin Will, eds., *Crescent of Conflict: International Relations in the Caribbean Basin (Boulder, CO: Westview Press, forthcoming).*

8. *New York Times*, May 20, 1982.

9. *The Times of the Americas*, August 1, 1984.

10. Jonathan Hartley, "The Dominican Republic, 1985–1986," Vanderbilt University, 1986, p. 25.

11. Antonio J. Colorado, "Puerto Rico Pushing Ahead with CBI 'Outreach' Program," *Business America*, November 25, 1985, pp. 2–9.

12. Jan Knippers Black, *The Dominican Republic*, op. cit., p. 127.

13. This attitude is further discussed in Howard Wiarda and Michael Kry-zanek, *The Dominican Republic: A Caribbean Crucible*, (Boulder, CO: Westview Press, 1982), p. 61.

14. For example, President Balaguer is reported as making an "impassioned plea" to the Reagan administration not to cut the sugar quota, warning that higher unemployment tied to the fallout from the cutback would create "social explosions." See Tom Wicker, "Disastrous Sugar Diplomacy in the Caribbean," New York Times, March 14, 1987, p. 27.

15. Personal interviews, U.S. State Department, Washington DC, July 2, 1986.

16. U.S. Agency for International Development, FY 1987 Program Highlights, The Dominican Republic, Washington DC, 1986.

17. Of special pride to the Dominican is the U.S. $90 million loan from the Inter-American Development Bank to enhance the agro-industrial sector. See the Santo Domingo *Times*, December 11, 1986.

18. As quoted in Tom Wicker, "Disastrous Sugar Diplomacy in the Caribbean," op. cit.

19. The Santo Domingo *News*, December 4, 1986.

20. Jonathan Hartley, "A Democratic Shoot-Out in the D.R.: An Analysis of the 1986 Elections. *Caribbean Review* XV, Winter 1987. Hartley comments on the prospects for the PRD, and in particular the prospects of Peña Gómez, in this article.

8

CONCLUSION: ASSESSING THE IMPACT OF DEPENDENCY, INTERDEPENDENCE, AND INTERVENTION

The enormous impact of the outside world on Dominican national development is often presented as a negative by those familiar with the sad evolution of this country from the days of Columbus to today. The history of foreign intervention and dependent economic relations has been so pervasive that this book has stressed these as its dominant themes: the role played by foreign governments, international agencies, multinational entitites, and even some individuals from outside the country—in shaping politics, social relations, and economic activity in the Dominican Republic.

But if this analysis is to be complete, it must move beyond historical presentations and the discussion of the interconnections between Dominican society and external forces to an evaluation in which judgments are made as to how the Dominican Republic and the Dominican people have been affected by the constant involvement of non-Dominicans in the internal affairs of their country. In order therefore to complete this study of the link between the outside world and the course of Dominican development, a series of questions will be posed which address key concerns about the influence of intervention and dependency on this country with some speculation on the prospects for facing these critical challenges in the future.

HAS ANY GOOD COME FROM THIS LEGACY OF INTERVENTION?

Determining whether the external sector has had a positive influence on Dominican development, it is essential to separate short-term results from long-range problems. Given the frequent evidence of internal disorder and political polarization in the Dominican Republic, policymakers in Washington, schooled in the tradition of stable government and hegemonic presumptions, felt confident that this country had an obligation to control events in a neighboring nation.[1] Using its considerable military might and its image as a country that must assume the responsibility for maintaining order and democracy in the hemisphere, the United-States either sent in troops and civilian administrators to "set the country straight" or let it be known that it would not tolerate political activity that conflicted with its own interests.

In terms of achieving the short-term objectives of stable governance, keeping out real or perceived hostile foreign powers, and support for U.S. interests in the region, the interventions were indeed successful. Moreover, U.S. consciences were often salved by the fact that these interventions were accompanied by assistance or reform programs that transferred money, ideas, and expertise to the Dominicans and contributed to a degree of economic modernization, institutional development, and democratization. In some cases these aid and development efforts were well-meaning and designed to address serious deficiencies in the Dominican Republic, but along with them there was also evidence of self-serving administrators, patronizing diplomats, and sometimes even racist officials, and other "ugly Americans" who saw intervention as a means of making money, "civilizing" the populace, and keeping the Dominicans in line.

But the assessment of foreign, particularly U.S., intervention in the Dominican Republic should not be based wholly on whether geopolitical objectives were met or on the goodwill gestures of U.S. occupiers. The critical part for determining the benefits and drawbacks of intervention in the Dominican Republic comes when the post-intervention period is examined. In the case of the earlier Spanish and the Haitian invasions and occupations the assessment is fairly easy to make, in that these two intervenors used the Dominican Republic as either a geopolitical pawn in a major power struggle or as a helpless target of conquest. When they left the Dominican Republic, the country was not only devastated in the economic sense, but without the capacity to organize its people or govern itself effectively.

In judging the impact of U.S. intervention, the assessment becomes a bit clouded. The 1905 receivership may have helped pay outstanding debts, but it did little to construct a viable and independent economic system in the Dominican Republic. The Wilson intervention in 1916 may have brought order to the country, but it eventually led to Trujilloism. The 1965 intervention by the Johnson administration certainly "saved" the country from divisive civil war, but it also caused devastating economic dislocation, produced extensive loss of life, and fostered an authoritarian regime that was not only repressive but became increasingly unpopular.

When the United States left the Dominican Republic after each of these interventions, economic life, social relations, and partisan politics had changed for the Dominican people, but not necessarily for the better. In most instances political reform and political development were sacrificed or ignored in order to ensure some often vague security interest or greater normalcy in the economic sector. From the perspective of benefits and drawbacks to intervention, the economic changes achieved during or after the several U.S. occupations were out of balance when compared to the political losses in terms of a healthy human rights climate, popular access to government, administrative accountability, adherence to the rule of law, and the encouragement of pluralism and interest group competitiveness.

The fact that today the Dominican Republic is a reasonably thriving democracy (although in the Dominican mold and not necessarily the exact same Western liberal mold of the United States) is proof to some apologists for past interventions that this country acted correctly if not nobly to guarantee order and build a more open governing system in a nation viewed as vital to U.S. security interests in the region.[2] And yet when one examines the periods of heavy U.S. involvement or intervention in Dominican affairs, such as the Trujillo era, the aborted constitutionalist revolution in 1965, and the not-so-benign authoritarianism of Joaquín Balaguer, in each case democracy was actually held back and political development was seriously retarded because the U.S. intervenors valued economic stability and/or regional security as higher priorities than good government and popular rule.

The democratic "benefits" that have accrued to the Dominicans from these interventions have come more as accidental by-products than as the result of any planned policy objectives or recognized commitment to established governing principles. It is only in the 1978 "passive" intervention of President Jimmy Carter, which forced Balaguer to reopen the balloting and accept the Guzmán victory, that U.S. policy departed from the traditional mold. For the first time the United States placed principle ahead of security interests or economic considerations and permitted democracy to develop on its own. As for the Reagan administration, it has made conscious efforts to avoid being described as intervening in Dominican affairs and has emphasized a relationship of cooperation and partnership.

Perhaps the best that can be said of this legacy of U.S. intervention in Dominican affairs is that, although we often did not act in a noble way or with any vision for the future direction of the country, our involvement never really closed the door on democracy and economic independence. In fact, if anything, U.S. intervention intensified the Dominican desire to break out of the cycle of authoritarianism, instability, and dependency. Although there are no assurances that the cycle has been broken or that the country is now intervention-free, the apparent strength of democratic governance, the presence of an emerging consensus on the need for social stability, and the growing signs of economic indepndence and interdependence point to a time when the "Colossus of the North" may become a benign and helpful neighbor rather than a bothersome meddler in internal affairs.

ARE THE DOMINICANS DESTINED TO REMAIN DEPENDENT?

Although the legacy of foreign intervention in the Dominican Republic has, at least for the moment, receded into the background of national consciousness, the other threat to Dominican sovereignty and control of its destiny—dependent economic relations—has moved to the forefront of public debate. Even a cursory overview of Domincan national affairs in the last few years would immediately reveal that government officials and other critical elites are more aware than ever of the dangers posed by dependent economic relations and more determined to develop strategies and initiate policies that free the nation from the so-called "rollercoaster" cycle of economic development.

But while the Dominicans work to free their economy, and indeed their country, from the grip of dependency, it seems essential to address an even more fundamental issue related to foreign economic control and national development. The Dominicans can certainly not be faulted for doing whatever they can to make their economy more diversified, independent and self-sufficient. The concern for the future, however, is whether there is a proper balance between independence and dependence that may best serve the long-term development interests of the Dominican Republic. Every nation in the world, and certainly some of the richest, have dependent economic relations. What differentiates the dependency of the richer countries from that of the Dominican Republic is that their reliance on such critical items as oil, natural gas, steel, and technology is usually offset by their ability to expand export markets in industrial and consumer goods. In the case of the Dominican Republic, the import demand for goods and services essential for modernization and expanded prosperity is not properly matched by its diversified exports since, in fact, the Dominicans have for too long relied on agricultural commodities such as sugar, coffee, and tobacco as their prime sources of foreign exchange.

Many economists and development specialists who have looked at the Dominican Republic agree that it is unlikely the country will be able to move quickly away from its agricultural dependency and replace sugar, coffee, and tobacco production with assembly plants for clothing, manufactured goods, and even semi-conductors. What will most likely happen is that there will be periods of growth in selected sectors of the economy, but overall the imbalances created by dependency will restrain the Dominican Republic from breaking out of the rollercoaster development cycle. Critical to the future of the Dominican economy is the speed and extent of the transition to a more diversified and industrially based economy. If this transition is limited or, worse yet, halted because of lack of investment capital, the Dominican Republic will certainly remain a largely agriculturally based economy dependent on world prices for its exports and overwhelmed by the costs of the imports it needs to maintain an acceptable level of social and political stability.[3]

While dependency may remain at the core of Dominican economic relations, there is nothing to restrain the country from modernizing and thereby improving its dependent position. The Dominicans can and indeed must work to recast their economic relations with the outside world. The Dominicans are already recognizing that dependency on revenue from the sale of sugar should be replaced by agricultural diversification and by further enticing foreign investors to build assembly plants in the country. There will still be a reliance on a foreign source of internal development, but the prospects for strengthening the economy, employing workers, and building an industrial base are far better with more diversified investment dependency than with sugar dependency.

Thus, despite the fact that economic and other forms of dependency in the Dominican Republic appear to be a permanent fixture of national life, it need not be or become a static condition. Just as the overall economy modernizes and reforms, so too can dependency. In many respects the severe economic crisis of the Guzmán and Jorge eras was the result of the Dominicans clinging to their old dependency relationships and failing to do enough to establish new and more beneficial ties to the external sector. Only in the last year of the Jorge administration, after the currency reform and increased efforts to entice foreign investment and tourism, did the Dominican economy begin to rebound.

President Balaguer may benefit politically from the strengthened Dominican economy, but only if he continues to develop export and productive sectors, while deemphasizing the traditional ties to foreign sugar markets. Privatization, consolidation and greater efforts to combat inefficiency and corruption in state enterprises like sugar must be joined by aggressive government programs to diversify the industrial base and continue the influx of foreign investors and tourists. Descriptive phrases like "the new Taiwan" and "the Riviera of the Caribbean" may exaggerate the real potential of the Domincan economy, but they do strike at the heart of what this country must become in order to survive. The future of the Dominican Republic is in its ability to modernize and change its dependency and move from an economy reliant on the sugar trade to one that establishes the country as a tropical vegetable "greenhouse," the assembly plant of the hemisphere, and the Caribbean vacation spot for the tourists of the world. In the process, the Dominicans could well change their status from that of dependency to a situation of much more complex interdependence.

WHAT ARE THE KEY DEVELOPMENT ISSUES FOR THE DOMINICAN REPUBLIC?

The word development is so laced with value judgments and eth-nocentric biases that it is difficult for an external observer to speculate on what may be a proper course for the Dominican Republic in the coming years. One way to approach the future of this country is to examine the successes and failures of the past and then point out the challenges that remain. Although it may be dangerous to do so, the fact is that the Dominican Republic in the last ten years has in a real sense achieved remarkable progress in both establishing a viable democratic framework and implementing a series of economic and financial reforms.

The fact that new ways of dealing with critical aspects of national life have been developed in no way suggests that the Dominican Republic has mastered democratic politics or is assured of a stable and prosperous economy. In fact it is safe to state that the Dominicans will continue to be challenged by internal threats to democracy as well as by external influences on its fragile economy. But what has happened is that the Dominican Republic has moved forward to a new level of political and economic organization and maybe even institutionalization, and along the way has changed the manner in which the Dominican people approach their government and their economic relations.

The last ten years have indeed been critical for the Dominican Republic. From the election of Guzmán in 1978 to the present the Dominicans have been engaged in a process of reordering their society. Power relations, decision-making practices, national priorities, economic arrangements, and financial structures have all undergone either reform or total reformulation. As we have seen, the process has not been an easy one, with numerous setbacks and crises as the entrenched interests in the country resisted what seemed an inevitable and unstoppable wave of change.

Given these changes, what is the policy agenda for the future in the Dominican Republic? The answer is surprisingly rather simple: to transfer the successes achieved in the political sector and the reforms established in the economic sector to the mass of Dominicans. The development of democratic governance and the painful transition to a more modern economy have only had a slight impact on the quality of life for many Dominicans. Granted that democracy has lessened the harshness of authoritarian rule that seemed always to prey upon the poor and the austerity measures instituted by the Jorge government have brightened the overall economy. But these accomplishments are strangely distant from the everyday lives of the Dominicans and on occasion have been the source of angry protest as the search for food, housing, and jobs has sometimes outweighed and overwhelmed the benefits of free elections and devaluation.

The development issue of the future for the Dominican Republic will undoubtedly be whether the political and economic elites in the country can create a process of social change that can match the systemic changes that have occurred in the political and economic sectors. The modest success that the Dominican Republic has achieved over the last ten years in addressing political and economic problems has created an expectation on the part of the people that they will begin to see some significant changes in their lives.

Just as the last ten years have been critical from the standpoint of political and economic reform, the next ten years may prove to be the real challenge to the stability and modernization of the Dominican Republic.[4] For it is in these years that Dominican leaders will face a more skeptical public who will ask whether democracy has lived up to its promises of greater access, participation, and human rights, and whether the economic sacrifices of the early 1980s actually did bring a greater level of prosperity. Initiating a social revolution that touches the large mass of poor Dominicans will unquestionably be the most difficult challenge faced by this country. In the last ten years, despite their goodwill efforts and ideological commitment, two reforms presidents failed to address the issue of social change and instead paid primary attention to political institutionalization and financial restructuring.

The onus for social change thus seems to lie on President Balaguer, who in an odd way may be capable of taking on this last great challenge. Despite his authoritarian-paternalistic background and unwillingness to be tied to past democratizing and social reforms, Balaguer is more conscious of the dangers that will be created if vast and far-reaching social reform is not attempted in the Dominican Republic—and soon. Some of the early initiatives of the Balaguer government demonstrated the president's recognition of the need for such reform, earning him grudging support even from his detratctors. Although we will have to wait and see to assess the accomplishments of Balaguer, the sense is widespread that the Dominican Republic must go forward quickly with social reforms or domestic turmoil, or even upheaval, is likely to result. It is still too early to determine the commitment of Balaguer to social change, but the level of domestic disorder and criticism of democratic governance emanating from the left may reveal whether the masses perceive change trickling down to them or not. Should the Dominican Republic not undertake such changes and thus become a nation plagued by turmoil during the next years, it is a virtual certainty that the advances made since 1978 in the areas of democratization and economic restructuring will be severely compromised or perhaps even destroyed.

NOTES

1. This theme is discussed at length in Jerome Slater, *Intervention and Negotiation: The United States and the Dominican Revolution (New York: Harper & Row, 1970)*, pp. 208–13. See also an editorial by Brian McGinn, "Diplomacy, Not Force, Nurtured D.R. Democracy," *The Times of the Americas*, March 11, 1987.

2. See, for example, Alfred Cuzan, "Balaguer in 1986 Vindicates Johnson in 1965," *The Times of the Americas*, December 10, 1986.

3. See F. Desmond McCarthy, "Macroeconomic Policy Alternatives in the Dominican Republic: An Analytical Framework," *World Bank Staff Working Papers, 649* (Washington DC: 1984). pp. 22–33.

4. For a Dominican perspective on the future, see Frank Moya Pons, "El futuro dominicano," speech presented to the Dominican Jaycees, Santo Domingo, August 27, 1980.

SELECTED READINGS

Atkins, G. Pope. *Arms and Politcs in the Dominican Republic*. Boulder, CO: Westview Press, 1981.

Atkins, G. Pope and Larman Willson. *The United States and the Trujillo Regime*. New Brunswick, NJ: Rutgers University Press, 1972.

Bell, Ian. *The Dominican Republic*. Boulder, CO: Westview Press, 1981.

Black, Jan Knippers. *The Dominican Republic: Politics and Development in an Unsovereign State*. Boston: George Allen and Unwin, 1986.

Bosch, Juan. *The Unfinished Experiment: Democracy in the Dominican Republic*. New York: Praeger, 1963.

Calder, Bruce. *The Impact of Intervention: The Dominican Republic During the U.S. Occupation of 1916–1924*. Austin: University of Texas Press, 1984.

Crassweller, Robert. *Trujillo, The Life and Times of a Caribbean Dictator*. New York: Macmillan, 1966.

Diederich, Bernard. *Trujillo: The Death of the Goat*. Boston: Little, Brown, 1978.

Gleijeses, Piero. *The Domincan Crisis*. Baltimore: Johns Hopkins University Press, 1978.

Kryzanek, Michael. *U.S.-Latin American Relations*. New York: Praeger, 1985.

Kurzman, Dan. *Santo Domingo: Revolt of the Damned*. New York: G.P. Putnam's Sons, 1965.

Logan, Rayford W. *Haiti and the Dominican Republic*. New York: Oxford University Press, 1968.

Lowenthal, Abraham F. *The Dominican Intervention*. Cambridge, MA: Harvard University Press, 1972.

Martin, John Bartlow. *Overtaken by Events: The Dominican Crisis from the Fall of Trujillo to the Civil War*. New York: Doubleday, 1966.

Moreno, Jośe, A. *A Barrio in Arms: Revolution in Santo Domingo*. Pittsburgh: Pittsburgh University Press, 1970.

Rodman, Selden. *Quisqueya: A History of the Dominican Republic*. Seattle: University of Washington Press, 1964.

Sharpe, Kenneth Evan. *Peasant Politics: Struggle in a Dominican Village*. Baltimore: Johns Hopkins Press, 1977.

Slater, Jerome. *Intervention and Negotiation: The United States and the Dominican Republic*. New York: Harper & Row, 1970.

Szulc, Tad. *Dominican Diary*. New York: Delacorte Press, 1965.

Welles, Sumner. *Naboth's Vineyard: The Dominican Republic, 1844–1924*. New York: Payson and Clarke, 1928.

Wiarda, Howard. *The Dominican Republic: Nation in Transition*. New York: Praeger, 1968.

Wiarda, Howard. *Dictatorship and Development: The Methods of Control in Trujillo's Dominican Republic*. Gainesville: University of Florida Press, 1970.

Wiarda, Howard. *Dictatorship, Development and Disintegration: Politics and Social Change in the Dominican Republic*. Ann Arbor: Xerox University Microfilms Monograph Series, 1975.

Wiarda, Howard and Michael J. Kryzanek. *The Dominican Republic: A Caribbean Crucible*. Boulder, CO: Westview Press, 1982.

INDEX

ABOUT THE AUTHORS

MICHAEL J. KRYZANEK is a Professor of Political Science at Bridge-water State College in Massachusetts. His major research interests have been in the area of Caribbean politics and U.S. foreign policy in Latin America. Professor Kryzanek has written *The Dominican Republic: A Caribbean Crucible* (with Howard Wiarda) and *U.S.-Latin American Relations*. He has written a chapter on Dominican-Haitian relations in Richard Millet and W. Marvin Will, *Crescent of Conflict* and a reassessment of the Dominican revolution of 1965 in John Martz, *U.S. Policy in Latin America: Quarter-Century of Crisis and Challenge*. Professor Kryzanek is currently the editor of the *Bridgewater Review*, a scholarly magazine published by Bridgewater State College, and also editor of the *Commonwealth Review*, a magazine of the Massachusetts State Colleges.

HOWARD J. WIARDA is a Research Scholar at the American Enterprise Institute (AEI) in Washington, DC, Professor of Political Science and Comparative Labor Relations at the University of Massachusetts in Amherst, Thorton D. Hooper Fellow in International Security Affairs of the Foreign Policy Research Institute in Philadelphia (1987–88), and Visiting Professor at the George Washington University in Washington, DC (1987–88). Before joining AEI, he was a Research Associate at the Center for International Affairs at Harvard University, a Visiting Scholar at Harvard, and a Visiting Professor at MIT. For several years he taught the Central America/Caribbean course for the Foreign Service Institute of the Department of State.

Professor Wiarda has been the editor of the journal *Polity* and served previously as the Director of the Center for Latin American Studies at the University of Massachusetts. He is on the editorial board of *World Affairs*, the *Foreign Policy and Defense Review*, and the *Journal of Inter-American Studies*. He is a member of the Council of Academic Advisers of the Inter-American Foundation. He was a Lead Consultant to the National Bipartisan (Kissinger) Commission on Central America and served by appointment of the president of the United States on the

Presidential Task Force on Project Economic Justice. He is a member of the Council on Foreign Relations in New York.

Dr. Wiarda has published extensively on Latin America, Development Policy, Southern Europe, the Third World, and United States foreign policy. His most recent books include *Finding our Way: Toward Maturity in U.S.-Latin American Relations; The Communist Challenge in Central America and the Caribbean; Latin America at the Crossroads: Debt, Development and the Future; The Iberian-Latin American Connection; New Directions in Comparative Politics; Latin American Politics and Development; In Search of Policy: The United States and Latin America; Rift and Revolution: The Central American Imbroglio; Ethnocentrism and American Foreign Policy; Politics and Social Change in Latin America; Human Rights and U.S. Human Rights Policy; Corporatism and National Development in Latin America; The Continuing Struggle for Democracy in Latin America;* and *Corporatism and Development: The Portuguese Experience.* He is currently finishing two books, *The Democratic Revolution in Latin America* and *Foreign Policy Without Illusion: How Foreign Policy Works and Fails to Work in the United States.*

POLITICS IN LATIN AMERICA
A HOOVER INSTITUTION SERIES
Robert Wesson, Series Editor

POLITICS IN CENTRAL AMERICA: Guatemala, El Salvador, Honduras, Costa Rica
Thomas P. Anderson

SOCIALISM, LIBERALISM, AND DICTATORSHIP IN PARAGUAY
Paul H. Lewis

PANAMANIAN POLITICS: From Guarded Nation to National Guard
Steve C. Ropp

BOLIVIA: Past, Present, and Future of Its Politics
Robert J. Alexander

U.S. INFLUENCE IN LATIN AMERICA IN THE 1980s
Robert Wesson

DEMOCRACY IN LATIN AMERICA: Promise and Problems
Robert Wesson

MEXICAN POLITICS: The Containment of Conflict
Martin C. Needler

DEMOCRACY IN COSTA RICA
Charles D. Ameringer

NEW MILITARY POLITICS IN LATIN AMERICA
Robert Wesson

BRAZIL IN TRANSITION
Robert Wesson and David V. Fleischer

VENEZUELA: Politics in a Petroleum Republic
David E. Blank

HAITI: Political Failures, Cultural Successes
Brian Weinstein and Aaron Segal

GEOPOLITICS OF THE CARIBBEAN: Ministates in a Wider World
Thomas D. Anderson

PUERTO RICO: Equality and Freedom at Issue
Juan M. Garcia-Passalacqua

LATIN AMERICA AND WESTERN EUROPE: Reevaluating the Atlantic
Triangle
Wolf Grabendorff and Riordan Roett

GEOPOLITICS AND CONFLICT IN SOUTH AMERICA: Quarrels
Among Neighbors
Jack Child

LATIN AMERICAN VIEWS OF U.S. POLICY
Robert Wesson

CLASS, STATE, AND DEMOCRACY IN JAMAICA
Carl Stone

THE MEXICAN RULING PARTY: Stability and Authority
Dale Story

THE POLITICS OF COLOMBIA
Robert H. Dix

GUYANA: Politics in a Plantation Society
Chaitram Singh